His²

His²

BRILLIANT NEW FICTION BY GAY WRITERS

edited by Robert Drake with Terry Wolverton

Faber and Faber   **Boston · London**

Library of Congress Cataloging-in-Publication Data

His 2 : brilliant new fiction by gay writers / edited by Robert Drake
     with Terry Wolverton.
       p.   cm.
     ISBN 0-571-19908-9 (paper)
       1. Gay men—United States—Social life and customs—Fiction.
     2. American fiction—20th century.   3. Gay men's writings, American.
     I. Drake, Robert.   II. Wolverton, Terry.
     PS648.H57H56   1997
     813'.0189206642—dc21
                                                                        96-37876
                                                                        CIP

Jacket design by Susan Silton
Jacket photograph by John Dugdale
Printed in the United States of America

We dedicate this book
to Gil Cuadros and Rick Sandford,
two unforgettable voices
silenced too soon

Contents

Introduction

"You confuse what's important with what's impressive."
—E.M. Forster, *Maurice*

What is a "community"? According to the dictionary[1]:
community (kə-myoo′nĭ-tē) noun:

1. A group of people living in the same locality and under the same government. b. The district or locality in which such a group lives.
2. A group of people having common interests: the scientific community; the international business community.
3. a. Similarity or identity: a community of interests. b. Sharing, participation, and fellowship.
4. Society as a whole; the public.
5. Ecology. a. A group of plants and animals living and interacting with one another in a specific region under relatively similar environmental conditions. b. The region occupied by a group of interacting organisms.

There's been much talk lately of the gay community. We exist when politicians want us to, for purposes of vilification or solicitude. We exist when we are perceivable demographically (for

[1] *The American Heritage Dictionary of the English Language,* Third Edition, is licensed from Houghton Mifflin Company. Copyright © 1992 by Houghton Mifflin Company. All rights reserved.

example, to justify a collection of new literary fiction by writers sharing a common denominator). We exist whenever there's a fundraiser; we exist in the form of the numerous and good-willed organizations trying to serve the community.

But without someone around to perceive us as such, *do we* exist as a community? Queer theorists debate this with enthusiasm, vigorously thrusting their lances upward into the rarefied air of academia, but I confess this has never interested me much. I have always been rather happily common and I am by extension something of a populist. Sure, I think theories are well and good— occasionally even fun to muck about in—but they are pointless if their ultimate effect is only intangible thought, without an eventual tangible impact upon the life of the common man, the average folk. In sum: It's all very impressive, but it's not very important.

Accepting in great part that homosexuality is biologically predetermined, we admit that other communities are granted clearer demarcation lines for their members: women and people of color, for example, in most instances have (literally) visible characteristics identifying them with their communities. Gay people do not. At a stretch it could be said we have mannerisms—and that ineffable "gaydar"—but this is a reach that falls short of its grasp. We have nothing *quantifiable* determining our membership in the gay community except the urges of our biology and our willingness to recognize them, and by extension ourselves, as gay.

In the old days this argument was about the ability to "pass," a drawback in that it allowed those who chose to pursue self-interest over the betterment of life for the whole an opportunity to slink away and do so; an asset in that it allowed us to walk, work, and in essence infiltrate the enemy without their knowledge. But we have fallen away from thinking of straight people as "the enemy"—it has proved an increasingly false perception as education efforts and MTV hammer away at the American facade of homophobia and, bit by bit, civilize this country.

So the ability to pass becomes less of a sinful temptation and more a tool employed by a Special Agent to seek the successful mission. The FBI attempted to infiltrate ACT UP meetings in the 1980s to get the dibs on subversives, only to find themselves hampered by their inability to pass. Suceeding where they failed, we infiltrate school boards, city governments, state governments,

Congress, and the halls of the White House, passing when it suits us—walking the walk, talking the talk—to obtain information and progress, and then reclaiming our queer identity as fast as we are able—sashaying the sashay, snapping the snap. Yet perhaps this is too elitist or rarefied an example. For most of us, we simply go to work, where we may or may not—at our discretion, as anti-discrimination laws entrench themselves—discuss our lives as queer Americans and live our lives outside of work as openly queer Americans. This is admittedly an urban perspective in great part, but as a West Virginia boy who returns home often enough, there are echoes of these changes soughing through the trees of the Appalachian mountains, imaginably equal in streaking across the Kansas plain.

Still, all of this leaves us wobbly. Where do we belong? We become increasingly vigorous in the reclamation of our history, an effort now more than a quarter-century old. Within the literary world, this is achieved vividly and personally in works like *Jeb and Dash,* the diary of a gay government worker—a common man—in the years 1918–1945, published by the publisher of these anthologies. We glimpse a more highbrow life in Farrar, Straus & Giroux's *Continual Lessons: The Journals of Glenway Wescott (1937–1945).* James Baldwin's nonfiction writings powerfully recreate for us the emotions and passions of the times that led to our present possibility; they also remind us that, despite the work thus far accomplished, we have only begun to mine the rich ore of our history, the better to build a sturdy framework for community in the present 1990s.

We are black, white, yellow, brown; we are male, female, transgendered; we are gay, lesbian, queer; we are Christian, atheist, Jew, Buddhist, Hindu; we permeate all nations and cultures. As the ability to pass proved both asset and liability, so does our diversity—we have the benefit of all cultures; we have none of our own.

Or do we? Does our culture, like our very identity, exist if we allow ourselves to perceive it and then, once perceived, exist with increasing certainty, gaining greater form much the same way a book passes from popular fancy to enduring classic—over time?

That is the question these stories brought me. In reading more than 450 stories for the second round of *His* and *Hers,* common themes began to emerge. Having edited previous volumes in the series, there was an opportunity to remember the themes of 1995 and compare them with those of 1997. What stood out visibly was surprising.

In the new stories considered for *His* in 1997, the two note-worthy and—at first glance—disturbing trends not noticeable in 1995 were: a lot of stories about men having sex with youths and not very many stories about AIDS. The former may be fueled by the success in literary realms of novels dealing so well with this topic: Scott Heim's *Mysterious Skin* fruit-loops to mind, as does the work of Matthew Stadler. Yet these men both boast a skill in artistry and talent that lifts their representation of men having sex with lads free from the muck of sordid fantasy—doing with words what Caravaggio did with paint—and do not make the mistake of relishing in the perversity of the act as much as indulging the per-versity of the reader, thereby turning the work upon its audience and flaying their readership alive. This is a vital reading experi-ence. In this collection, William Mann's "Say Goodbye to Middle-town" joins their company, and provides an incredible story about intergenerational relationships and truth.

And what of AIDS? Does it no longer capture our imagina-tion's fancy? Does its horror no longer serve our muse? Can it be that we are bored with AIDS, tired not just of red ribbons but of the cause they represent? Are we ready for something new, some fresher disease-of-the-day?

I hope not. For writers of talent addressing AIDS within their works are providing some of our richest reading experiences. As with stories involving men loving boys, bright writers who do tackle this difficult subject matter with the full force of their talent spawn something not only surprising, but surprisingly different: "Storm," by G. Winston James and "Birth" by Gil Cuadros stand as a testament to the remarkable power of AIDS to disturb the very fabric of fiction—of life—and to render us certain that what we once thought we knew, we do not; what we once thought we con-trolled, we never did.

A liability emerges if we focus on these two themes without ac-knowledging the remarkable breadth of the stories received in full. Although these themes may surface as a thread in the submis-sions for the anthology, they are only a thread. What remains, and what reflects the community when considered with the themes evinced, are stories diverse enough to include, among others, game-show contestants ("Parting Gifts"), drag queens ("Dyanna

Ross"), young love ("Drinking Water Lilies"), and a hunger for role models fed with the desire for escape ("Evesham Encounter").

All the stories herein speak to our lives or the lives of others embraced by our community. Ultimately I believe it is this that signifies and establishes our community: Not the ability of others to recognize and define it for their various purposes, but our ability to define it for ourselves, as a part of ourselves, as a part of our lives. We do not inherit our community and its traditions as much as we invent it, and create them. Queers are to the gay community as God is to Man in the opening of Genesis—hungry for something made in our own image. We create it in our art, and in our art we recognize ourselves.

We recognize further that our community is a diverse beast, yet we recognize we are a part of that diversity, we are the muscle of the beast. As it shows through in our art, so it manifests itself visibly when we joyfully gather together, during afternoons like that of the 1993 March on Washington's Mall-sprawl.

Yet such manifestations are fleeting, a moment out of a movie, and we break from them to find ourselves returned to the daily busy-ness of our lives, where it is easiest to forget that we are all part of one community by choice and by recognition. We yammer instead about our differences, often being so busy with the infighting that we forget what we should be fighting for in the first place. We accomplish little if not nothing, when we could have accomplished so much if we maximized our strengths instead of tearing each other apart over perceived weaknesses.

This is a frequently voiced complaint, most often spoken by those who should be hearing it, but it is valid nonetheless: there is a sense of camaraderie we seem too ready to forget when we slip free of the group euphoria found in Pride Day celebrations, political rallies, or joyous nights of clubbing. It's damaging in that it ruptures important positive self- and community-esteem with impressive angst, trading something needed for something useless. We lose sight of the fact that (queer) Pride is more important than blame. We become allies with the heterosexual supremacists then, trading our truth of dignity for their conspiracy of shame. Shameful. But even in these self-inflicted, hapless moments:

The truth is out there.

Terry Wolverton and I have been called the "Scully and Mulder" of queer letters. We mirror their crossed gender lines pretty well: Terry's the organized and methodical one, hunting down the real world; I'm the one continually chasing flying saucers.

Only in my case, the flying saucers are little bubbles of our community, the "aliens" aboard them musclemen, or drag queens, or GOP true believers, or barflies, or writers—who are all of the above, and any other possibility you might concoct. As for those cliquish saucers, they're flying about; and they bump into each other. Sometimes they fly in formation—more often than not they take potshots at each other—but they're all headed for the community mother ship.

But of what is this mother ship built? What enables it to exist?

Art, stretched tautly across a sturdy foundation of history. It is its own creation story: The artist creating the art creating the community creating the artist creating the art. Panels of dance, literature, music, painting, and film form the skin of the community, its ability to speak to us, acknowledging our diversity and providing in its fine glimmer the mirror of reclamation where we may recognize ourselves, recognize our culture, recognize each other. It is our recognition that fuses these panels of art against their beams of history, over time. Indivisible, in the greater picture, we weather mainstream societal indifference and aggression, establishing a *quantifiable* home that may know no one country without knowing all, no one race without knowing all, no one faith. Man's law is its fist, history bone, but Art is the mother ship's flesh and heart.

It is important. It is impressive. And this book is a part of it.

By virtue of reading it, so are you.

Welcome to the mother ship.

:-)

ROBERT DRAKE, 1997

His²

Stealing
Memories

RICHARD C. ZIMLER

In September of 1931, the French painter Fernand Léger visited the United States for the first time. He was fifty years old and already famous for his darkly outlined, colorful figures. In early October, while in New York, one of his lower molars became infected. At the time, my father did all the dental work for Marcel Berenger, the Madison Avenue gallery owner. One evening, Berenger called our home. Could his close friend and compatriot Léger come by that night?

Near midnight, Léger arrived wearing a tweed coat and cap. My father told me years later, "He had panicked eyes, and I knew he was going to be a difficult patient." In fact, he sat frozen in the dental chair and mumbled in French when my father didn't have his hands in his mouth. Was he cursing? Praying? My father spoke little French and couldn't say for sure. He told me, "I remember that he sweated a lot and that he smelled of some peculiar floral soap." The problematic molar was easily cleaned and filled. Léger shook my father's hands exuberantly and thanked him with great praise for his dental skills. In his awkward English, he confessed that the toothache had made him forgetful, and that he only had two American one-dollar bills in his wallet—just enough for cab fare back to his hotel. Of course, he had no checking account in America. If my father were willing to wait till the next day, he would mail a check drawn on Monsieur Berenger's account. My father said not to bother, that it was his pleasure to work on the molar of so talented an artist. Léger reluctantly agreed and parted a happy man.

Exactly three days later, however, a small flat package arrived by messenger. It was twelve inches square, wrapped with brown paper and tied with red and white bakery string. "I thought your Aunt Rutya had sent us some of her strange Rumanian pastry," my father told me with a laugh. Inside the package, however, was a small painting Léger had apparently just completed and a signed, two-word note: *Avec gratitude.*

As children, my brother, two sisters, and I called the painting, "The Woman with Stone Hair."

It is a portrait of a young woman seated on the ground with long black tresses done in such a way as to make them look solid—like polished obsidian. She has the soft pink skin and dreamy face typical of Léger's female portraits at the time.

The painting was my introduction to modern art. It used to hang in my parents' room, above their bed. Years later, I realized that it must have been a study for Léger's famous work, "The Bather," completed in 1932.

Both my parents adored the painting, and after my mother's death it seemed to take on the importance of an icon for my father. Sometimes I'd find him sitting on the green armchair where he piled his dirty clothing, holding the canvas, daydreaming. Once, late at night, I found him asleep with the Léger on his lap. At the time, I had no idea why.

My mother died on June 6, 1954, of breast cancer. By the time the lump was detected by our family doctor, the disease had spread to her lymph nodes. I was thirteen at the time. I didn't understand why her hair was falling out. My dad explained that Mom was really sick but that I shouldn't worry about her; she was getting the best possible care.

Before I realized that she was dying, she was already dead.

My mother and I had been very close. During her illness, we played endless games of gin rummy after school. Sometimes she liked to draw portraits of me. I'd sit in her bedroom by the windows facing Gramercy Park where the light was strong. She'd sit on her bed with her box of colored pencils. She wore a bright blue beanie to keep her bald head warm. Her eyes were large and brown. She smiled a lot, as if to encourage me. As she sketched, she nibbled bits of Hershey chocolate bars; it was the only food she could keep down.

Sometimes, she and I would clear off the dining-room table

and paint together with the sets of Japanese ink which my father found for us at a tiny art supply store on Hudson Street. Mostly she'd paint finches nesting in pine trees. I have two of these studies hanging in my office at Barnard College. Visitors always say, "Oh, so you've been to Japan. . . ."

One strange little painting that she did hangs in my bedroom, however, over my bed. It's a finch, but it has human eyes— my eyes.

My mother was buried at Mt. Sinai Cemetery in Roslyn, out on Long Island. I refused to go to the ceremony and spent the afternoon alone, eating the rest of her chocolate bars in front of the television until I got sick and threw up all over an old Persian rug we had at the time.

After she died, I felt as if I'd been left behind on a deserted planet. It was my father who rescued me. He let me come into his bed at night for a couple of months after her death, never uttered even a single complaint for my disturbing his sleep. Nor did he listen to my older siblings' warnings that a fifty-one-year-old man shouldn't share the same bed as his adolescent son. "Forget what they say," he used to tell me. "They don't understand." To get me to stop shivering and fall asleep, he'd rub my hair gently and tell me stories of his youth back in Poland. He spoke of seductive demons from Gehenna, shtetls turned magically upside down, chickens with angels in their eggs. He took great pains to make all the endings happy.

On my insistence, he wrote down two of these stories and tried sending them to children's publishers, but all we got back were mimeographed rejection letters. Editors didn't regard dybbuks and Cossacks as fitting for American children. I still have the manuscripts at the bottom of my linen closet.

My brother and sisters were off on their own by the time my mother died; they were all in their twenties and married. So for the next six years, till I went off to college, my father and I lived alone in our apartment at the corner of Irving Place and East Twentieth Street. He was a good man, heartbreakingly lonely and prone to distant silences, but attentive when I needed him. After my mother's death, the pride that she had taken in my smallest accomplishments was magically transferred to him, just like in one of his crazy stories. When I won my high school English award, he sat in the front row of the parent assembly with the tears of an immigrant father streaming down his cheeks.

When my father turned sixty-five, he sold his dental practice and moved permanently into a cottage in Hampton Bays out on Long Island. He gardened, watched New York Mets Games, and scratched out Bach suites on his violin. I spent every other weekend with him.

In later years, when New York winters forced him indoors for weeks at a time, he spent all of January and February with me at my apartment on Ninety-first Street and West End Avenue. He'd read his South American novels in the bed that I set up in my living room, snooze, water my plants, browse in the local bookstores. When I'd get home from classes, he'd make me verbena tea. I used to make him jambalaya, his favorite dish, every Saturday.

In February of 1984, he suffered a minor stroke. In the hospital, he developed bacterial pneumonia. Then, something seemed to snap inside him and he grew delirious. One specialist said Alzheimer's disease. A couple of others suggested various pathogens which could cause brain lesions. Tests were ordered, but none proved conclusive. It was agreed by default that Alzheimer's had set in—that he'd managed to keep it hidden until illness weakened him. He was eighty-one years old. I was his only child still living in New York. That spring, I took a leave of absence from my post in the Art History Department at Barnard and spent long afternoons in his cottage, feeding him and watching him snooze. He grew progressively weaker and would sleep most of the time, in the most cockeyed positions, legs and arms dangling over the side of his bed, his head twisted to the side and mouth open. One day, I dared to straighten him out. He was pliable, like a rag doll. I gingerly moved his legs together and placed his head straight back into the valley of his down pillow. He looked as if he were prepared for burial. So I took his right arm and laid it over the side of the bed and twisted his head. He looked much better that way.

Anyway, the important thing is that after I arranged my father in his bed, I noticed out his window that the crabapple in the backyard had become a cloud of soft pink. And that a male cardinal had alighted there. Red feathers and pink petals. Life doesn't get much lovelier than that.

Now, a decade later, I still associate the cardinal and the crabapple with my father's illness. When he wasn't sleeping, he'd sometimes kick and scream, froth at the mouth, rant about being held hostage. Toward the end, during the few moments of lucidity which gave him peace, he would reach for me. "Paulie, you're still here," he'd say. "When will it end?"

His grip was that of an eagle. Talons biting into my flesh.

Then he would begin to shout again. "I want out! Out! You can't keep me here against my will. I want to see the manager! Where's the manager?!"

Pieces of the verbal puzzle I put together made it clear that he often thought he was being held captive in a hotel in San Francisco. At other times, he was convinced he was being dunked underwater. I found out that an eighty-one-year-old fights like a teenage boxer to keep from drowning. His doctor recommended low dosages of tranquilizers. Half a five-milligram Valium on his bad mornings did the trick. That explained his pliable limbs, of course.

Once, during a calm moment, I found him sitting on his bed facing the Léger, just like in the old days. We held hands without talking, and then he got up to make us verbena tea as a treat.

All of us who loved my father knew he had been constructed of more fragile materials than most people—a man of balsa wood with a rubber-band engine flying off to foreign lands inside his head. So dementia was not totally unexpected. In fact, my two sisters and brother all told me—independently of one another—that they were only surprised he'd stayed sane for so long. They said it easily, as if they were discussing a family pet who'd been gently weakened by an invisible cancer.

My own interpretation of the visions my father had that spring is that there was always a kind of fairy-tale landscape inside him which in the end engulfed him completely. It was a world of inns hidden deep inside the forests of Poland, a land of Talmud scholars and white magic; but also one of Cossacks and pogroms.

For many years, he escaped such a world successfully, but then, when he weakened physically, it claimed him back.

As we reach the end of our lives, do we all return to our ancestral landscape? Will I, too, return to the threatening forests of Poland even though I've never set foot inside that country?

After he died, when I was sitting alone by his side, listening to the room exhale with relief, I began to tremble. There was no one there to make me verbena tea or rub my hair. No cardinal perched in the crabapple tree.

For about a week, I didn't feel anything but the gaping absence left by his death. My brother and sisters flew in for the funeral. They were helpful then because there was no one to nurse. They brought me barbecued chicken from the deli in Hampton Bays, cookies to nibble on in bed, dropped me at Westhampton Beach where I could walk down the strand and think about the past.

I didn't go to the funeral itself; that morning, my body seemed to give out, and I woke up shivering with a high fever and stomach cramps. I was not sorry; I was dreading having to share my grief with people who didn't help me take care of him.

The only thing I could keep down was chocolate. Real food tasted thick and stale.

Two weeks after my father died, I was alone in his house, beginning to inventory the tchochkes that he and my mother had accumulated. It was then that I discovered that the painting by Léger was missing. "The Woman with Stone Hair" had been in his bedroom, of course, above his bed and my mother's worn and ragged blood-red blanket. I'd seen it there every day for three months while nursing him. All that was left of its presence was a tawny square where the sun had not been able to bleach the wall.

I didn't panic. I called up my brother and two sisters to see if they'd seen it; they were the only people who'd spent any more than a few minutes at my father's house since his death.

I called each of them in turn, and each denied knowing anything about the painting's disappearance.

I don't believe that the particular personalities of my siblings will help anyone understand why they lied to me. What is important to know is that they hated my father for things that had happened many years before, during their childhoods. After his death, they each made a point of telling me that he was a very different person when they were growing up: strict, unfeeling, vindictive. He didn't listen to them or our mother, liked to humiliate the kids by slapping them in the face when they misbehaved.

They all mentioned these things to explain why they weren't visibly upset at his death. They spoke forcefully and slowly, as if I were a prosecutor spending my time gathering evidence against them.

Although it's hard for me to believe, I suppose that their portrait of my father may be accurate; after all, children sometimes grow up in different families according to their ages. Also, parents often grow more tolerant as their youthful self-righteousness fades, and very possibly my father had changed his whole attitude toward child rearing by the time I came along. Another possibility is that his relationship with my mother improved over the years; when I knew them, my parents were affectionate and playful with each other. Apparently, that was not always the case.

When I told my older brother Mark about the painting, he acted real poised and said, "I didn't even know Dad still had it."

Hard to believe he could forget a painting worth a few hundred thousand dollars, but I didn't say anything.

When I called Sarah, next in line in our hierarchy, she screamed at me: "You lost it?! You lost the Léger!"

I replied, "It was right there all the time. And then it was gone. Someone stole it."

She shouted, "How could they steal it?! You were living in the house."

"I wasn't watching every minute. Someone could have walked in, just picked it off the wall and carried it off. If you'll remember, I was pretty depressed at the time and wasn't thinking about such things."

"Well you should have been thinking about them, because now you've really screwed things up! You should have put it in a vault, goddammit!"

Then I called Florence, number three in our line of descent. When I was a kid, I was close to her. She played baseball with me, took me to foreign films, taught me how to roller skate in Gramercy Park. She had been bright and daring, had had thick, dark hair, a quick smile, long and elegant hands. After my mother died, however, she hardly ever came to visit me and my father. Now, she considered herself the only intelligent member of our family—the scholar. She taught anthropology at Oberlin and spent her summers digging up Hittite tablets in Turkey. She had neither a lover nor husband—no children, no friends. Her conversations with me had grown more and more bitter over the years. She was like a never-ending winter whose days grow darker and colder with each coming year. Her particular brand of contempt for our father had mostly to do with him supposedly belittling her for pursuing an academic career. She hated me because

I didn't hate him. "That's just great," she told me when I informed her about the missing Léger. "Do you know how much money I make a year?"

"More than me, probably."

"Clever," she said. I could see her sneering. "I need that money," she continued. "We could've auctioned it and made a fortune. I was counting on it."

"So what do you want me to say?"

"You could start with you're sorry."

I let an angry silence spread between us to let her know that she had reached the limits of my patience. She understood, and she spoke more gently now, "Did they leave any clues?"

"None that I can find."

"So who could it be?"

"The only people who ever entered Dad's bedroom were me, you, Sarah, and Mark."

She suddenly shouted, "If you're making this up . . . if you've hidden it so you can sell it later, I'll kill you!"

"Florence, what the hell are you . . ."

She was screeching at the top of her lungs: "I swear I'll kill you, I'll cut out your heart, and I won't give it another thought."

That was the first time I thought that something might be seriously wrong with her.

The police came twice to my father's cottage to dust for fingerprints and interview me. Florence even insisted on hiring a private detective. We each chipped in $750. But the painting didn't turn up.

Till three weeks ago.

Meanwhile, by that time, we'd all stopped talking to each other. At first, Florence suspected me, Sarah suspected Mark, and Mark suspected Florence. It was like a bad imitation of Shakespearean comedy. Then things got really wild; Florence convinced the others that the villain could only have been me. After all, I was the only one who'd been at my father's cottage all the time. Hence, I had far more opportunity to take the painting and find a buyer. As for my motive, that was harder for her to concoct, since I had never been known to care particularly about earning more money than I made as a professor. But she managed to come up with one.

According to Florence, I needed the money to pay secret debts. Her diabolical reasoning went as follows:

1) I'd been promiscuous during the 1970s and had thereby caught AIDS.

2) I'd stolen the painting because I didn't want to admit that I had the disease and desperately needed to make hospital payments. Of course, I could have used my Barnard medical coverage, but I didn't want to confess my illness to administrators for fear of being ostracized, even fired. She claimed that she'd actually searched through my garbage and found huge bills from Roosevelt Hospital stamped overdue. Naturally, she said, I couldn't admit that I'd stolen the painting or even had such hospital bills because to admit either would be to virtually confess that I was tainted with plague.

I found all this out from Sarah's eldest daughter, Rachel, the only person in the family with the courage to call me up and ask if this scenario was true.

Thanks to Florence's creative storytelling, my three siblings have never talked to me again.

It has always been hard for me to believe that reasonably intelligent adults could behave like this, especially if they really thought that I had AIDS. But, as I found out, such things happen. Since 1984, I've never even received so much as a Christmas card or birthday call from any of them. And until three weeks ago, I really did believe that they bought Florence's story. I figured that they must have regarded it as an absolute miracle that I managed to live this long.

During kind moments, I used to say to myself that when Florence started these rumors everybody was in a panic about the new plague striking America. And my father had just died. None of us were behaving rationally.

Occasionally, however, I speculated that Florence had stolen the painting and had accused me to cover herself. But mostly, I didn't care. My father was dead. I had a tenured teaching job which fulfilled me, good health, and close friends. At a time when people really were starting to die in the long, drawn-out viral war that was just then beginning, these were the important things. As for the painting, I hoped that it had been sold to a museum where people could appreciate the nobility of the peasant girl with the obsidian hair. If I gave in to anger at times, it was only because I thought that the loss of the painting had somehow ripped out the very last page of my father's life story.

Then, just three weeks ago, I was attending a series of lectures on French twentieth-century figurative painting at the Serralves Foundation in Porto, Portugal. Martin Roland was there, the mural painter and professor of art history at McGill University. The title of his talk was "Léger, the Female Nude and Solitude." I didn't know what this meant exactly, but I liked the way it sounded. During his lecture, he showed slides to illustrate his theory that Léger's women were fundamentally more isolated than his men—that they inhabited what he called *espaces fermés*— closed spaces. Additionally, Roland suggested that such an attitude was fundamentally new; the Classic and Romantic attitudes being that women were far more in touch with the world—connected to the cycles of birth and death—than men. One of the slides illustrating Roland's thesis was of my father's painting. When I saw it, it was as if a loved one had risen from the grave. Frightened, confused, I thought: so is she still here? I realized then that I'd thought for many years that the young woman in the painting had died at the same moment as my father. Strange what the mind comes up with.

More importantly, I also realized that the young woman in the painting looked like my mother. How I could have missed this before is beyond me. Perhaps it was denial—a block produced by the trauma of losing her. Or maybe I needed to be older to see the subtle correspondence in their *attitudes* rather than their physical forms. There was no denying, however, that they had the same serene look in their eyes, the same inner elegance manifested in their graceful postures. Was this a coincidence? Or had Léger met my mother that night when he came to have his molar filled? Had he, too, recognized the similarity of attitude and offered the painting in tribute?

When Roland's lecture ended, I ran to him to ask about "The Woman with Stone Hair."

"I got the slide from the Fondation Maeght," he replied. "I suppose the painting must be there, but I've never actually seen it in person."

I called up the Fondation Maeght outside Nice and spoke to a helpful young woman who told me that the painting in question was owned by a private collector in Princeton, New Jersey. She was a miracle worker and called me back later the same day with his phone number and name—Carlo Ricci.

When I spoke to Mr. Ricci, he was friendly. Yes, he had the painting. It was hanging in his living room, over his couch. He remembered very well the circumstances under which he'd bought it. He voice was deep, his accent slightly British. He said, "At the time, I was collecting Léger, everything I could find. I was in love with his scope, his size. A dealer in Boston called me. Jensen . . . Richard Lloyd Jensen. Do you know him?"

"I'm afraid not."

"Well, he called me up one day, out of the blue, and he said he had a lovely portrait in the style of 'The Bather,' and that the people who owned it wanted to get rid of it quickly—that I could get it for a bargain price."

"Did he say who it was who was selling it?"

"Not that I recall."

"You wouldn't have Mr. Jensen's number, by any chance?"

"I have his gallery number. If you'll wait just a moment . . ."

But Ricci couldn't turn up the number; he'd stopped buying paintings years before and had moved on to antique cars. He said, "I began to lose patience when museums started exhibiting cement phone booths and calling them works of genius."

I managed to find Mr. Jensen the next day through a series of phone calls to the Fogg Art Museum in Cambridge and some gallery owners whom the curator recommended as having been in business in the Boston area for many years. A man named Levine with a gallery in the Back Bay area told me that Jensen was now retired, but still occasionally dealt in paintings. "His house is a treasure trove," he said.

When I got Jensen on the phone, I said, "Let me tell you a crazy story," and I proceeded to tell him about Léger's toothache and the history of the painting.

When I'd finished, he said, "I remember it very well. Personally, I didn't like it. But I knew Ricci, and I knew I could sell it."

"Do you remember the name of the person who offered it to you?"

"I'm afraid not," he replied. "Ten years is a long time. But I still have my files. If you'll hold on . . ." I waited twenty minutes on the line. Twice he came back to tell me, "Don't hang up, I'm coming closer," then, the third time, he said, "Got it . . . Mark Kumin and Sarah Halper."

"Both? You're sure?"

"It's right here in my own writing. They both signed the forms."

"And no one else?" Of course, I was thinking of my youngest sister Florence.

"No one."

"Do you have the date of their contract with you?"

"June seventeenth, nineteen eighty-seven."

So they'd hidden away the painting for three years before putting it on the market. "Do you mind telling me the price?"

"Oh, it was a bargain. Two hundred and seventy five thousand. Of course, they didn't keep it all. I got my commission."

After I hung up, I sat for a long time just thinking. For maybe a hundred thousand dollars each, Mark and Sarah had stolen our father's painting; been willing to let lies about me go unchallenged; and never spoken with me again. It didn't make much sense. And Florence? Had she been involved behind the scenes? I suspected so. She was clever enough to have developed the plan and found a way around actually signing anything.

I couldn't sleep that night. The sheets were icy, the bed too small. I put on long underwear, watched TV, and thought about the past as if I were searching for clues to a murder. At nine the next morning, I called Mr. Ricci back and asked if I could see the painting. He explained that he was an old man, seventy-seven, and was no longer in the habit of receiving guests. I said, "I'll come whenever you want and I'll only stay a moment." He simply sighed, so I added, "I'll pay you five hundred dollars just to stand in front of it for a minute."

"Oh dear, that won't be necessary," he answered in an apologetic tone. "How about tomorrow, say early afternoon?"

His granddaughter got on the phone to give me directions to his house. That night, I took a tranquilizer in order to sleep. In the morning, I rented a big American car and drove to Princeton. I'd never been there before. Ricci lived in a wealthy neighborhood with towering oaks and perfect lawns about a mile west of the university. His house was English Tudor. When I rang the bell, a young woman answered. She introduced herself as the granddaughter I'd spoken to. She was tiny, with short black hair. She wore jeans and a baggy woolen sweater. I thanked her for giving me directions. She smiled warmly and said, "My grandfather is in the living room."

I'm usually quite observant, but I couldn't say what the foyer looked like or how exactly we got to the living room. I suddenly couldn't seem to get my breath, and I was worried that I was going to faint. All I remember are my feet pounding on a wooden floor for the longest time. Then I saw Ricci seated in a wheelchair at the center of a large, brightly lit room. He was bald and shrunken. A blue blanket was draped over his shoulders. He was holding my father's Léger in his skeletal hands. He smiled, and I remember his teeth were too large. He asked, "Is this the painting, Professor Kumin?"

I nodded.

Objects must soak up memory and become aligned to certain events; looking at the Léger, I was overwhelmed with the feeling of being in my mother's presence. It was as if we were about to play a game of rummy on her bed.

The connection, of course, was loss. My mother had disappeared from my life when I was thirteen; "The Woman with Stone Hair" was stolen some thirty years later. Below my consciousness, apparently, there had always been the connection of never understanding such irreversible separations.

It was then, too, that I understood why the painting meant so very much to my father, and why I'd discovered him once sleeping with it on his lap; for him, the memory of my mother must have soaked into every brushstroke.

"Professor Kumin, is it the same painting?" Ricci suddenly repeated.

"Yes, that's it."

"Would you like to take a closer look?"

When he held it out to me, a hollow ache opened in my gut. I wanted to run my finger over her hair. I wanted to cry. "No, thank you," I whispered. "I think I should be going." I turned and rushed past Ricci's granddaughter out of the living room. I ran to my car. I cursed myself for having visited.

At home I went through old photographs of my parents. I kept looking at my mother as if there were a mark I needed to find—later, I figured I was looking for the first sign of her cancer. Then I had this overwhelming urge to see her grave. I felt like a character

in some feverish detective novel. But I couldn't help myself. So I
drove out to Roslyn and found the Mt. Sinai cemetery. It was past
closing time. The sun was setting, and the gates were locked. But
the brick wall around the cemetery was only four feet high. I
climbed over, found tailored lawns, pink azalea bushes, and neat
rows of white marble. I rushed around like a trespasser till I found
my parents' graves. It took less time than I thought, maybe a half
hour. By then, dusk had veiled everything with gray.

Isadore Kumin, January 12, 1903–June 18,1984
Gnendl Rosencrantz Kumin, December 4, 1906–June 6, 1954

I gathered pebbles and put them on their headstones and kept
putting them there till there was no space left for anything. Then
I put some more stones in my coat pockets till they felt heavy
enough for me to leave.

When I got home, I typed notes to each of my three siblings consisting of only one line: "I know now for sure that you stole Dad's
painting."

It seemed important to let them know that I had found out
about their treachery.

Florence was the only one to write me back. She sent a typed,
single-spaced, seventeen-page letter. She wrote about all the bad
things my father and I had ever done to her. Everything was distorted, and a lot of incidents were totally invented. *How you and
Dad abandoned me after Mom's death . . . The time you told the principal
of the school that your older sister was a whore . . . When you belittled me
for having an abortion when you knew I had no way of raising a baby. . . .*

In reading her accusations, however, I learned why she, Mark,
and Sarah had stolen the Léger. She said that when she was in
high school, she'd pleaded with our mother to leave our father
and divorce him. *Mom was so good and kind, you weren't old enough to
know. And Dad was evil, a secret man of silent plans whose very presence
was toxic. . . .* When Florence's effort failed, and when our mother
died, she realized that she couldn't bear to see our father keep
"The Woman with Stone Hair." *We had to get the portrait of Mom
away from him. He had her in life, but would never keep her in death. I*

had to make sure of that. And we knew you wouldn't agree, so we never
told you. . . .

Florence's style was garbled, but perversely methodical; wild, ser-
pentine sentences snaked through a hundred different accusations in chronological order. Eleven times she told me that I was a
"queer without balls" and that if I had had any courage I would
have admitted years ago that I'd done everything I could to ruin
her life.

I had the feeling that she typed the letter with a hammer in
each hand.

When I was growing up, I always thought that as an adult I'd be
friends with my siblings, particularly Florence. I also thought that
as we age we must each inevitably grow more accepting of our parents and their failings. The complete destruction of these illusions has given me insomnia for the last two weeks. It usually be-
gins with a dream of Florence trapped in one of Léger's *espaces*
fermés, trying desperately and unsuccessfully to break through the
thick black border around her by slashing at it with a knife. In the
early morning, sitting up in bed, frigid with fear, I remember her
predicament. I begin thinking that she's going to break into my
apartment while I'm teaching and steal both my mother's painting of the finch with my eyes and my father's children's stories. I
suppose it's crazy, but workmen are coming over in the morning
to install a security system.

Beneath
the
Planet
of the
Compulsives

EITAN ALEXANDER

*I have never made but one prayer to God, a very short one: "O Lord,
make my enemies ridiculous." And God granted it.*

—Voltaire

I have this problem. And one of the things I'm doing about it is
going to these meetings. I'm in this program called Coitus and
Anal Compulsive Addicts Anonymous. That makes the acronym
for it C.A.A.C.A.A. At first, I never even used to mention that
name to anyone outside of the group. It doesn't bother me that
much anymore. Still, some people in the program are really hyper
about the "anonymous" part, so don't tell anyone else about this.

I guess it would help if I gave you some background on what
C.A.A.C.A.A. is all about. Basically, it's a program to get you sober.
Not from drugs, at least, not from what most people think of as
drugs, like alcohol, cocaine, or heroin. It's for people who are
addicted to sex or love. Or drama. Until recently, if I was with
another homosexual, it was mostly stuff like jacking off in a car or
a blowjob in a porno booth or getting reamed, bent over a trash
can in an alley. It's hard to break the habits you develop as a child.
About three years ago, I got arrested by an undercover transit
cop. The big ape came on to me in an empty Metro Line car at
3 A.M. It was either jail time or a fine, community service, and
mandatory attendance at a twelve-step group for sexual recovery.
There are actually a lot of different programs that deal with this
issue, but I picked C.A.A.C.A.A. because it's almost all gay men

that are involved with it and that's a big part of my problem. Being involved with gay men. I fulfilled my debt to society after a year, but I'm still showing up.

At some meetings we read from *Redemption and Healing*; it's the main piece of literature for the group. We pick a chapter, then one person reads the first paragraph and passes it to the person on his left, who has to stop squirming in his metal folding chair long enough to read it before passing it on again. After the chapter is finished, we discuss it. It's kind of like bible study, although it's not supposed to be religous at all, it's supposed to be "spiritual." But all the references to God and prayer make that a little difficult to figure out. Some people in the program still haven't, or don't want to.

Like this guy from the program that I dated once. C.A.A.C.A.A. doesn't encourage dating between members, but it's acceptable if you've been in the program for a while; you're just supposed to discuss it reasonably first. His idea of a date turned out to be a service at this "nondenominational" church. It wasn't an ideal first date, but it was okay. There was an incredible choir. I was really enjoying them and then they got to a song where they had choreographed these little movements. The choir was singing about new beginnings. Every time they sang about the sunrise in the chorus, they raised their arms in big circles above their heads and when they sang about turning your life around, they made a 360-degree turn where they were standing, holding their arms up and wiggling their fingers. It reminded me of a third-grade recital. I said so to my date while we were swaying back and forth and clapping and he smiled back at me.

After the service we went for a walk on the beach. I saw some people I knew and made introductions. My date told them about the church service, all teeth and enthusiasm. While he talked, my friends kept on turning to me and squinting. When he started talking about the choir, I kind of nudged him with my elbow and imitated the choir's choreography, making a little circular trail in the sand. My friends giggled a little. The guy I was with turned around and walked away.

So I spent the rest of the day with my friends. One of them had just bought the complete collection of "The Simpsons" on disc. We were all laughing as we talked about our favorite episodes and moments. I gave my flawless vocal impersonation of Grandpa

Simpson after the minimum of prodding. Then I told everyone the details of my afternoon and we laughed some more.

The next night I was at a meeting; my church date came in late and almost immediately shared about the whole incident, no names mentioned, and thanked God for letting him love himself enough to take care of himself and set boundaries. I still see him at almost every meeting I go to. Expecially at the study meetings, the ones where we read from *Redemption and Healing*.

It's this study meeting that I went to a short while ago that I want to tell you about. It was pretty crowded. I got there in time to grab the last available seat. The chairs were arranged in concentric circles, and there was an empty one in the small circle in the middle. Sitting across from me was this guy that I've never seen in the group before. Another ape. I'm no specist, but I know the correct term is Simian-American. It's just that this monkey was really fine, a lot better looking than that cop on the bus. I started looking around the room, I didn't want to just sit there and gape at him. In the meetings, guys will share about how they sexualize the other men that are in the room with them. They're always thanked for their honesty afterward, but you don't want to be caught in the act. Besides, I didn't want to make my monkey uncomfortable. He was the only simian in the room. I saw some familiar faces and nodded hello. I didn't see my church date anywhere. Wherever I looked though, my eyes always came back to that ape.

He was big. Huge really, he obviously spent a lot of time at the gym. You know how those guys get once they start pumping iron, they look like superheroes. I can't believe people ever thought they could impose some sort of control over that. I remember the pictures I would load down from the Grid when I was about ten. Shots of street arrests, three or four cops hauling off a domestic, usually a chimp or an orang, some scattered groceries or dry cleaning on the ground. If Animal Control had cornered a worker, an ape or a gorilla, there was usually a dozen or more officers circled around them, pointing their stun rods toward the center. I didn't realize until later, after I had seen the documentaries they made for Public Mandate Videolink, that the simians always had their mouths closed. You can see it in all the pictures. Their lips are pressed tight and drawn to their ears from clenching their teeth. They had decided in their underground meetings not to make any noise if they were arrested. They thought sapiens would think of them as wild animals if they heard them yelling or screeching. I guess they were right, some people still do. There were also pictures of the camps: chimps, apes, baboons mixed into small barracks and warehouses. The government thought they would kill each other off if they crammed all the different species together. The riot shots were my favorites. I printed up hard copies of the ones where they were using high-pressure hoses for crowd control. All those wet hairy bodies, I used to lock the door to the bathroom and masturbate to them. I finally burned those pictures, to commemorate one of the times when I had thirty days of sexual sobriety.

The ape sitting across from me was wearing a really tight white T-shirt and I could see how incredibly defined his abs were. You know, a lot of simians do those stomach exercises, mostly to straighten their spines. That's why in all those infomercials for home ab machines and tapes, there's always a bunch of chimps and apes in the audience standing up and testifying about their posture. Well, this guy's spine was as straight as it can get for a monkey. It almost negated his neanderthal hunch. Almost, but not quite. He had on a pair of gray sweat shorts and some white Converse high tops. They must've been about size nineteen.

The meeting began and after some announcements, this guy a couple of seats to my left started reading the chapter. He was hunched over, his right elbow on his right knee, the fist of that arm supporting his chin. He held the copy of *Redemption and Healing* open in his left palm, resting on the other knee. He looked like Rodin's Thinker and when he read the text, he made it sound like he was seeing it for the first time, even though I'd seen him in meetings since I started coming three years ago.

Some of us did not want to believe in God, in fact, some of us still don't. And that's all right, this program is open to all who have a desire to be cured of their compulsion. If, for example, a newcomer is firm in his faith of science and can not see how God or a higher power can fit in the plan, we can offer him a scientific approach. We can show him that C.A.A.C.A.A. evidenced prodigous results. In the recovery equation then, the newcomer could then substitute the group itself for the higher power. How often have we heard, perhaps from ourselves

even, 'But that's so easy, will that really work?' 'Yes,' we can answer. 'It can, and it has. . . .'

It was the chapter about accepting your higher power. Not only
is this chapter as boring as the rest of the book, it's the longest
one. It's not that I don't appreciate the recovery I've gained since
I've been in these rooms. Since I'm not jacking off and cruising so
much anymore, I have a lot more free time on my hands and
more stuff to fill it with. Like hiking and writing and holding
down a job, things you can't get arrested for. But it doesn't make
this stuff any more palatable. I couldn't be bothered to concen-
trate on the text, and I was already really distracted by the monkey
sitting across from me. I didn't want to spent the meeting obsess-
ing on the ape; then again, I wouldn't have been in that room if
that sort of thing was within my control, or better yet, not even an
issue in the first place.

One topic that the guys in the program always talk about are
the sexual thoughts that constantly fill their minds, triggered by a
look, a movement, a drop in the humidity level. Among the confessions of sexual thought crimes, there's a lot of talk about how
fast they fall in love. I think I've heard the phrase "I was already
picking out china patterns" in the last three years more than I
heard "What are you into?" in the fifteen before that. But I've
never heard anyone mention one of the things I fantasize about.
If I'm fiending on someone, I start imagining that I'm at their funeral, that I'm the bereaved lover. So, at this meeting I was creating this scenario where I'm sitting graveside watching the large
ebony casket containing my beloved monkey's remains being lowered into the ground. They usually die a few years after I meet
them too, so they still look the same. I see myself sitting rigid and
silent, wet eyes concealed behind tortoise-shell Vuarnets. My
grieving friends surround me. They clasp my hand, squeeze my
shoulder. And even within my fantasy, I'm reminiscing. Remembering the sensation of his leathery ape lips pressed against mine,
he was such a good hard kisser. Remembering the way he would
pick at his fur while we were watching TV, he would never do that
when other people were around. Even with all his talk about moving beyond tolerance to appreciation, he was so vigilant about fitting in, but I understood. How he loved to fuck in the shower and

he knew the taste of his freshly scrubbed monkey asshole drove me wild.

I stopped daydreaming when the book was finally passed to my ape. He started reading.

> Some of us believed in God once. We may have lost our faith for many reasons. We may have been disgusted by the acts we witnessed 'religous' people committing like hypocrisy or bigotry. We could quote the numbers of people killed in the name of "God" and supply you with the dates. But to the disenchanted we can say, 'We too felt superior, but God is God, no matter who prays to him. . . .'

What I noticed most of all was that every time he said God or religion, his top lip would turn up at the left. It was the beginning of that feral snarl that I can't imagine being supressed by any amount of socialization. Right at that moment I knew, my monkey was an atheist.

It's one of the central issues of the simian value system. Mostly I learned about it from TV. When I was a little kid there was this thing on Sean Lennon's talk show, "Simians—Saviour vs. Science." And there was the Cody Gifford special for Public Mandate, "God, Darwin, and the Species Next Door." It's a real touchy subject for most monkeys, what with all the churches treating them as everything from devil's spawn to ignorant savages in need of salvation.

I guess my obsession about simians has made me a little more knowledgable about them than the majority of sapiens, but I hardly knew any until a few years ago. One night some of us were downtown looking for this new club but we didn't have the address. We saw a couple of gorillas assuming that familiar bouncer stance outside an unmarked door. At the time, the latest clubs were just starting to use simians for doormen and bouncers, so we thought we were at the right place. It turned out to be the Monkey Bar. It was pretty underground then, even apes hardly knew about it. And sapiens, forget it. They weren't going to let us in at first but there was this chimp working the door and he said it was okay. It turned out he was totally queer. Some of the monkey population was just starting to get really retro about the homo thing; it looked like it was going to get nasty and I think he was just surrounding himself with comrades. I realized I'd never seen simians socialize away from sapien influence. Most of the younger simians were fed up with the "tame yourself" attitude of their parents. That club was wild and it was loud. We had a blast, though honestly I was really intimidated at first. Later that night, me and the chimp that had let us in, we had gotten really drunk and were dancing together and that's when he told me about Hollywood Jungle.

Hollywood Jungle is kind of an infamous bathhouse. And the thing it's infamous for is that it caters to the inter-species crowd. Back then, it had just opened up. Sometimes I tell the story like I went there on some multicultural sexual goodwill mission. But by that time I was already hitting the baths whenever I could get away from my job or my friends.

I was at the Hollywood Jungle the night after the Monkey Bar. The first thing that blew me away about the place was how it looked inside. I've been to a lot of baths and sex clubs and at the best they were kind of industrial and depressing. They always make them look like a warehouse or an abandoned building. I've had sex in warehouses and abandoned buildings. There's no cover charge. This place looked organic, all curved and layered.

I was standing there taking in the architecture and this big chimpanzee came up and started talking to me, you know, "I haven't seen you here before," the usual. He offered to show me around and when we got to this one room on the top level, I followed him inside and he shut the door behind him and he started handling me and kissing me. Pretty soon we were down on the ground and he started nailing me. My first monkey. After a couple of strokes, he started howling and his whole body started shaking like a clothes dryer with a pair of sneakers inside.

When I've talked to other recovering addicts a lot of them have said that the most potent drug for them was adrenaline. I know it's true for me. I would get most excited when the hunt was on, when I was at a bar and it looked like someone was going to come on to me, my heart would pound and my whole body would tingle. Nothing else mattered then, I felt so focused, kind of hyper-aware. It was the same if someone was skulking around the door to my room in a bathhouse or following me around in a park. But when we got to the sex, after a while I'd have to really work my imagination to keep up that level of intoxication. Usually I'd just make some lame excuse, if that, to get away and start looking for it again. But monkey sex is different. The noise and the physical frenzy, it's kind of unpredictable. From what I've seen, sex is one of two things that makes simians totally lose control. And I know all about being out of control, which I guess brings me back to the meeting.

When my monkey turned to the person on the left to pass the book, I could see that my boundary-setting church date was sitting right behind him. Up until then the huge form of the simian had completely blocked him from my view. But when I saw him sitting back in the second row, with his eyes closed and a half smile on his face, I got this idea.

While the next few people read, I kept my face toward the floor, but I rolled my eyes up as far as I could so I could see the bottom half of my monkey's head. Every time one of the readers would mention God or faith or a higher power, his lip would curl and quiver. I just waited for the copy of *Redemption and Healing* to be passed to me.

When the person on my right was finished, I looked up at him, smiled, took the book, put it in my lap, and bowed my head toward the text.

Some of us came to the program with our faith still intact. But we were confused, frustrated, because we didn't know how our compulsion and addictions fit into God's plan for us. Why wasn't our higher power helping us, giving us some sign? But it wasn't faith in God that was the problem, it was our approach to it, the quality and the honesty of it. . . .

That part I read as it was written in the book in front of me. But some of what I was about to say next wasn't in *Redemption and Healing*. I had thought of it while I was watching my monkey man's mouth, rehearsed it silently while the last few people had read. I was a little worried that I wouldn't be able to make it sound enough like the original text. There were a few people there that night who I was pretty sure would know the chapter almost verbatim. And there's a tradition in the program that if someone speaking during a meeting says anything inappropriate, something too suggestive sexually or something that disrupts the format of the meeting, that you can knock, on a chair or a wall or a table, to alert them, and anyone else who didn't catch it, to their transgression. I didn't think what I was going to say would take long enough for one of them to react if they wanted to, but you never know.

> We were just waiting, often inactive, other than the activity spurred by our compulsions, waiting for Redemption to find us. It could have been right outside our door . . .

I rolled my eyes up again so I could see my ape. I was wishing I could see my church date too. I wanted to see if he still had that contented grin on his face.

> We wouldn't have noticed it even if Jesus Christ himself came to our door, held out three nails in his hand and said . . .

And then I broke out my trusty Grandpa Simpson voice.

'Hey, can you put me up for the night?'

I stopped talking and there was a moment of silence. Then the ape started cracking up. I'm not sure, maybe he'd had a real stressful day. Maybe he was a big "Simpsons" fan. Or maybe he actually thought that old joke was really funny. Whatever the reason, he started laughing. At first it was that startled bark that just flies out of you when you're not expecting something funny. I remember thinking "Perfect!" because that was exactly what I was hoping for. I was already imagining that during the break he would come over to speak to me, we would get along so well we might even skip the rest of the meeting and go out for coffee or a walk. But I had forgotten one thing. That besides sex, the other thing simians have trouble keeping under control is laughter.

All of a sudden my ape doubled over and shook silently for a second or two. Then he snapped upright in his chair, threw back his head, and started howling. Tears were streaming from his eyes and his mouth was pointed at the ceiling and it just kept on snapping open and those screeches kept on coming out of it. The other guys in the room, a lot of them had been at least chuckling before, now they were all just staring at my monkey. Most of them had this look on their face like they were in a zoo or at a circus. I should have known better. A lot of people haven't been around this before. I just forgot, that's all. And the ape, he was still laughing. It seemed like a long time before he stopped screeching. Before his body stopped shaking and jerking. By then most of the other guys had stopped staring at him, they were just staring at the floor. I was still smiling, even though I didn't much feel like it. I just didn't want him to think I thought he was some freak.

When the ape noticed everyone staring at the floor, he tried to keep the rest of the laughter inside and nearly choked in the process. He looked at me for a second and then bent forward to rest his head between his hands. I caught sight of my church date then. He looked at me briefly too, and then closed his eyes and turned his head to the floor, shaking it slowly from side to side. I looked away as he started to put the palms of his hands together as if in prayer.

I didn't know what else to do, so I started to reread the paragraph as written. When I finished I passed the book to the guy on my left and I looked at that beautiful monkey. He was staring at the floor just like everyone else and I watched his chest heave up and down as he tried to control his breathing. The skin under his eyes was really damp and I wasn't sure it was all from his laughing fit anymore. So I looked at the floor too, but no matter what part of it I focused on, I could always see that big pair of Converse high tops. I gave up and let them fill my vision, until the spaces between the treads of the soles were big enough for at least one metal folding chair and a large ebony casket.

Say Goodbye
to Middletown

WILLIAM J. MANN

His hands, as I remember them, were like the twisted apples left on the trees after the apple pickers were through.

Not like the hands of the boys I'm watching now: soft hands, smooth, cupping each other's hard pink butts. They don't know I'm watching them. They think they're hidden, but they're wrong. I'm sitting in my car, pretending to be asleep. They think the bushes around the cold asphalt lot protect them from being seen. But they're wrong.

It's their hands that fascinate me: hands so unlike the ones I have come here to find, hands that remain forever twisted in my mind. They are the hands of the man who first loved me, who I rewarded for a such a gift with a stretch in jail, simply for teaching me the secret of the apples left behind on the trees. I can see the orchards now, finally, after driving the last three hours, leaving the city before the sun was up, eager to get here while it was still morning. Now, here at the rest stop on Eagle Hill just outside of town, my contemplation of the orchards and the town they embrace has been disturbed by the sight of two boys fucking each other, with all the vitality I once had in this place, except my passion had been met not by a boy my own age, but by a man, many times older than I.

I reach into my jeans with some difficulty. The steering wheel is cumbersome to get around, but I manage. I touch myself just as the older boy drops to his knees and takes the younger one into his mouth. They are beautiful. The older one, on his knees, is dark and thin. The younger one, with his head thrown back and his eyes now closed against the cold sky, is fair and stocky. There is nothing about them that reminds me of the boys of New York: no goatees or sleeveless flannel shirts, no clunky Doc Marten boots, no black leather jackets with crack-and-peel slogans accusing the government of having blood on its hands. No, these are the boys of Middletown, simple boys, the milk under the cream, not the ones who will be siphoned off, stolen by the lure of the city. These are the sons of the boys I once knew, the sons of their experience if not of their flesh, boys who remained in the place where I was born long after I had left it—and them—behind.

We are the only ones here, these boys and I. They lurk behind a cluster of wild rosebushes, stubborn orange leaves shielding them from the lot. But not from me. The younger boy now grabs his partner's hair, fucking his face. I stroke myself, watching the scene, like a porno film with the volume turned down, the way I usually have it. But this is even better: this is an unexpected welcome home.

"Yes," I whisper, watching them. "That's the way."

I hear the younger boy moan, even at this distance. I moan too.

The younger boy comes, and I notice with a queer mix of unease and envy that he does not pull out, that the older boy eagerly drinks what has been offered. There is no hesitation, no negotiation. The boy merely comes, the other swallows, and then they stumble out from the bushes, pulling on their jeans and their sweatshirts, mounting their respective bicycles and pedaling away with as much energy as they have just fucked, in opposite directions, of course.

I come into my hand, a sorry excuse for a climax, frothy semen bubbling over my fingers.

I take time to breathe. The air is sharp in my nostrils, sharp and cold, sharp and clear, sharp and blue, very blue, the hard blue of a cloudless sky. I look out over the orchards, barren of fruit. It's past time, and the leaves on the trees are red-tinged gold. The ground is becoming hard. I take a deep breath and exhale slowly, thinking about the trees. The apples have been packed into crates and shipped into stores, baked into pies and dropped into lunch bags. All gone, except for the few twisted ones left rejected on the branches, tiny deformed apples that cling desperately to the cold limbs, ugly little children who have aged too quickly, abandoned by their too-beautiful brethren, picked over and left to rot.

But that is not the whole story of the twisted apples. Below me is Middletown, and I look down at it like a map memorized: I know these streets which crosshatch through the meadow, ending by the river. I know who walks them, who comes out by day and who by night. When I lived here, back in another time, I knew everything there was to know about this town. I would listen to my mother standing at the clothesline, sharing the gossip with the lady who lived next door. I stayed after school to hear the secretaries in the office trade stories about the nuns and the priests. I listened to the clerks at Britta's Grocery, to the waitresses behind the counter at Henry's Diner, to the old men who sat out on the steps of the post office. I listened, and watched. Watched old Mr. Smoke steal a pack of cigarettes at South End News. Watched Ann Marie Adorno make out with Phillip Stueckel in the choir loft. Watched Eddie Piatrowski's father beat off in his basement to a greasy pile of *Penthouse* magazines. Watched Miss Aletha take off her wig when she thought she was alone. Watched, without ever being seen, without ever being heard.

In the town where I grew up, the factories still stand: big old husks of brick and steel and journeymen's ghosts. I stand now at the edge of Eagle Hill, where I doubt an eagle has roosted for more than a hundred years, and gaze out over the valley at the ruined castles below. They have decayed ignobly for decades, many of them since before I was born. I once played among those ruins: a King—more often a Queen—a knight, a mad monk, the hunchback of Notre Dame. "Stay out of those places," my mother scolded, but what child ever paid his mother any mind when the iron claws of a rusting factory awaited his imagination?

My father, many years before, had worked in one of my castles: as a young man, as a young husband, before he finally moved on to better things, like selling shoes—before the factories themselves moved on, leaving the town behind. "Middletown was once a thriving place," the old-timers in front of the post office would say, "till the factories shut down." As a boy I'd listen to them, not comprehending their melancholy.

For as a boy, what was there to be sorrowful for? For grand adventures in ruined palaces? For long and twisting walks along daisy-covered railroad tracks, for discovering forgotten tunnels and

the occasional overturned caboose? For the tall, ivy-covered spires
of the university, where I would climb and peer out of the green
stained-glass windows, imagining myself to be Rapunzel, trying to
follow the river all the way past the great bend? Then the watch-
man would arrive, shouting after me to get out, barking at me that
townies weren't allowed up here. I'd run out as fast as I could,
back to my own castles, where no one dared to chase me away.

They've boarded up the factories now, I can see, even from way
up here on Eagle Hill: posted signs to keep out. Those who dare
to enter are no longer boys or imagined queens, but rather hard-
eyed addicts with maps of the world etched upon their faces—
men who, like my father, may have once worked in these ruined
places in days gone by. Today, the children of Middletown do not
venture into the crumbling fortresses of my youth; the moat has
gone dry and the drawbridge has rotted into pulp. The sadness is
now—even to children, I suspect—palpable.

It was in such a place that I first had sex with Alexander Reefy.

He is the man I have come back to see, the man who first
touched my trembling skin, the man whose life I ruined and who
I sent to jail. He is the man whose hands live on so strongly in my
memory, hands that first touched the pink buds of my nipples,
hands that stroked my hair and spanked my innocent butt.

It is the morning of Halloween, his favorite holiday. I remember when he dressed as Marilyn and it shocked me. It was the first
time I'd seen a man in drag. Now, twenty years later, I remember
that night, the party and the costumes, the Richard Nixon masks
and the man who came dressed as H. R. Pufnstuf, and how after
everyone had gone home, Alexander Reefy took me up into the
night-blackened orchard and taught me the secret of the twisted
apples left behind on the trees.

Gnarled apples like his hands. Knuckles like tumors. On my
skin. Big hands. Rough hands. Soft, baby skin. His hands, and
then his breath, hot and smoky, against my face.

He fucked me in the factory behind St. John the Baptist, on
the edge of Dog Town, where he lived in a two-floor brick house
with a wooden front porch. "Don't go down there," my mother
had warned me. "That's the bad part of town." And it was, indeed:
beyond the crumbling factories the old tenant housing remained,
housing built by rich WASP factory owners for their immigrant

workers at the turn of the last century. Houses built over swamps, where the river swelled its banks twice every spring, where skunk cabbage grew plentiful and tall, where velvety cat-o'-nine-tails enticed children to wade across the muddy, stinking water that licked the edges of the tenements. "Don't go down there," my mother had pleaded, but although I listened intently to every conversation dropped in line at Grant's department store, I had long since stopped listening to her.

When I was a boy, the immigrants had moved on from Dog Town: the Irish and the Poles and the Italians lived in Middletown proper, as proper Middletonians. When I was a boy, Dog Town consisted of the blacks and the perverts, those strange, leftover hippies in VW vans and patchwork-covered, bell-bottom jeans. "Don't go down there," my mother warned, time and again. But I turned a brazen shoulder to her pleas, hopping upon my bicycle—the very cool 1974 banana bike with the long shiny purple seat, the newfangled handlebars and the tall silver bar behind my back—and pedaled with every ounce of strength I had all the way from our quiet little subdivision into the swamps of Dog Town.

"Todd," she says now, her arms outstretched, welcoming me home.

Not my mother. My mother still lives in her quiet little subdivision, in the same house where I grew up all too quickly—that is, until the summer I turned fifteen, when I left my mother's house forever and came here, to Elsa.

"Todd," she says again, encircling me.

How old she has gotten. How unlike my memories. But it is her, just the same: Elsa, the woman who took me in, who set me right, whose roses every year win first place in the Middletown Flower Show. Or at least, used to. I do not know if she still competes. We exchange cards maybe once, twice a year. After I first went away, she would come and visit. She came to my college dorm room once. We had a party. We got her high. But I haven't seen her in seven years. She knows little about my life today. As little as I know of hers.

"Elsa." I look down into her soft blue eyes. How strange it feels to be taller than she is.

A teakettle whistles. "Join me?" she asks.

I nod. Her kitchen, unlike her, is exactly as I remember: cluttered and odoriferous, with a tanginess underneath, as if something in the refrigerator has gone bad. But it's not an unpleasant smell: the candied scent of overripe fruit or the tempting promise of old wine.

She pours me some tea and we sit at the table overlooking her yard. A few roses, a deep red-purple, cling to the vines along the trellis. I point this out to her.

"Yes," she says, smiling. "Some of them last this long. But tonight there will be a frost." She sips her tea.

"Will you bring them inside?" I ask.

"I can't save them all," she says.

One of her cats rubs against my ankles. I reach down to stroke it.

"Your letter came as quite a surprise," she says to me.

"I'm sure it did."

"You don't even know if he will want to see you."

"No," I admit. "I don't."

"I was sorry to hear that your lover died," she said.

I look back out the window, at the purple rose on the vine trembling against the cold wind.

"Had you been together long?" Elsa asks.

"Just a year," I tell her. A year of many dreams. I turn my eyes to her. "Do you know I turned thirty-three this year?"

She smiles. "A babe."

I smile back. "Thirty-three. Christ's age when he was crucified."

She shakes her head. "Since when did you become religious?"

"I'm not. It's just a strange age, that's all. I remember the nuns talking about it, at Saint John the Baptist. As if it were magical or something. The double threes. The Holy Trinity." I smile. "There are a lot of threes in Christianity."

She shrugs. "I don't believe in symbolism."

"And I asked myself: what has my life been like in thirty-three years? What have I done, compared to Christ?"

Elsa gives me a stern look. Even with her pure white hair and thousands of wrinkles, it is still the same look she gave me all those years ago—a look much more serious than any my own mother ever gave me, a look that said: "You are being foolish but I love you anyway." I receive that look for what it is, and I smile.

Elsa lives on Oak Avenue, in a great old Victorian house that was her grandmother's. It's in an old part of town, just up from Main Street, and some of the houses are not as well cared for as Elsa's. Many of them are now subdivided into two, three, or even four apartments. University kids mostly and a scattering of black families, taking their first halting steps out of Dog Town. Elsa's been here as long as most folks can remember, and for just as long, everyone has known that she's a lesbian. She's been harassed—not often, but sometimes cruelly: it comes and goes in waves. Right now it's quiet. She thinks maybe she's getting too old for people to care anymore.

"You think thirty-three is an age to be reckoned with," she says to me now. "I'll be seventy next year."

Elsa at seventy. It boggles. Seventy used to seem so old to me. So did thirty-three. But being with Elsa, despite the wrinkles and white hair, is the same as it ever was, sitting here across from her, just as I did years ago, telling her my dreams. "Elsa," I say, "it feels good to be here."

She smiles. "I'm glad."

"I didn't know how I'd feel," I admit. "Coming back here . . ."

". . . is difficult," she says, finishing my sentence. "But you'll write about it?"

I shrug. Perhaps she assumes that is why I've come back. To be sure, it would make a great piece. *Boy returns to face the man he accused of rape.* But I'm a news reporter. I don't do features. I deal with facts. And there are no facts to explain why I have returned.

"Do you still work with the kids?" I ask.

"Sometimes. There's a center now. The Community Health Collective. There's a regular Friday night gathering."

I'm surprised. "For queer kids?"

"That's what you call them now," she says. It's a statement. Nothing else. "There are about six or seven every Friday night."

"That's so hard to imagine. *Here.* If only—"

"Yes," she says, understanding. "If only there had been such a thing for you." She laughs. "Or can you imagine for me? You didn't have it easy, but think about me. Forty years before you came along, needing help."

"But how much had really changed between your time and mine?" I ask. "In nineteen seventy-six, as compared to anytime before? How much was really different for me? Who had heard of Stonewall in Middletown?" I've thought about this a great deal, working as a reporter for a New York alternative weekly. I've written about it, in fact: interviewing a dozen New York transplants from places like Mount Pleasant, Michigan, and Wilming-

ton, Delaware. Stonewall came to the provinces much later than it
did to the big cities. "Strange how it seems sometimes that mine
was the last generation, the last of a long line of invisibles, that I
have more in common with you than I do with these kids who
gather every Friday night, even though forty years separates you
and I and less than fifteen stands between me and those babies."

"You could be right." She pours me some more tea. "But we're
still invisible here."

"That's not so. There's a center, there's a room, there are pink
triangles on pick-up trucks, I saw two as I drove down Main
Street—"

Elsa shakes her head. "I'm talking about *us*. Not the children.
Hurray for the children, and God save them all. But who will
teach them? Who is left? There is me, an old lesbian grandmother, and a handful of sick old queens."

I understand. "So they will leave. The kids. In their time."

"As they all do. As you did."

"But I had to."

"Yes," she says. "I suppose you did." She stands up, shifting on
tender joints to find some balance, and opens her old refrigerator. "Do you still like cheese sandwiches?"

"Sure," I tell her.

She makes me lunch. How often I once sat here, especially in
the beginning, sat right here at this table, watching her there, at
the counter, preparing a meal, not wanting to ever leave this
warm, fragrant kitchen.

"So who's died?" I finally ask.

"All of them," she says.

"All?" I ask.

"All of those you'd remember." There's a pause, very slight.
"Except him, of course."

Her back is facing me as she makes the sandwiches. "Do you
see him often?" I ask.

"No," she says. "Nobody does."

"He doesn't ever come to the center—?"

She turns to face me, as if I had just said something completely
absurd. And maybe I have. "No," she says, turning back to the
cheese. "He has never come down to the center. Not since he
started it."

"He—?"

"Yes," she says. "It was him."

"Even after he'd been in jail? He came back, and still was involved?"

"As much as they'd let him."

I ask her what she means.

"He spent a year in prison, but that's not what was really so bad," she says. She opens the refrigerator, pours me a glass of orange soda. "It was afterward. You know, things started happening here in Middletown after you left. Some of us tried to put together a community center. And we got a political group going. Did you know we got a civil rights bill passed in the state?"

"Yes," I say.

She places the sandwich and the soda in front of me. "We did some good things. But then ten years ago somebody came along, some do-gooder from down from the state capital, and he says that it's not a real good idea to have a convicted child molester playing such a public role. Bad for the image. The *community*, he said. Think of the *community*."

I look up at her.

"Do you want a pickle with that?" she asks.

"No," I say. "Tell me. What did Zandy say? How did he respond?"

"I'll always remember it. He stood up at the meeting, the very first one we had at the community center. 'Child molester?' he said. 'Is that what I am?' And Miss Aletha, God bless her old heart, she stood up and said, 'Well, I guess you don't think drag queens should be part of this community either?' And the do-gooder got all flustered and said, 'Oh, drag queens are okay. You know, Stonewall and all—'"

"Miss Aletha was always ready to stand up and be—"

"But he won, the bastard." Elsa turns away, back to the sink. "They voted to expel him from the board. Only Miss Aletha and I voted in favor of keeping him."

I'm quiet for a long time, watching the day get colder outside her window. I can tell the temperature is dropping: the purple roses shiver on their vine, and big gray clouds now obscure the sharpness of the blue sky. I decide I want to walk to his house, not drive. I want to feel the air, breathe in its coldness.

"He was the first to tell me stories of New York, of Greenwich Village, of Christopher Street, of Fire Island—and now I live there." She knows this. She lets me talk. "San Francisco and Provincetown, too, he told me about these places, places where gays could walk in the street, holding hands. They were like fairy tales." I take my first bite of the cheese sandwich. It's as good as I remember. "He taught me about gay liberation, about how we were going to change the world—"

"He was a leftover hippie," Elsa says. It's just a statement. Nothing else.

"I use the stuff he taught me every day. In my work. The way I see myself, the way I see us, as a community—that all came from Zandy. He was never ashamed of who he was or what he did. Never. Not even when—"

I don't continue. "No," Elsa says. "He was never ashamed."

"He taught me so much," I tell her, more softly now. And I think of his hands, on my body.

"You tell him that," Elsa says, "when you see him."

It was my statement to police that caused Alexander Reefy to be arrested for statutory rape.

I gave it willingly. To say otherwise now would be a lie. My parents did not coerce me. I walked into the police station ahead of them, and even spelled his name for the officer sitting behind the desk. I can remember him still: Officer Joseph Garafolo, a big man with eyes that never looked at me. He had been eating a pear when we came in, and bits of it clung to his bushy black mustache all through our conversation.

And then he sent out a cruiser to arrest Zandy, and never again did Zandy touch me.

I was fifteen years old.

Alexander Reefy first touched me when I was thirteen, back in 1974, the year I got my banana bike. The year I was first allowed to stay up past nine o'clock and watch "Rhoda." I was in love with Joe. I'd jerk off into my underwear as I lay in front of the TV set, humping the braided rug. There was this terrible urgency in my groin at all times. There was no community center then, no gay characters on "Rhoda," as there are on TV today. I'd flip through the card catalog at the school library, only to find nothing between *homoeans,* a fourth-century Christian heresy, and *Homs,* a city in Syria. Occasionally there was something on the news—"Gay rights marchers paraded down Fifth Avenue in New York City today"—reports that caused me great distress if my mother happened to be in the room, shaking her head silently as if to ask: "What *is* this world coming to?" All I had, really, were the whispers of my classmates: the whispers about a world none of us knew anything about except somehow that it existed, in the dark, marshy fringes of our own world.

The boys in my eighth grade class at St. John the Baptist knew the word "homosexual." Those who lived in the neighborhood closest to the school, the neighborhood that bordered the swamps of Dog Town, told me tales of Alexander Reefy, how he would leave his front-porch light on whenever he was free and available, how men would stop by and go inside and the light would be turned off for the duration. "They're *homosexuals,*" Eddie Piatrowski would whisper, and all of our eyes would grow wide. Mine especially.

I was a loner in school. I would watch, I would listen: I knew all their secrets. But none of them knew mine: my private thoughts, my private parts, how my body was changing, how I had learned to do strange and fascinating things with it. No one had prepared me for the changes that were taking place in my body: the hair under my arms and around my dick, the white stuff that would shoot out of my slit if I pulled on myself long and hard enough. No one had told me how good that would feel, or how it would make me think of Joe Gerard, his big hairy chest crushing into Rhoda's face. How it would make me obsessed with that front-porch light on a house I had never seen, with a man whose face I had never glimpsed, but whose name conjured up images and thoughts that consumed my days and the dreams I endured at night.

It was a cold November morning, and Eddie Piatrowski, the closest I came to having a friend, asked me if I wanted to join him and some other boys who were planning on skipping school. We were in the recess yard, before the first bell. Eddie wanted to head south, down along the river, where we could smoke cigarettes and look at the dirty magazines he'd stolen from his father and carefully hidden in his knapsack. Michael Marino preferred the university, where we could maybe bum some beer from a student. I cared about none of those things: I hated the taste of cigarette smoke, hated more the taste of beer, hated most the big fleshy knockers of the women held captive in Eddie's bag.

"Let's go into Dog Town," I suggested.

"Yeah," Eddie said, gleeful. "We can go find the *fag.*"

Only a few abandoned factories stood between us and Dog Town, and these were places well known to me, every nook and broken board, my private after-school clubhouse since the third grade. I led the way. For once, I felt important, as if the other boys looked up to me. It was Eddie Piatrowski and Michael Marino and Craig Warzecha, and they were all following me. We crept past an abandoned car, inexplicably hauled into the ruins of the factory and left there to rot. Craig Warzecha wanted to stop and explore, but I urged him on: much more of interest lay ahead.

"There," Eddie pointed, when we climbed out of the last of the factories and stumbled into the marshy field that led to Dog Town. "His light's on."

And it was. We approached like warriors, but there was no plan beyond getting here. No words were spoken now. Eddie picked up a stone and threw it at the window. We followed suit. The tiny pings of the stones against the glass were the only sounds along the street.

He emerged finally, awakened by the stones: sleepy-eyed and disheveled, not shouting as we had expected. From his lair he crept dizzily, not stealthily, not threateningly. "Hey, what—?" he asked, rubbing his eyes, and I tried desperately to get a glimpse. But Eddie barked: "Run!" So we ran, turning on our heels and plunging through the swampy field, foul-smelling mud soaking into our shoes as we tripped over rusting casements of the old factory and dove back into the darkness.

But this I saw: Alexander Reefy, shirtless, a mat of mysterious black fur on his chest, in checkered pajama bottoms, standing on the steps of his house under the dull golden glow of his front-porch light, and he was smiling. "Hey, peace and love, you little hooligans," he said, and then he went back to bed.

I walk up Oak Avenue to Pearl Court, crossing over to Washington, the wide boulevard that connects Main to High and to all the new shopping plazas and condo developments out past the orchards. It's these new places that have sapped Main Street of its life, drained away its business. Once there were dozens of shops along Main Street, lined up between South End News on one end, where I bought every issue of *Action Comics,* to Schafer's Shoes in the north, where Dad once worked. I remember Schafer's Shoes with one of the few good memories I have of my father. He'd sit me up on the chair like a little prince and let me try on all the new pairs of Buster Brown shoes. But even back then, back in the days of bustling shops and a regular Main Street bus line, the old men who sat on the post office steps would lament what had become of Middletown. What might they say now, with South End News paved over and Schafer's Shoes boarded up? With a Subway Sandwich Shop in the place of Henry's Diner? With the benches along the street occupied not by fellas with their girls but by the homeless and the mentally ill?

On the corner of Pearl and Washington, I see from the mailbox that the Piatrowskis still live in their big yellow Victorian. There, in an upper room, they used to keep Eddie's retarded older sister, a big-faced girl with pop eyes named Helen. I wonder if she's still there. Helen was always screaming. There was never any reason for it that was obvious. Sometimes poor Helen seemed genuinely terrified; other times, it just seemed as if that was all she knew how to do. Mrs. Piatrowski spent all her time tending to her. I was the only kid Eddie ever invited to spend the night at his house. I remember all through dinner—a feast of cabbage and sausage—Helen screamed upstairs. Her screams unnerved me for weeks—all my childhood, in fact, and whenever I was at Eddie's house, I'd come home shaken, waking up in my own bed convinced I could hear her still. There were times when Helen Piatrowski's screams seemed to echo all through the town: from the brownstone spires of St. John the Baptist through the abandoned factories right into the streets of Dog Town.

Now, as I turn onto Washington Street, the traffic gets heavier. Zandy doesn't live in Dog Town anymore, Elsa had told me. He lives here, on Washington, just before the street ascends the hill to wind its way past the large white homes on High Street, past the stoic, ivy-covered university, ending finally at the shopping plazas, where, behind a Shop Rite, my mother still resides in her quiet subdivision. My father had been very proud to finally buy his own home after renting for so long, even if it was a modular one-story behind a grocery store. Now my father is dead and my mother a vacant memory. Zandy's apartment is as far down Washington Street as I will venture. Going further is not the reason I came back.

And what is? I ask myself, raising the collar of my coat against the wind.

Where Zandy lives now is unremarkable: an apartment complex I remember being constructed in my youth, over the remains of a small park where once a rusted jungle gym had enticed children. One of those children—a boy or a girl, I don't remember now—darted into the traffic on Washington Street and was run over by a garbage truck. So they closed the park and built the apartments. Boxy red brick. Stone Estates. This is where Alexander Reefy ends up. A square, small apartment on the side of a busy street, with no front-porch light to flick on and off as his libido wills.

The wind bites my cheeks. I imagine children are preparing their outfits for tonight. Mothers are sewing on sequins for their daughters' ballerina costumes. Little straight boys are planning to go out dressed like Power Rangers. Little gay boys are turning up their noses at such absurd masquerades, preferring to apply their own hideous make-up to transform themselves into witches and devils and similar creatures of the night. Or at least I would have, anyway. I feel as if I am in costume now. My costume is that of an adult, of a man who has lived long and hard, who has claimed his part of the world as his own, who has lived with some manner of integrity and decision since leaving this town, who has come back to say goodbye to a part of his past. This is the costume I am wearing. This is not who I am.

When I find his name on the list beside the door, I press his buzzer and wait.

When he first fucked me, I cried. There was pain, such pain as I had never known, before or since. He held me around the waist, my face away from his. I felt his smoky breath at my ear as he lifted me up off my feet, holding me in front of him, pushing his dick up inside me, causing me to squirm, to writhe, to cry like a little baby.

I was fourteen.

And how he comforted me after. We built a fire, in an open section of the old factory, where the roof had caved in. There was a pool of oily black water beside us, where he rinsed off the Vaseline from his hands. I sat in front of the fire, feeling my sphincter still contracting, feeling as if I needed to shit, to piss, to pass out. And he came up behind me, wrapped his big arms around my frail, shaking body, and held me tight, kissing my neck as I'd seen Joe do to Rhoda.

I loved him immediately.

Alexander Reefy was not a handsome man. His nose was too long and his eyes too small. And his hands: but I've already mentioned his hands. I never knew exactly how old he was. Not quite thirty, but close to it. Younger than I am now. The thought staggers. To me, he seemed much, much older than I, and in truth, he was: but he also seemed ageless, like a genie or an old elf out of Tolkien. And yet, what did I care how old he was or what he looked like? He was a *man*—a man with a penis and a chest like a bear, a man who recognized the urgency within me, and affirmed it.

I had made anonymous phone calls to him in the days after we'd pelted his house with stones. I asked: "How would you like to suck my dick?" and he answered: "I might be interested." *Might be interested.* It blew me away. Here was a man acknowledging he *might be interested* in sucking dick. Even though Eddie Piatrowski had told me that Alexander Reefy was a homosexual, to hear it confirmed was almost too much for my senses. I jerked off to that phrase for days: "I might be interested."

One night, coiled up like a slinky ready to shoot across the room, I called him. "Can I come over?" I breathed. How I found the nerve, the appalling guts, to ask such a thing I still can't fathom. My father was snoring in his chair in front of the TV in the living room. In the kitchen, my mother was packing lunches for my sister and I to take to school the next day. It was a Sunday afternoon. I was in my parents' bedroom, my hand cupped around my mouth as I whispered into the phone.

"How old are you?" he asked.

"Sixteen," I lied.

It was an age pulled from the air. Something told me it held some magic. I did not know it was the age of consent in this state. But Zandy did, and he said, "All right. Come on over."

I don't remember much of the ride through town on my purple banana bike, except that it was the longest ride I'd ever taken. I assume I came straight down Washington Street, dodging the traffic, then headed north on Main, around St. John the Baptist and past the factories along River Road. I do remember that his front-porch light was on.

That first day all he did was touch my dick. With those hands.
No sucking. No fucking. But that was enough. I came in ten seconds, flat. Then I was out of there, pedaling back home as fast as
my frightened little feet would take me. But I was back the following Sunday, and that's when he gave me my very first blowjob. He
took me upstairs to his room and sat me down on the edge of his
bed, kneeling in front of me and unzipping my fly. He didn't expect me to reciprocate.

Afterwards, I didn't run, but hung around for a while. He gave
me some apple juice. He was nice to me, nicer than anyone had
ever been to me. We sat in his living room, papered with posters
of Karl Marx and Janis Joplin and Barbra Streisand, and I cried. I
didn't say anything. Just cried. He sat there, nodding his head.
"Yeah, yeah," he said softly. "I know."

The next time, I met his friends, people who would become
well known to me over the next year and a half. A tall man everyone called Miss Aletha, who wore a blonde wig and purple eye
mascara; Bertrand, his (her?) boyfriend, a shy young man in his
twenties with tattoos on his arms; and Cisco, a dark-skinned kid
not much older than I was who always looked at me strangely, as if
he resented me.

It was Cisco who said, finally: "That kid ain't sixteen." And Miss
Aletha had gotten up and walked out of the room. Bertrand
smiled. Zandy reached over to me where I sat on the couch, sipping my juice, and tousled my hair. He winked at me. It made me
feel better.

Zandy taught me the things my father should have: why I had
to shower more frequently now that I was sprouting hair, how to
wash my dick to keep it clean, how to get rid of an infestation of
crabs he said was inevitable for any teenage boy. He taught me
that the feelings I had shouldn't be cause for shame or concern.
He said being gay was just the most natural thing: "And don't you
ever let anyone tell you otherwise," he said. Of course, there was
more. He taught me how to give pleasure and how to receive it:
the best way to handle a man's dick, the best way to show your
partner what turned you on.

But I never sucked his dick. Not once in all that time. He
taught me how to do it only through demonstration, never asking
me to practice what I had learned. Later, with others, I was eager
to get down on my knees and serve. To Zandy I offered my ass

without hesitation, but never my lips. And he never asked. In all of our lovemaking, which was considerable, I never gave him a blowjob.

Zandy told the judge later that he had wanted to stop, wanted to send me away. But there was something in my eyes, he said, something that wouldn't let him. Elsa would say, even later, that that was no excuse, that he shouldn't have put the onus on me. "Maybe there was nothing wrong in what he did," she always asserted, "but it was him doing it to you, not the other way around." But she was wrong, one of the rare occasions when she didn't get it right. It *was* me. There *was* something in my eyes.

"Someday," Zandy promised me, "we won't have to hide. We won't have to pretend." The days had become longer for me, the weeks interminable. I lived for my Sunday afternoons, listening to Miss Aletha sing show tunes from her days as a performer at the Follies Cafe, long since closed. Bertrand could perform magic tricks, and he did lots of them. I still remember the parakeet coming out of his old black hat and how astounded I was. Cisco was always sullen, sometimes (I learned) slipping outside to sell his body to the men who would drive very slowly with their lights off along River Road. Zandy didn't like to talk to me much about that.

That's how I met Elsa, when she came into Dog Town to counsel Cisco. She was a social worker back then. She worked with street kids and poor families. She met with Zandy, who was putting together an organization he called the Gay Liberation Project of Middletown. He was really into it, making up fliers and brochures. Elsa allowed her number to be listed on the handouts as part of a hotline service. She was a nice lady, and clean and very respectable. I didn't figure she was like Zandy or Miss Aletha or Bertrand. But she was.

"Yes," she said to me one afternoon, after I'd met her on the sidewalk in front of Zandy's. "I'm gay, too."

That really just knocked my socks off. Here was this well-dressed lady saying she was just like me. After that, whenever I'd see Elsa on the street passing out her literature or knocking on the doors of poor families' apartments, I'd always hurry up to greet her. And she always seemed happy to see me.

I dreaded the prospect of high school: my classmates were all clamoring to join the Middletown High football team. No, not me, I'd say, backing off, and already the taunts were beginning. *"Fag,"* the boys would whisper, "queer boy." I looked forward to Sunday afternoons more than I possibly could have expressed at the time, because that's when I felt the most real: sitting in that living room in Dog Town, listening to Miss Aletha sing, watching Bertrand pull parakeets out of his hat, hearing about Zandy's trips to Greenwich Village or his summertime jaunts up to Provincetown.

"Someday, kid," Zandy told me, "I'll take you to a gay pride parade in New York City. It's fabulous. Lots of balloons and banners and great music to dance to. As soon as you're a little older, we'll go and we'll watch all the hundreds of homosexuals walk down Christopher Street. You'd never believe there were so many. Drag queens like Miss Aletha, and dykes on their big old motorcycles, and big hunky guys with lots of muscles. And we'll stay out all night. I'll take you dancing and we'll go into the back room and boy, will you be popular there . . ."

On Halloween night, Zandy opened his door dressed like Marilyn Monroe. I was shocked, appalled. But Zandy sat me down and explained all about Stonewall, how drag queens have always been the ones on the front lines. "You like Miss Aletha, don't you?" he asked.

I nodded my head.

"Well, she was leading the fight here in this town long before any of us arrived. We've got her to thank for a lot."

He was always teaching me these things. "From here," he said one afternoon, seated in his overstuffed, frayed armchair, beneath a tattered American flag pinned up to the wall with a large peace sign painted over it, "I can see the very edge of the rainbow."

"The edge?" I asked.

"You've got it made, kid," he said. "You and all the little ones to follow. We're making such progress. You'll see. Even here in Middletown."

I couldn't imagine.

"Look. It's 1975. In San Francisco, there's a guy running for supervisor. That's like the City Council here. And he's gay. And people don't care. His name is Milk. Strange name for a fag, huh?" Zandy laughed. "And he's gonna make it. Looks like he's really going to make it. How about that, huh?"

I raised my eyebrows.

"You just imagine twenty years from now, kid. Just you imagine."

I tried, but couldn't.

"Don't worry," he said, "take my word for it. It's going to be *grand.*" And I remember how he kissed me then, his smoky breath in my mouth, putting his hands in front of my lips afterward, letting me kiss them and lick them and suck each one of those knotty, twisted fingers into my mouth.

That night, or a night shortly thereafter, he took me out to the old abandoned factory, just as spring began to thaw the cold earthen floors, and fucked me for the first of many, many times in my life.

Why not me? I asked myself, when my lover died in New York. *Why not me?* I asked again, when Elsa told me that all of them—Miss Aletha and Bertrand and Cisco, too, I imagine—were dead. *Why not me?*

Maybe that's why I've returned. Maybe that's why I press his buzzer now, and wait for him to answer.

There's nothing. I wonder if he's gone out. But he's too sick to go out, Elsa told me. That's what she had heard. Maybe he's too sick to open the door.

In the street behind me, a motorist slams on his brakes, causing a terrible screeching sound. An angry horn blares. I think of the child run over by the garbage truck here, long ago. I remember how we prayed for—him? her?—in church, how terrified I was of the thought of being run over in the street.

A young woman is suddenly behind me. She smiles shyly and I step aside, allowing her to unlock the door and go inside. I hold the door for her. She's carrying a bag of groceries. She says, "Thank you." I nod and follow her inside. She does not appear to be uncomfortable with my presence and I follow her up the first flight of stairs. At the landing, she turns and unlocks the door to the first apartment on the right. When she is inside, I hear a chain lock quickly slide into place.

Zandy's apartment is 311. Third floor. I climb another set of stairs.

It smells of mold and mildew in this place. The gray carpeting is stained in places. At the far end of each corridor on each floor a fingerprint-covered window lets in cold blue light. Cigarette butts litter the stairwells, despite the "No Smoking" signs.

I find 311 on my left, at the end of the corridor. The last apartment on the last floor. I knock. I hear nothing. I decide he's gone,

perhaps in the hospital. I fear my whole trip here has been in vain.
But then I sense a shudder from inside, as if a hibernating animal
were just stirring back to life. There's a sound, a noiseless kind of
sound, as if from under something: a pile of blankets, maybe, or a
mound of pine needles and soil.

"Zandy?" I call.

There's the sound of air, a strange sound, like the flurry of
wind in the eaves. Then it's quiet again.

"Zandy? It's Todd O'Riley."

I swallow hard. Why should he want to see me? Who's to say if
he's even read the letters I sent? Who's to say he doesn't hate me
with all the passion my parents once hated him? And who would
blame him?

Then I hear the scuffing: footsteps approaching the door. And
then a voice, softly entreating: "Go ahead. Come in."

It was the day Schafer's Shoes closed its doors. Dad hadn't been
forewarned. Old Mr. Schafer just told him it was over. "Go on
home," he said to my father, handing him his severance pay.
"That's what I'm going to do."

The men on the steps of the post office would have something
else to cluck over. The little store just couldn't compete with the
new Shoe Town that opened up on North Washington, one of the
first of the new stores out there, not far from our house. "There's
a big parking lot there," my mother would say, by way of explanation, as if parking lots could explain the entire world. Later, my
Dad would blame Jimmy Carter, and the Arabs: I'm not sure why,
but it was all due to inflation somehow, and Carter and the Arabs
were to my Dad the root causes of most of our problems.

But on this day, Dad said nothing. He just sat on the couch not
moving, just staring into the air. I was fifteen now, and when I got
home from yet another harrowing day of high school, fending off
the taunts of the upperclassmen and the guys who had once been
my classmates back at St. John the Baptist, I found him tight-
lipped about the whole thing, unwilling to look me in the eye.
"Leave your father alone," my mother commanded. "Go to your
room and pray."

For what? For Shoe Town to close? For Jimmy Carter to resign?
But my younger sister obeyed. I still remember looking into her
room and seeing the sad little Sign of the Cross she made that day

sitting on her bed, her feet in their black patent-leather shoes not even reaching the floor. But I simply flopped down on my bed and stared at my ceiling. It was a dark day. At least, I remember it that way. I'm pretty sure it was raining. Or maybe I just think I remember the rain, because my life had become a drizzly blur, a damp mist shrouding everything I did. Who can explain teenage angst, particularly queer teenage angst? The very last completely happy time I can remember with Zandy was a night shortly after Halloween, when he took me up into the orchards and we filled a basket with the picked-over apples. "Miss Aletha taught me a secret a long time ago, when I first came to Middletown," he told me, and it struck me that I didn't know he had come from anyplace else. "The secret is in these apples. Everybody leaves them behind. But they're the sweetest of the bunch, and they're *free.*"

He was right: they *were* sweet. And we picked as many as we could, stumbling in the dark, shivering and laughing and biting into the hard sweet fruit, oblivious of the threat of worms or the chance of being discovered. We went back to his house and baked Miss Aletha a pie and I remember how she cried, the mascara running down her cheeks, and that was the last completely happy time I ever had with Zandy and his friends.

Because after that things started changing: the taunts at school got worse, my father began to suspect I was becoming somebody he didn't want me to be. "Why aren't you on any sports?" he griped, now that I was in high school. My mother's face simply went tight, abandoning me to his suspicions. But I no longer found solace in my Sunday afternoons with Zandy. Instead, I wanted to appease my tormentors. I wanted finally to be like them, especially the handsome jocks whose images I would jerk off to at night, after a day spent fending off their taunts and insults. I wanted friends my own age, *normal* friends: I wanted to hang out with Eddie, and Craig Warzecha and Michael Marino, as I had on that day when I led them through the factories, the day I first got mixed up in all of this. I was weary of being alone in the hallways, lugging my books spiritlessly from class to class, occasionally having them knocked from my arms by a band of roving jocks. I no longer desired the refuge I found in the arms of Alexander Reefy—that *man*, that *old* man, how dare he do the things he did to me?

This is how I was thinking, in those last several weeks, sitting in

Zandy's living room, listening to his stories now with a feeling of revulsion. My Sunday visits became fewer. Zandy never asked why, which made me even more resentful. I became hostile to him, refusing sex. I even told Miss Aletha that she looked foolish one day: "Everyone knows you're just a guy." I wanted to take the words back instantly, because I saw how it hurt her. But Zandy never asked what was going on with me. If he didn't care, I reasoned, then neither did I.

I had stopped riding my banana bike: too faggy. So I'd ask my father for an occasional ride to the center of town, from which I'd walk the mile into Dog Town. Once he turned to me and asked, not expecting an answer, because I never offered one: "What do you *do* with your time, anyway? You don't go out with girls. You don't play football. I don't understand you at all. You can't be a kid of mine."

Maybe I wasn't. Then whose kid was I? Certainly not Zandy's, because by then I hated his hands on my body as much as I hated my father's words. Maybe that's why I went directly to his house the day my father lost his job. Maybe somehow I figured my father would follow. Maybe I wanted what happened to happen. My father *did* follow, and he must have driven real slowly and deliberately because I walked all the way there and yes, I'm sure now that it was raining, because I remember being cold and damp when I finally got to Zandy's, and Cisco was there, on the front porch, with another kid I didn't know, and I ignored them and walked right on inside without knocking. Zandy came out of the kitchen with a towel in his hand and without his shirt—freshly showered, I think, because the hair on his chest was all alive and shiny and not at all matted. He said, "Hey, kid, what's up?" and that's when I heard my father behind me and he was shouting, "We're going to have you arrested, you pervert!" and he did just that: he got Zandy thrown in jail. No. *I* got Zandy thrown in jail, because I told my parents and the police everything. Every last detail. To shock them, perhaps. To repulse them. To drive them out of my life. Them and Zandy, too.

My father smacked me across the face that day in front of Zandy's house. Zandy tried to stop him, but then he hit Zandy too, and I remember Zandy's mouth bleeding and Cisco running off down the street with the other kid and I think they were laughing, the little shits. My father pulled me outside by my hair and shoved me into the car and by this time I was crying and denying I'd ever been there before, little coward that I was. That was the last time I ever saw Zandy: bleeding mouth and open eyes, listening to me deny he'd ever meant anything to me. I didn't have to see him in court, because I was just fifteen and didn't have to go. There was a big scandal and the local newspaper wrote a story using Zandy's name, although mine was not revealed. Still, everyone knew it was me: it went all through school, and the taunting just got worse. So did the beatings at home.

When my father kept hitting me, I ran away. To Elsa's. Somehow she got my parents to agree that I could live with her, even though there were rumors in town that she was a dyke. But I think my parents just wanted to be rid of their faggot son. Elsa was good to me. She got a dentist to cap the tooth my father had broken and she even sent me to a shrink. But school became unbearable, and Elsa figured it was better if I went away. She arranged for me to go to a prep school in New York. She chipped in to help pay because my father still didn't have a job. If it weren't for Elsa, I'd probably be dead now. But she gave me a chance to start over, and that starting over began the day she drove me out of Middletown in her big brown station wagon to catch the train in New Haven. When I looked out the car window at Middletown receding behind me, I saw my life there just disappear, as if it had never happened, fading away to just a muddy background on which I could paint the rest of my life.

I remember the train ride to New York as vividly as I remember anything. Watching out the window as the train passed the backs of shopping centers and the backyards of suburban, lower-middle-class homes, I felt like a voyeur, seeing parts of people's lives I'd never seen before, parts of their lives I wasn't supposed to see. Yet instead of guilt, I felt privileged to have such a glimpse: the backyard swing set, the garbage cans, the flower pots and the tool sheds. People didn't often have the opportunity to see someone else's backyard, littered with bikes missing wheels, forgotten toys and broken wheelbarrows.

I remember, even now, especially now, the little girl I spotted, swinging dispiritedly on an old rusty swing set behind a one-story house. She seemed lost in thought, oblivious to her surroundings. She didn't even look up as the train whizzed past her house. It must have become so routine for her: the clatter of the tracks, the blowing of the horn. She didn't raise her eyes in excitement at the approach of the train, as most children would: it was something she heard every day, several times a day, and it brought her no particular joy. I wanted to call to her, to tell her to look up, to hop on the train with me. "It can take you away, too," I wanted to tell her, suddenly feeling responsible for her, wanting with all my might to grab onto her and take her with me.

But I couldn't, of course. All I had with me was one small bag, all new clothes that Elsa had bought for me. I went to school, and did all right. After graduation, I got accepted at Columbia, and took up journalism. I came out. There was a gay and lesbian group on campus. Some of the older guys would go out dancing at the Saint, or spend all night at the Mineshaft, but I never went with them. Too scared, maybe, after all the shit I went through. By the time I wanted to go, no one was going out anymore—it was 1983, the year of the Big Scare. So I never went dancing all night in New York as Zandy had prophesied. I didn't have a lot of sex. I never did drugs. The promise of gay life being one long, never-ending party failed to materialize for me. I admit to being somewhat disappointed: Zandy had made it all sound so dazzling. But gay life had never been that way for me: why should I have expected anything else?

I *did* have expectations, though. "It's going to be *grand,*" Zandy had said. But the first man I fell in love with died—not from the plague, but at the hands of some teenage boys from New Jersey, boys not much different from Craig Warzecha and Michael Marino and Eddie Piatrowski. They thought it was a joke: "Let's beat up a fag." They kicked his brains out, left them in a grisly, watery stream all the way down the pier. It made me write to my mother, finally, after all those years. I don't know why. I told her Zandy had been no molester, no aberration. She sent me back a long letter, quoting the Bible. She'd never been religious before, but now she listened to Jim and Tammy Faye with all the passion of a convert.

When I graduated, I got my current job. I like it okay. I fell in love for the second time, and then he died, too. This time it *was* the plague. I haven't had sex since, unless you count watching at the piers or at the rest stop outside Middletown. Then, a few months ago I got the letter from Elsa: "I thought you might want to know that Alexander Reefy is sick. He's not doing well. Just thought you might want to know."

"Todd O'Riley," he whispers now from the darkness of the shuttered room behind the door.

"Zandy," I say.

He steps aside to let me in. The apartment is dark, cast with a strange blue light. The Venetian blinds are pulled tightly shut on all the windows. The smell is foul: cigarettes and urine and bad milk. A mix of staleness, sweetness, and sour. He's dressed in a big floppy flannel shirt, untucked, way too big for him, though it probably fit him when he was healthy. His gray sweatpants are stained and torn. He's barefoot.

"Todd O'Riley," he says again.

His face has the skeletal look I've come to recognize as a last sign of the plague: deep hollow cheeks, wide eyes, protruding teeth. His breath is rancid; how well I remember Steven's breath, at the end, how repulsive it was, as if all his organs were decaying inside of him with the stench making its way up through his mouth. In Zandy's case, the odor is made worse by the decades of cigarettes: his teeth are yellow and chipped, his lips a stained brownish green.

He's unshaven, with big tufts of black hair on his cheeks and his chin. I remember for a while he had grown a beard, and how I thought he looked magnificent, back in those days when facial hair was still socially affirmed among gay men. But now the hair on his face is patchy and ragged, as if whole clumps had fallen out all at once.

"Zandy, I wanted to see you," I begin.

He smiles. His teeth frighten me. "Well," he says, gesturing, "here I am."

I reach over to touch him, shake his hand, something. He folds his arms across his chest. I brush his wrist as he does so. I feel nothing. It's as if I've just swept through smoke, not flesh.

"I want you to know—" I try again.

He laughs. "How sorry you are? Is that it, kid? Is that why you've come back?"

I don't know what to say. "Yes," I try. "Yes. That's part of it. How sorry I am."

For a flash I see the old Zandy: the face hidden behind the

death mask. I'm transported nearly two decades back into time, and I feel a strange stirring in my loins.

"And what should I tell you now?" he asks. "What is it that you've come back to hear me say?"

"I don't know," I admit.

"How about 'I exonerate you?'" he asks suddenly, his eyes lighting up, as if the idea had just occurred to him. "Isn't that why you came back? To receive absolution from a dying man?"

"Zandy—"

"Well, you're too late. I'm already dead."

"Look, Zandy, I don't need you to forgive me. I've had to do that for myself."

He just looks at me, and for a minute it's as if I can see right through him: lungs and heart and ribcage, and then the wallpaper beyond.

"I just wanted to say that I was sorry," I tell him. "That I was a fucked-up kid who nonetheless loved you very much. And still does. There was so much, so very much you taught me. I am who I am because of you. Everything I know about being gay, about our history, our traditions—you taught me. You taught me not to be ashamed. I owe you enough to at least come back here and tell you—"

"You don't owe me anything." Zandy puts his hands over his face. They're as knotty as I remember, but thinner, so much thinner. He takes a deep breath, and then lets it out. He uncovers his face and looks hard at me. "You've become a mere peddler of words," he says at last.

His words take me by surprise. "How do you know what I've written?" I ask.

"You're a reporter. A reporter writes only what he *sees*. Not what he feels. Not what he *knows.*"

I don't understand.

"You *do* understand," he says, reading my mind. "Don't pretend you don't. You know what to do."

"Tell the stories," I say.

"Yes," he tells me. "And not from your eyes. Your eyes are only part of it. Your heart, kid. Your heart and your soul and your head and yes, kid, your dick. You write the book I will never get to write."

But I don't know if I can.

"Sure you can," he says. "You tell 'em for me. It's *still* going to be grand."

Then he laughs. "Hey," he asks, "do you remember the secret Miss Aletha taught me?"

I hesitate for just a second. "About the apples?"

"Yes," he says. "How sweet are the twisted apples that they leave behind." Zandy turns to look at me. We hold each other's gaze, and I can see through his eyes.

I know what he means.

"Don't worry," he says. "You can't get infected by a dead man."

And then I understand. Fully, for the first time. I'm not frightened, standing here with a ghost, the ghost of a man who loved me, who I loved in return, the ghost of a man I could have been, and still might be. I approach him, falling to my knees in front of him. I gently pull down his sweatpants, my fingers caressing cold, cold flesh. His dick, shriveled and blue, nests in a stinking mat of pubic hair. I take the icy shaft into my mouth. He moans, and for a second I remember that voice: the soft cooing in my ear, the soft promises of a world yet to be explored. And I give him the best blowjob that I know how, a skill I learned from him. And when he shoots, I take his cum down my throat, drinking every last drop of that sweet freezing liquid that burns all the way down, purifying me.

"He's dead," I tell Elsa.

She's not surprised. She's clipping the purple roses from the vine. "Some warm water," she says. "That'll keep these for a few more days."

The sun is setting in a watery mix of reds and purples. The ghosts and the goblins will all emerge now, going from house to house, collecting their treats and delivering their tricks.

"I want to head out tonight, get back to New York," I say. Elsa understands. "I had thought the dying was hard there," I tell her. "Here, how do you go on?"

She holds me tight for a few moments, then lets me go. "I love you," I tell her, and she smiles.

Her, too, I think, as I drive out of town. Her story, too. I pull off the road to watch the sunset on Eagle Hill, this time oblivious to the boys in the bushes. I can see her house from here, standing out in the red glow cast by the setting sun among the long purple shadows. I can see the factories, the deserted shops of Main Street, the cold brownstone steeple of St. John the Baptist Church. I can see Stone Estates, too. I shiver, wanting to get back to New York before it gets much later. Before I forget the job I have to do. Before I forget what I have to say.

Before I hear Helen Piatrowski scream.

Yellowtail

VIET DINH

It's not every day that I'm called a gook. It happens occasionally, in passing, but it doesn't hurt anymore. Hits like a bullet, but doesn't penetrate. I get assaulted by words every day. What gives this word special power over me? I should be insulted, but I'm not. The insult, like so many other things, passes. It's not worth a response.

The advantage of working as an assistant sushi chef is that everyone thinks I'm Japanese. No one takes an Asian seriously if he works in an Oriental restaurant. I call myself, always out of earshot of the management, the sushi slave. The nigiri master is an ancient man, like a blurred watercolor emperor hanging from the wall in bamboo slats. The owner is his wife, the little woman who shuffles around in white gym socks and sandals, wearing a kimono, her hair in a bun, chopsticks poking out like the arms of a drowning man. She smiles to the customers, brings them their checks without a word, feigning ignorance of the language, but, after closing time, she shrieks at me in stuttering English, then turns to her husband and laughs at me in Japanese.

She would much rather have another Japanese working for her, I know. All the other waiters are Japanese. She hired me hesitantly, but without other applicants she had no choice. I know how to cut meat quickly from my previous job. She would treat me better if I knew the language, but I'm not going to learn it for her sake. I won't be her little Vietnamese geisha boy.

I'm trying to find another place to work.

It's hard. No one wants to hire a college dropout. I apply to an office position, but they ask, What sort of experience do you have? and when I tell them, they raise their eyebrows and say, That's all? as if they expect me to be a computer programmer. They stare at me, with their big eyes, as if they want an explanation, and when I don't offer one, they say, Thank you, that will be all.

Until I can find a better job, a sushi slave I will be. It's not bad all the time. Nice people make the world bearable. One man, he is white, comes in once a month when we offer all-you-can-eat and sits near my end of the bar. He always wears a red cap with a blue *S* in the center, curly brown hair squatting across his forehead. He dresses colorfully, in shirts with stripes running up and down, making my eyes dizzy, or plaids that switch patterns halfway to the buttonholes. I think he is about my age. He is polite and orders in a quiet, kind voice.

He knows the names of the different types of sushi without stumbling over the pronunciation, and orders the same every time. Two kappa maki and two California rolls. I wince when people order the California rolls, because they're sticking to something that sounds familiar. White businessmen order California rolls as they drink themselves blind with sake. But I think he orders it because he likes the avocado. I slip him an extra sliver in the roll when Kaneda isn't looking. He smiles as I serve him, and I smile back. I wonder if he's a vegetarian, but I correct myself. California rolls have crab. It is Yurie who comes and breaks the reverie, the cloth near her legs going swish-swish against the sash as she walks with a handful of orders, and I have to turn away.

I wish that I didn't have to wear the uniform. It makes me look like a cartoon samurai. All I need to do is pull my hair back in a ponytail and tie a katana next to my belly. The robe is long and sometimes my feet get caught in the bottom. Yurie hisses, Clumsy! at me. I hate it. It's white with blue prints of fish, waves, pagodas, and seashells. I wear a shirt under it, but when I get home after work, my arms are red from the coarse fabric.

They keep me later than I need to be, ordering me to wipe the bar a second time or recheck the fish in the freezer. I want to get out, but they send me to the men's bathroom to make sure the toilet seats are clean. When everything is done to their satisfaction, she waves her hand to dismiss me, then speaks Japanese to everyone else, the strange syllables poking like skewers. I cover my ears, because I don't want to hear it anymore. I don't.

I go home and wash the smell of fish off me. The robe I throw with the dirty laundry sitting in the corner. I cannot afford a large apartment, so I live in one room. I have a bed, desk, bookshelf filled with bent-eared books, and a nightstand. All my clothes I keep in the closet. I don't invite people here. It's too small and it's all I can afford.

My mother hasn't called in two weeks. She can't go too long without hearing from me. I can already hear my mother's voice saying, "Giang, Giang, you need to find direction. You think you can go much longer living like you do? You will live a hard life until you die." She says this once again in English to make sure I understand: you will live a difficult life, Giang. I have memorized her speech, can repeat her word for word, match her inflections, even the words I don't comprehend. She sighs, "Ai-ya," and I hear her rubbing her face. I was born as I was born, and I live my life as I live my life. Even if I do not like it, I go to work. It is an honest job. My parents do not see that. If I were a drug dealer, my parents see me in the same light, a dim light.

She tries to get me to come home, but I know that will make things worse. I cannot live under their roof, and they do not understand me. I expect to hear from her soon. They have their house, safe, calm, emerging only to go to work or to go shopping, and because bombs are not dropping on their doorstep, they think that they no longer have to fight. Every month, they gather with their friends, a houseful of aging couples, eat dinner, and gossip.

"If you only knew how life was back home," she tells me. I do not know what life was like and will never know. I was born there, but they brought me here days before the South fell to the Communists, when I was young, a child without memories. My father says, "That man looks like a Communist," when he suspects he is being cheated at the grocery store, or when he sees a man he does not like.

He believed they were everywhere, in the streets, in the stores, in the soup restaurant he took me to. It was his favorite food, that soup. Pho. We spent hours there, he and I, from when I barely came up to his waist until I finished high school. After the college, he didn't want to talk to me anymore, as if I had become one of the Communists he hated so much.

I grit my teeth. I do not want to talk to her tonight, not tonight. I watch the phone, in case it rings. I do not know if I would pick it up. It might be her, I tell myself, if I am lucky. If I am not, it will be the one I will never speak to again, even to hear his apologies, as if he had any to give. I will not speak to him.

The robe still itches. I launder it every day, to wash off scraps of fish and other smears from work. I pour two capfuls of fabric softener to the wash, the baby blue liquid brand which is more expensive, to try to get the robe to be kind to my skin, but the material never relents. The rest of my clothes smell of flowers and perfume, overpowering, and come out of the dryer limp; my shirts, my pants, my underwear. I smell like a girl. But the robe is rough and carries the never-ending stink of fish.

I scratch as I enter work, and Yurie gives me a dirty look and barks what must be prepared before the customers come. The lunch dishes must be cleared, the tables must be wiped, the floors must be swept, the food must be ready. She sits in the kitchen and sips plum wine from an earthenware cup. Her husband comes and helps me, but does not say anything. He never does.

One by one, the customers come in. Tonight will be busy; it is all-you-can-eat night. She greets them graciously, always the hostess, and they are charmed to be in such an authentic Oriental restaurant. They sniff the soy sauce bottle and wrinkle their noses. There are placards at each table, describing the different pieces of sushi. Edible art, it says, and they laugh. They break their chopsticks unevenly at the bottom and wonder if they will get fortune cookies at the end of their meal.

I go through their orders, slicing the fish, rolling the rice, wrapping in seaweed. Over and over. I could do this in my sleep, no matter what the fish: tuna, salmon, yellowtail, octopus, eel, shrimp, crab; they all fall victim to my knife. I pack the brownish grey sea urchin mush into a log and shape the wasabi with my fingertips. Cut, wrap, roll. It has become habit now. I put paper cutouts of bamboo trees on the tray for decoration and drop a fluttering lump of ginger on the side. I do all these as fast as I can, because these things must be done before the customer has put down his bowl of miso soup, done before the salmon roe begin to hatch, and done before I can rest, even for a second.

The order comes, and I almost do not recognize it in my haste. I finish the order, then realize what is on the tray. Two California rolls, two kappa maki. I look up and he is smiling at me, the same, kind smile, not like the other one. When the other one smiled, I could see the water behind it, dark and churning, with secrets sunk deep into his face. This one, he smiles and there is nothing but lightness in it.

I watch his tray as I hand it to him, the chunks of fish. He looks at me with flattering eyes, but I do not want to be caught there. It is too easy to get lost. I can feel his smile on the back of my neck as the tray leaves my hands. When I glance up, he looks like a new schoolboy in class, bright and hopeful, a bit bashful. It is almost more than I can stand.

Kaneda nudges me in the ribs with his elbow. Hei! he grunts and continues working. He has not missed a step. It is my signal to stop daydreaming. The man has a sympathetic look on his face and shrugs as if to say, What can you do? I smile back. A word appears on his lips, and I think it might be his name, but I can't quite make it out. I think the word is *Robert*. I must return to work and let him enjoy his meal.

Not long afterward, a brawny man walks in, his arm strangling the arm of his girl. She is bleached blonde; the dark roots are starting to grow in. They sit at the bar, in the center stools. He spreads his legs wide, as if he were at a saloon, and she puts her purse on her lap. Her bosom flops up and down as she giggles, and I watch the man's eyes track the nipples poking through the stretched cloth. She picks up the placard and tries saying the names, carefully, as if in kindergarten, learning to speak for the first time. Every time she completes a word, she looks at him for approval, and he nods, even when she is wrong.

Hey, he yells at Kaneda. I dislike them already. Kaneda asks, Yes? The man starts pointing, I want one of these, one of these, and what do you want, baby? She squeals, I don't know. The octopus sounds good. He points at another one, This too.

Kaneda works on the sit-down orders, I work on the orders at the bar. I add more rice and reduce the amount of fish. Yurie should be proud of me. I save her money. They want inari? I give them egg instead of eel, and they will never know the difference.

Then, where appropriate, I squeeze a thick strip of spicy mayonnaise, more than is usually put in. Perhaps, I think, that will curb their tongues.

The woman asks, Do you have any forks? I am busy, so I do not hear her at first. You know, she says louder, a fork? I look up and she is holding up three fingers, the nails red and shiny, and makes a thrusting motion with them. I glower at her, reach under the counter, and bring up a fork. She places it next to her, then leans over and whispers something in her boyfriend's ear. I'm still glaring, I think I hear the words *slanty eyes.*

What do you got to drink? demands the man, and I nod and point to the list. Good, I want a—His voice trails off as he defers the decision to the girl. She chooses, and he shoves the list across the counter. That one, and I must trace his finger to the proper brand. Does he not think I speak English? There should be a sign on the door announcing that good, grammatical American is spoken in this establishment.

The couple are loud, even as they eat. They raise their voices, competing with one another, end up roaring. The woman squeals, waving a half-bitten piece of sushi on her fork, tuna chunks oozing out of one end. I snicker once, when the man gobbles a piece and snorts like a pig from the burning rush of wasabi going up his nose. He holds his nose, stamps his feet, slams his fist against the counter, eyes spinning to the back of his head. Ron, honey, are you all right? asks the girl. God damn! he exclaims, shaking the restaurant, that was strong! as he reaches for his half-empty glass.

I make another roll, yellowtail, my personal favorite, and make it inside out, tiny salmon roe sticking to the rice like orange pearls. I grasp the four pieces in my fingers and drop it on Robert's plate. He has a surprised expression on his face, surprised and happy. He places the first piece gently in his mouth and closes his lips around the end of it, until it is entirely engulfed. He looks funny with his cheeks bulging out, and I want to laugh.

The moment is short, because the loud man is yelling again. Hey, you, he says to me, I want some more. I break away from Robert and turn my attention to the belligerent one. I bristle at his words. He exasperates me more and more, his pointing, his condescension. This one and this one, he says, and don't make it so strong this time. I nod dumbly, putting on the act of no-speakeede-Engrish and I ready the largest slab of wasabi ever to be placed in ebi maki.

Robert only has one piece left on his plate. I want to make him another roll, but I wonder if he would misunderstand my intentions. He looks nice enough, but I want to be careful. Nothing like last time, I tell myself.

I stop paying attention to what I am doing and don't notice the filet knife go through my left index finger. I feel the cool edge of the blade, then, a few seconds later, the pain. I look down and I see that I've begun to bleed. Without a word, I finish the roll and plop the pieces in front of the man with my right hand. I stride into the bathroom, thinking, Does slanty-eyed blood taste different?

I rub the white creamy soap into my hand and onto my finger. It stings, the soap, hurts more than the cut itself. The cut is not deep, but goes along the length of my finger, the cut flesh forming a red coastline. I want to make sure the wound is completely cleaned out. The flap of skin continually opens as I rinse and it drips its contents profusely. The iridescent sheen of the bubbles have a base of blood. Ashamed, they run away, hide down the drain.

Opening the cabinet underneath, I take a bandage from the first-aid kit. Then another. The cut is long and is not easily covered. I dry my hands carefully, trying not to aggravate the wound. The flesh-colored bandages look pale, obvious against my skin. I wrap the bandages tight, as tight as I can, until I can feel my fingertip start to swell, so that the bleeding stops. I can't have the bleeding go on.

I walk back outside, and Kaneda has given me no mind, although Yurie shoots me an angry glance. Behind the counter, I cut away the piece of tuna I was working on, in case there are traces of blood on it. It is cool to the touch, slightly slimy. I am running low on fresh tuna. I look for a place to dispose of it, and toss it, behind Kaneda's bent back, into the garbage.

I pick up my knife, come from behind the counter, and head toward the kitchen for more tuna, I don't notice that the man has bitten into my special ebi. For a moment, he only winces at the taste, then, as the wasabi rises, he yells, displaying the half-chewed rice in his mouth. It is the sound is of a Kappa bowing and losing the potent water in the dent of its head. Even the girl is taken aback and flinches away from her bellowing man.

Son of a bitch! he yells, you did this on purpose! The words come out as if he has no tongue. I'm trying my hardest not to laugh and to act normally, because it is unbearably funny, until his hand reaches over and grabs the front of my robe, pulling me nose to nose with him. I can smell the horseradish on his breath.

Listen, you Nip, and I interrupt him. I'm not going to stand for this, this guy pushing me around like this. I'm not Japanese, I say, as if instructing an unruly five-year-old, I'm Vietnamese. This I say proudly, not afraid of him, just as proudly as he would announce that he hails from Alabama, anywhere the Confederate flag waves on Independence Day.

He grows silent, but it is not a good silence. The girl now has her eyes open wide, as if in horror. I see red streaks creeping around his dilated pupils, blood vessels bursting, I can almost hear them popping in his forehead. From beside me, the steady sound of the knife's edge on a cutting counter stops.

What did you say? are his first choked words. Then again, but this time deafening, What are you? He yanks me and for a moment, I feel like I'm flying in a helicopter, moving vertically. He throws me onto the floor, knocking out my breath. The girl screams. He hovers over me, on his hands and knees, his hands pinning mine to the floor. He is very strong. The muscles bulge from underneath his shirt. My head hurts from where it struck the ground. A chair scrapes the floor, and I know that Robert is on his feet, probably thinking of ways to defend me. The rest of the restaurant is hushed, watching expectantly in fearful submission.

I can't move, struggle in vain. He says, Don't try any of that kung fu shit on me, I'm going to tear your ass apart. This man is caught in anger, malaria-induced violence in his eyes. His breathing, I feel it in my face. I am thinking of ways to get out from under him. Maybe I can get my feet under him and kick or knee him in the groin. I have a knife in my hand, the filet knife for fish. Maybe I can slash his hand, get him off. I start spinning the blade in my fingers like a baton twirler, slowly, so that he doesn't notice what I'm doing. He is breathing hard, almost on the verge of tears. The girl is at his side, tugging at the back of his jacket, saying, Let's go, Ron, please? Let's go. Yurie is standing in a nook, with the rest of the wait staff, powerless.

Hey, man, get off of him. A voice I've only heard ordering cu-
cumber rolls. Robert, very evenly, trying not to provoke him. The
man growls, Stay out of this, faggot, and I hear Robert bristling,
the hairs standing up on his nape. The man puts his face close to
mine, huffs and puffs as if he will blow my house down. Yurie
screams something in shrill Japanese. I don't understand what she
is saying, but she is white as a sheet and sees something, maybe
the knife. The other waiters must see the same, because they have
looks of dread dangling on the sides of their mouths.

I set my face. It is impassive, and I clench my teeth. I am familiar with this face, from once before. The knife is in place. I will
not allow myself to smile as I do so. I am going to cut him.

I remember the time. It was with Arthur, his name was, and I
remember the hurt as he slapped me. I told him that I wanted to
get away for a while, for myself. I was confused, and the blow was
dumbfounding. He had gotten angry before, but never hit me.
Never. It was so sudden, catching me off guard, his hand had flown
out too late for either of us to stop it. Why? I asked then, and immediately wished that I hadn't. I knew his answer. Deep inside, I
knew his words even before he spoke them. Because, he hissed,
you're nothing more than a whore. A fucking yellow whore. You
want to go suck some more white cock? Do you know how many
Asians are waiting to jump me? *You* come in boatfuls every day.

The words turned me cold. I became a stone, flat, crackless, im-
pervious. I knew what he wanted, the smooth, hairless body, the
legendary tightness, the naïveté, the subservience. He cried, I'm
sorry, I didn't mean it, but I no longer heard him, not with my
ears of granite. His tears did not melt me, acidic as they were.
"Please," he whispered in Vietnamese, and I regretted teaching
him the word, insisting that he repeat it over and over until he
had every inflection and nuance exact. He hated me back then,
making fun of him not being able to pronounce it correctly. I only
wanted him to impress my parents when they finally met. I hated
him using it against me. I wouldn't play up to him, not this one,
not any more. No more begging to my white master.

Afterward, he tried calling. Once. Maybe to cajole his way back
into my life, I didn't know, maybe to shout more, maybe to apolo-
gize. I let the phone drop back into its cradle without saying a
word. I had gotten the last word in. He could not hurt me any
longer. My heart was already closed to him.

Ronald, get off of him! The girl pushes him, palms flat against his side. The man is shaking, his arms, muscles, every bit of his body is quivering. His strength is waning, leaking out. Go to the car, now! She cries, Please. He looks at her, at me. He turns and staggers out, one hand on his face and the other held out in front of him, like a man suddenly struck blind by a magnesium flare. I hear the fading howl, a low, descending whistle.

I'm sorry, the woman says, but not directly to me. She is saying it to my race. She is upside-down and walking backward toward the door. I'm sorry, she says again. Her make-up is running, revealing the sallow skin beneath. His brother, she starts, looking around, his older brother was killed in the war. She looks at me, as if her explanation excuses everything. It doesn't. She follows her man, Ron, whatever his name is.

It's funny, and I'm laughing because I've just discovered that the point of the knife is digging into my own skin, not breaking it, but nearly there. No one else finds it funny. They move slowly, like ghosts, around me.

Here, let me help you up. Robert again. Why is it always him? I have an arm around his shoulder, but I don't want to stand any more. The floor was very comfortable. I could spread out my robe as a mat and sleep there, in the fish and the heat. The knife bounces against the carpet.

We're moving in waves, up and down. The flatfish has both eyes on one side of its face and both look at me, swimming through this crowd. We stop by Yurie, the big cahuna. They are talking, Robert and she, and I hear the word *home*. Ah, yes, I'd like to go there, but it's a bombed-out shell, overrun by Communists. The Communists will get me one of these days. See, they've drawn up tactical maps, and there's no way to escape. Yurie nods, and as we move away, calls out, You stay at home tomorrow, okay?

I can't tell where I'm going. It's nighttime outside. I feel drunk, because I'm stumbling, leaning against things. My skin feels tight, stretched burning across my face and body, like I'm going to rip. I don't have a car, I tell him. He says nothing, and I feel myself being put in a back seat. Can't think straight. I lie on my back and look up at the velvety ceiling. Looks like a coffin.

The driver's seat has a disembodied cap floating above it, Robert's head. He must be picking me up. Well, it was bound to happen sooner or later. I want to laugh, but my sides hurt too much and I end up coughing.

You all right back there? he asks. I nod, but don't know if he can see me. Where do you live? I mumble my address and hear the engine rumble. What's your name? This conversation is taking us nowhere.

"Giang."

He looks behind, puts his arm on the headrest. Must be pulling out. John? he asks.

Close enough, I mutter.

A little later, he says, "Giang?" and I tell him, yes, that's *my* name.

When we reach my apartment, I can walk by myself, but Robert has his hand on my back. I'm afraid it's going to smell like fish inside, but it doesn't. It smells of dust. *I* smell like fish. Through the dark, I see my bed, inviting. I collapse onto it.

Robert is uncomfortable, he paws the floor with the toe of his shoe. Are you going to be all right? he asks, and I sit up in bed and see his outline. The cap, the shirt, him, I can feel him there. If only for tonight, then I'd be all right. I know it. I guess I'll be going now, he says. He doesn't turn right away, but I sense him looking at me looking at him. We look and we look, but what do we find?

I say, very simply, Stay, and close my eyes.

Footsteps, and then I feel him wrapping himself around me, in darkness.

The ringing telephone wakes me. The brightness hurts when I open my eyes, but the ringing is insistent. I unravel myself from his arms and clatter on the floor. Robert murmurs, not even half-awake, and turns over.

"Lazy American," I say. Then I smile. I pull on the robe, discarded by the side of the bed. The smell of fish is gone. The phone wails again.

Hello? My voice drawls.

It's my mother. "Giang? Did you just wake up?"

"Yes, mother."

"Just now? Why so late?"

"I had—" My Vietnamese is rusty and I finish—"a hard night, mother."

She has listened to my bilingual hybrid long enough to understand and doesn't respond. "Well, I was calling to check up on you, and…" I try to listen, but I'm too drowsy to pay attention. I'm acquainted with this routine anyway. She probably learned it from her mother, and it had been passed down like that, mother to daughter, generation to generation. A long heritage of nagging. I say, "Yes, mother," at the appropriate points as she tells me the latest gossip from her friends, but I'm watching Robert instead. He sleeps with his mouth open, and I remind myself to yell at him for drooling on the pillow again. His hair, freed from the cap, has fluffed to enormous volume. I reach up and find that mine has done the same.

". . . maybe come home for a visit?"

I think about this, about having a bowl of home-cooked soup, maybe talking to them. I haven't spoken with them in such a long time. I don't even remember what Dad's voice sounds like.

"Maybe," I respond, when everyone's ready.

"You need any money?"

"No, I'm okay." I hold my finger up to the sunlight to check its progress. I think it's healing well, cleanly, with only a hint of a scar.

"You go back to work then. I'll call you next week."

"Okay, Mom."

"You remember to pray, don't you? Every day? You don't have to say it aloud, but in your mind, at least. To relieve stress and . . ." The religion lecture.

"Yes," I lie. "Three times every day." To prove that I know what she means, I say, "*Nam mô A Di Da Phat.*" Then, in my head, I repeat it twice.

"Good. That's good. I'll talk to you next week, then."

"Okay, Mom."

"Have anything else to say?"

The words are on my tongue, "No, good-bye," but this time, they don't come out. Instead, "Tell Dad that I love him."

There's a short sigh on the other side. "I will."

"I love you too, Mom."

A pause.

"Good-bye," I say.

"Good-bye."

"Good-bye," I say again, then hang up the phone.

I climb back into bed, and Robert, eyes half-opened, asks, "Where do you want to eat for lunch?"

Is it time for lunch already? I look at the clock. It's almost one.

I think I want some soup, I inform him. After some thought, I add, Vietnamese soup, have you ever had any? He smacks his lips. They are dry, and I wet them for him. No, I don't think so, he declares, does it have fish in it?

I laugh, No, it doesn't have any fish in it. Are you tired of fish already?

You're the one who should be tired of fish, he says.

Not all fish. Some I still like.

Yellowtail? he asks.

No, that's something that *you* like, and I poke his sides. He yelps, fidgets, and grimaces. I put my head on his chest. The hairs tickle my ears, and I can hear his heart pump blood to and fro, a soothing sound. You should try this soup, I say, I think you'd really like it.

Later, he says, and closes his arms around me. I am pressed against him and his warmth. I am going to fall asleep here. One day, I will teach him the words "*Yêu thoung.*" But I won't tell him what it means until later, much later, on a day when we are sitting across from each other, big bowls of pho steaming before our faces. Then, right before we start eating, as he pushes the thin, raw beef into the soup and stirs the vermicelli to the surface, I will whisper in his ear, and he will understand everything, long before the beef re-emerges, cooked and ready to be eaten.

The
Loneliest
Gentleman

MARK A. SHAW

"Is he late or am I nervous?" Claiborne left the kitchen while re-moving a white apron from his tasteful ensemble—black tie again.

"He still has five minutes." Nancy sat at the table in the dining room, not concentrating on her drink. She pulled a glittering object from her lap and waved it at him. "I found your watch."

"Where?" He strapped it on gleefully.

"In the pocket of the trousers you wore the other night. I re-membered that you had placed it there, imagining the crowd at the Carlyle were sailors and thugs, dressed up to fool you. You are the most paranoid drunk."

"Why do we remember these details only days later? It would be more convenient if we could remember what we had done the next morning."

"It is probably best we don't, but someday we'll indulge in a crime which will call for our flight from the Empire state, and we will probably be the last to know."

"I used to wonder, after participating in some Bayou Bacchana-lia and remembering nothing, where do I go and who takes over?"

"In your case, you become equal parts Cole Porter and Caligula."

"When did you first begin to lose telling portions of your memory?"

"At the cotillion on my eighteenth birthday. I broke the record held by Priscilla McMillan of nineteen sixty-three for my con-sumption of Southern Comfort and Coke. Remembering nothing the next day, I faced the silences at the Club with stupid confidence. I've never known how I lost my date, but he was never again seen in those parts."

"Perhaps you killed and consumed him." Claiborne observed as he moved to answer the ringing telephone.

"Hello. What's the matter, did you chicken out? Are you wearing something wildly inappropriate? Well, what on earth are you doing there? All right, I'll be there in ten minutes." Chuck had explained that he didn't want to see Nancy and if Claiborne still wanted to get together, he was waiting down the street. "He's in the coffee shop on the corner of Varick. He wants me to meet him before he comes over."

"Did he tell you why?"

"No, he didn't."

"You lie like a gentleman."

Her companion shrugged.

"Well, go meet this misogynist but don't forget I'm sitting here all dressed up with no place to go."

"I promise we won't be more than fifteen minutes." He lied again.

As he approached the coffee shop, he realized he did not remember this gentleman's features. He had nearly asked, on the telephone, what Chuck was wearing, but he was unwilling to confess this characteristic lapse and hoped to be guided by providence.

He was pleased to be meeting Chuck alone. Nancy's presence reminded him that they had made a place for themselves outside the world and communication would leave them injured. His curiosity pushed him into the world as his desire pushed him toward men and he hoped that by explaining himself to a man who epitomized homosexual desire he would find the world's embrace.

Very few customers were present in the early evening. One man, apparently finishing a life-risking jog, stood at the counter gasping for breath, unable to summon the breath necessary to order a restorative beverage. The other customer, seated at a booth in the back, was obviously the man for whom he was looking.

His features were large and thrown together in a cavalier fashion; his nose had obviously been broken, his black hair stood in uneven tufts. He was lightly tanned and wore a formidable black moustache. His thick arms were left bare by a USMC T-shirt. His black eyes met Claiborne's and gestured him into the booth.

"You're overdressed."

"I'm properly dressed for dinner, not a snack."

"You didn't remember what I look like, did you?"

"Of course I did."

"What was I wearing last night?"

"I don't have time to analyze the West Village fashion system. Nancy is waiting and dinner will spoil."

"I thought I was supposed to meet you at the Chelsea."

"I couldn't very well serve dinner in the Chelsea, unless Virgil Thomson wills me his place, and The Old Girl refuses to go there, bless her heart."

"Let's go eat somewhere alone. I don't want to spend the evening with your fag hag."

"You're not properly dressed."

"I'm properly dressed for gay. You're dressed for closet queen."

"I am not a closet queen. Everyone has known that I sleep with men since I was twelve."

"Sleeping with men doesn't make you gay."

"Precisely my point. I'm not gay and Nancy is not a fag hag. She has even less affection for gay culture than I."

"She made that clear last night."

"You spoke with her last night? What did you two discuss?"

"The fact that she obviously wasn't your sister. Then we talked about Doreen's."

"Doreen's? In New Orleans? How do you know about Doreen's?"

"I lived there for a couple of years. Your hair is different."

"It was much longer. Since I was treated like some down-home Duc de Bourgogene, I wore my hair tied with a ribbon. The urge to wear a powdered wig was often overwhelming." He paused, engulfed in a fog of panic common to those with a firm commitment to scotch. "Wait a minute, have we met before?"

"You'll never know, will you?"

"You mustn't tease drinking men like that."

"I used to watch you and your drunk boyfriend stumble from bar to bar."

"What boyfriend?"

"He was bigger than you—tan, big nose. You always dressed alike."

"How in the hell did I get hooked up with you?"

"You picked me up."

"I didn't pick you up. I was merely courteous. Any gentleman would have done the same."

"Any gentleman wouldn't be here now, sweating like a girl."

"I know I've been piling up sin upon sin, but never in my sickest dreams did I imagine this penance."

"Do you still believe in that shit?"

"What shit is that?"

"The Catholic Church."

Claiborne was unaccustomed to explaining himself. He grew up in a world where everyone knew all there was to know. He came North to escape the encyclopedic knowledge of the nodding old ladies who ringed the ballrooms, cataloging every indiscretion, comparing his latest outrage to those of his great-grandfather. He was surprised to find himself equally uncomfortable with someone who knew absolutely nothing about him and wished a few of the great matrons of New Orleans society were present to put him in perspective. He hoped that by telling a few well-chosen stories, he would be fully heard, seen, understood.

"The Church is bound up with family, and my family has a reach over five generations. I grew up with stories about my ancestors the way most children hear of the lives of the saints. I heard stories about how we tamed the wilderness of the Louisiana Colony for France; we survived cholera, malaria, fires, and floods; we triumphed over the humiliation of the defeat by the Yankees; all the while keeping our land, supporting those that depended on us, ultimately maintaining a sheen of respectability against the temptations of the tropics." He searched Chuck's face for an indication that he understood, but Claiborne was uncertain what it was he wanted understood. "I admit the use of the word 'we' is problematic. I, of course, did none of those things, yet I reap the benefits and must accept the responsibilities."

"What does that have to do with the Catholic Church?"

"I can't imagine why this interests you."

"When you do your Scarlett O'Hara routine, your accent comes back."

"That was in *Georgia* and she was *Irish*. Only a bunch of crackpot Southerners would adopt something as ludicrous as Tara as their Jerusalem, looking to a petty, imbecilic Irish fornicator for redemption. The French Church, especially the colonial French Church, cared very little about the sins of the flesh. The great sins were sins against society: dishonoring the family, abusing the land and the people who depended on us. One of the most burdensome sins of my fathers occurred after the war. Instead of freeing their slaves, who they felt could never exist without their beneficence, they murdered them, explaining to the Reconstructionists that they had died of a particularly virulent strain of cholera."

"So do you feel guilty because your family were murderers or because you aren't making babies?"

"My grandfather and grandmother had certain expectations. My grandfather expected me to follow his example: marry, produce sons, have discreet relationships no one has to talk about. My grandmother, who never accepted my grandfather's hypocrisy, counseled honesty and exile."

"I'll bet you had one of those huge old houses in the Garden District."

"Of course not, that's where the Americans live. My grandfather had an apartment in the Pontalbas. My grandmother's house had been in her family for one hundred fifty years, on Esplanade."

"They didn't live together?" Chuck asked.

"No, they each lived their own lives. My grandmother lived with Cora Mae, who got her out of bed a couple of times a week. My grandfather lived with a succession of male secretaries of whom he was unnaturally fond."

"How did your parents die?"

"They didn't. They live in Africa. My father was disowned for marrying a Protestant from Kentucky. I was raised by my father's parents."

"Did your grandmother know that your grandfather was gay?"

"Why must you use that word. He wasn't gay, certainly, and yes, my grandmother knew of his liaisons. Everyone did although my grandmother was the only one indelicate enough to mention them, often, to anyone who would listen. Which is, I suppose, why she went out so seldom. To survive in New Orleans society, it's best to keep your mouth shut about the vices of others or nothing else would ever be discussed."

At the age of twelve, Claiborne's relationship with his grandfather changed. They had always spent Saturday and Sunday together, roaming the streets of their city while his grandfather told stories about the old families to whom they were related, families that had apparently once inhabited every building in the Vieux Carre.

He no longer walked the few blocks from his grandmother's house to his grandfather's huge, dark apartment in the Pontalbas, which bore the uncomfortable burden of being the first apartment building in North America. His grandfather had a new secretary.

His grandfather's secretaries never lasted for more than one season. They did not accompany Beauregard LeMoyne in society, but waited demurely for his return. They did not, officially, exist.

This particular young man, Nick, had a tattoo, a beard, and an earring. He did not follow the established rules of dress, which meant seersucker suits in summer and gabardine in winter. He wore football shorts and cropped T-shirts. He spoke loudly. He did not drink whiskey or wine as did the other young men in his grandfather's employ. He drank what he called sody pop with foam on top, and showed a marked preference for inexpensive Jax beer, brewed just a few blocks from his new home.

Claiborne arrived at his grandfather's apartment and let himself in with his key. His entrance usually required a few moments for his eyes to adjust to the dim lighting. On this occasion he was dazzled by the light peculiar to New Orleans, a light both purple and gold. The heavy damask curtains had been removed from the french windows surrounding the room on two sides leaving it exposed and somehow shameful. The doors onto the balcony were open, admitting the sounds of tourists at play; their nasal awed remarks at the light shining off of St. Louis Cathedral. A more melodic cacophony found its way into the civilized chamber from the bars on Bourbon Street.

The room emitted its own smell of dusty books, bourbon, and stale cigarettes. This aroma blended with the smells of the city: decaying passion flowers, ripe honeysuckle, roasting coffee, and sizzling tourists.

Claiborne approached the piratical young man seated in his grandfather's armchair. "You must be Nick. I am Claiborne LeMoyne."

"Figured that. You're too pretty to be a delivery boy." He wiped away a bead of sweat which descended from the area covered by the T-shirt, cut off at mid-chest, just below the faded word "Tulane."

Another rivulet of perspiration was loosened by this action, and flowed freely into the baggy shorts. "While you're up, swing your behind into the kitchen and get me another Dixie. Get yourself one while you're at it."

Claiborne did not move for some time, studying the hairy brown flesh.

"Scoot, pretty boy." Nick commanded.

He returned with the requested beer and an old fashioned. "Don't call me that."

Nick grabbed the beer from the boy's hand, stashed it between his large, brown thighs and pulled the boy onto his knee. "What're you drinking?"

"An old fashioned. It's made with scotch or whiskey, bitters, sugar, mulled fruit, and seltzer."

"Too good for beer, are you?"

"Where is my grandfather?"

"Maybe I killed him so I could have my way with you." The boy made an effort to rise, but was stopped by a hand searching between his legs. "That's what I thought. You kind of like sitting on old Uncle Nick's lap, don't you?" Claiborne's attempt to rise only placed him more firmly in the man's lap. "That's it baby, shake it, but don't break it."

"I didn't know people actually said these kinds of things."

"The old man don't mind it—makes him whimper like a hungry dog." The man's hands pulled the boy down firmly. "Can you whimper for me, pretty boy?"

Claiborne turned at the waist, flicked his wrist, and deposited the contents of his drink in the man's eyes. The man shoved the boy off his lap and stood with a roar, rubbing his burning eyes.

Beauregard LeMoyne entered the room to find his grandson lying at the feet of his companion, who was roaring like a wounded bull.

"Claiborne, what have you done?" he asked, as he moved to comfort his secretary.

The boy was on his feet and out the door before the question could be repeated.

One week later, he waited for his grandfather in the dining room of his grandmother's house, where his grandfather had arranged to meet him.

The large room was dimly lit and was never used for its original purpose. It existed merely as a showcase for family history. Large, dark portraits of his ancestors for the last two hundred years were hung on three walls. Claiborne removed a small lamp from the large mahogany table and examined each dignified face, finding precursors to his own—two hundred years of the same long, thin nose and large, aquamarine eyes—only the hairstyles changed.

He heard his grandfather enter the house. Cora Mae directed him to the dining room. He did not visit the second floor and speak to his wife as he had each Saturday morning of their adult lives. Claiborne busied himself studying the face of his great-great grandfather and comparing it to the most recent painting of himself. He ignored the man in the doorway.

"I am sorry about the events of last weekend. I do not know what occurred, and I do not wish to know. Nick refuses to discuss it, which I think very decent of him. I will not demand an apology, as you are still very young, but I think it best that, in the future, we meet here each weekend. Do I make myself clear, young man?"

Claiborne did not turn, but studied the paintings more closely. "Why is there no painting of my father?"

"Your father was not wildly attractive."

"I would have thought his portrait was necessary to document the endless repetition of the LeMoyne features. Isn't there a portrait of him somewhere?"

"He left home when he was seventeen and he never returned. He broke your grandmother's heart."

"I would like a picture of him."

"I can't imagine why. He's never expressed any interest in yours."

"Nick certainly must have put you through the ringer."

"What goes on between my friend and me is no concern of yours or anyone else, unless you've already discussed this with your grandmother."

"No, your secret is safe with me. You know, of course, I did nothing to excite your friend."

"I wouldn't be surprised if your mere presence was excitement enough."

"Am I wildly attractive?"

"To many, I would imagine so. You and Nick will not meet again."

"I'll probably run into him in Doreen's."

"What would you be doing in a place like that?"

"The same thing I've seen you doing there."

"I can see to it that you aren't allowed in there again."

"I wouldn't recommend any interference if you wish to maintain your secrets."

"Secrets are a man's only weapon. You must learn that if you hope to survive in this city. As long as you marry and produce children, you are allowed to live your own life. Provided, of course, no scandal ensues."

"How do you prevent scandal?"

"Caution. Discretion."

"I am incapable of caution."

"It is a skill you will acquire."

"I will never marry."

"Yes, you will. It is not your choice, unless you care to follow your father's example, and I find it difficult to imagine you penniless. With your pedigree, mothers will overlook almost any impediment to marriage to their daughters."

"I will create such a scandal no respectable girl will dare approach me."

"That will be quite an undertaking in this province. Where would you like to have lunch?"

"Let's just pick up a couple of muffulettas on the street and watch the Tulane track team sweat through their shorts."

"I suggest you change into respectable clothes. We're lunching at Brennan's."

"Does Nick cook?"

"Not for you." Beauregard left the room.

Claiborne spit in the face of Florent LeMoyne, his great-great-grandfather. Spittle struck the canvas above the left eye and was left to follow its natural course as the boy ran upstairs to say goodbye to his grandmother.

He found her swathed in netting. She had pulled the elaborate system of mosquito netting down around her and was thrashing around, cursing the tropics.

"Darling, you resemble a particularly cranky mummy." Claiborne calmed her and unwound the netting, draping it once more over the frame of the bed of her ancestors. "I'm off to lunch with the old man."

"Why didn't the fool come up here?"

"He seems to be in quite a hurry."

"Where are you going?"

"Brennan's, he says."

"Then he's not in any hurry. He's been there every Sunday for eighteen years. They're hardly going to give his table to anyone else. He must be afraid to see me. What has he done?"

"He doesn't confide in me. He still thinks I'm a child."

"It does you no credit to lie for him. He's probably ashamed of that particularly horrible new boyfriend of his."

"How could you possibly know about that? You haven't left this house in eight months."

"That man has no secrets from me or anyone else in this village. We all pretend ignorance because he seems so ashamed of his liaisons, although we couldn't care less. It's not like he enjoys keeping things from me, it absolutely tortures him, and does no one any good." She popped her wrinkled head out of the netting for a kiss, which was lovingly bestowed. "Remember, young man. You needn't follow the example of your grandfather. Honesty is always an option."

"Yes, ma'am." Claiborne paused at her door.

"And I think you'd better skip the oysters this afternoon. I've been told they are not to be trusted."

"I wonder if I will remember any of this tomorrow?" Claiborne asked.

"You haven't had that much to drink."

"Don't tell me you've been counting."

"I'm very observant." Chuck smiled with satisfaction.

"Well, it won't work. If I'm aware of your censorious eye, I'll only drink more."

"Why do you think that is?"

"Don't act knowing."

"If you don't remember, I'll remind you in the morning."

"Will I see you tomorrow?"

"Yes."

"You take far too much for granted."

"You don't grant much."

The two men were seated at a table in the front window of John's Pizzeria on Bleecker Street. Claiborne concentrated on Chuck, resembling a player in a poker game with very high stakes.

Chuck frequently ignored Claiborne to examine the young men filling the sidewalk.

"Let's go to Paradise." Chuck suggested.

"Aren't we scheduled to tour the Inferno first?"

"Paradise is a bar. You'll have to change."

"Into whom?"

"You'll have to change your clothes."

"What is wrong with what I'm wearing?"

"People will think you're a society victim, or an opera queen. You'll ruin my reputation."

"You are more than welcome to find an actor/dancer/model to play lumberjack/cop/marine. I'll stay home until gentlemen are once again held to be desirable."

"You're a very hot man."

"I'm a great deal more than that."

"But that's the most important."

"What's the most important?"

"Being hot. Getting hot. Staying hot."

"I've no idea what that could possibly mean. To whom is this imperative important?"

"The men who share our world."

"It is not my world."

"Doesn't she let you go to the bars?"

"Her name is Nancy. She would never forbid me anything. Neither of us relishes spending an evening with hundreds of professional faggots."

"Don't use that word."

"I'll use any word I like. "

"What makes you think your life is any better?"

"I didn't say my life is better. I have never found a place for myself in the gay community."

"But you are a gay man."

"I'm not, you know. At least not as presently defined."

"Are you and Nancy honest with each other?"

"We know each other too well to have to tell each other the truth."

"Which is?"

"That neither of us will ever find anyone who suits us as well."

"Then why the other men?"

"Because we enjoy it."

"Who enjoys it more?"

"How would I know?"

"Whose idea was it?"

"Mine."

"Is that fair?"

"To whom?"

"To her."

"She has no illusions."

"You're in trouble if you believe that."

"Her illusions and mine still mesh."

"And when they don't?"

"We'll worry about that when the time comes."

"Why do you drink?"

"Because I like to drink. I like to be drunk. What business is it of yours?"

"You're not very happy, are you?"

"Why should you care?"

"Because I like you."

"How generous of you."

"Yes. I suppose it is."

"Do you want to take me away from all of this?"

"I want to make you happy."

Claiborne found the man and the conversation maddening. He remained because it was maddening in a new way. He hoped Chuck would provide an escape from the past. "Don't ever promise me what you can't provide."

"I'm not asking that much from you."

"I haven't figured out what you're asking."

"Come dancing and then come home with me."

"I don't understand what you want from me."

"I want to take you out, show you off, take you home, and show you how nice I can be."

"Good luck. I suspect that you find the prospect of rescuing me from my life of bitter dissipation even more attractive."

"These men you bring home, do they kiss you?"

"No, they have to draw the line somewhere."

"Do they tell you how pretty you are?"

"That is not an adjective appropriate to my age."

"Trust a trained eye." He pulled Claiborne to him over the top of the table, where they met in a kiss, both half-standing, half-sitting. "We'll find you something to wear at my place."

"I look ridiculous."

"You don't look ridiculous. You look hot."

"My disaffection with that word grows ever more pronounced. I resemble a nine-year-old trying on the apparel of his eccentric uncle."

"Everyone will be dressed like that. Stop worrying."

He did, in fact, look ridiculous. The black dungarees belonged to an acquaintance of Chuck's, apparently much larger than Claiborne, who had left them behind after a torrid encounter.

"What did this large young man wear after escaping your clutches?"

"I don't know. Put on this T-shirt."

"What color would you call this?"

"I don't know."

"Yes, you do. I feel certain that there is a word for it."

"I guess it's puce. I dyed it myself."

"No one in the history of the Louisiana Colony has ever worn this color. If they were foolhardy enough to brave the censure of the Southern Yacht Club in this abomination, I suppose they could always move to Oklahoma."

"You aren't going to the Southern Yacht Club. You are going to the hottest gay bar in New York."

"Do not sneer at the Southern Yacht Club. It holds many a surprise."

"This color does great things to your eyes."

"I would have been far happier never knowing that." He submitted to the inevitability of the undergarment. "Do I get to wear a jacket?"

Chuck tossed a leather motorcycle jacket at him.

"Why does this jacket smell like goats?"

There was no response other than a sheepish shrug.

"Chuck, what are these stains?" He had placed the jacket over his shoulders, but attempted to prevent any physical contact, which involved a modicum of squirming.

"I don't think you want to know."

"Is it toxic?"

"A couple of guys from the USC varsity swim team jacked off on it."

The jacket was shed with fantastic speed. "I may have what some would consider an unnatural attachment to my great-great-grandfather's cuff links, but that is as close as I intend to come to wearing anything that could be considered fetishistic."

"All right, you can wear one of my roommate's." He handed Claiborne a much larger leather jacket.

"Has it been squirted upon?"

"I wish you would trust me."

"Give me a few years."

He examined the jacket closely before putting it on. He was not small, but once placed on his shoulders, this jacket more closely resembled a trench coat. "This jacket is huge. Does your roommate sleep in a cage?"

"Only if the money is right. You can check it when we get there."

The line outside of the club consisted of hundreds of identically dressed men in jeans and T-shirts. A few wore leather vests and caps. They looked like the products of an assembly line of a firm that produced a generic man. As Claiborne was unaccustomed to waiting in lines, he moved to the front, which was held to be a considerable faux pas.

An enormous man with shaved head, bare chest, and gold rings through his nipples glared at him. "Back of the line."

They waited for some time, while Chuck chatted with those in back and front of him. Claiborne noticed immediately that no one else was wearing puce.

They were again before the dungeon master, who waved Chuck past but stopped Claiborne with a scowl. He appeared to be particularly offended by the lurid shirt, the baggy jeans held up by a leather strap, and the enormous jacket. Chuck remained at his side, hoping that Claiborne would not be inspired.

"What are you doing with a guy like him?" the doorman asked Chuck.

"I'm rich. I'm really, really rich," Claiborne answered.

"He has a really big dick," Chuck offered.

"I most certainly do not."

"Oh, let her in," yelled a voice from the crowd.

"Spare us the fag vaudeville," yelled another.

"I'll let you in this time, but if you ever come back, wear something else." The doorman gestured them inside.

Hundreds of men, with gleaming chests bared, streamed past them. A few paused in their rounds to glance at them in an obvious fashion. Claiborne smiled and nodded at them, which, from the change in their faces, was the incorrect response.

"What do you think?" Chuck asked.

"I don't understand. Why do they all look alike?"

"These are the hottest men in the city."

"Maybe they aren't people. Who decided that this is what we are supposed to look like? Everyone looks plucked and dipped in Caucasian paint."

"There are plenty of bars we could go to that are filled with ugly men."

"Why didn't you take me there?"

"They wear sweaters."

"There are no black men here."

"Sure there are, somewhere."

"I expect more from the gay community."

"You shouldn't."

"I could not wait to get out of the South and take my place in the gay world, only to find a microcosm of all the things I hated in New Orleans. Gay men found attractive in me all the things I loathed about myself."

"You've read too many books."

"Everyone is tan and beefy. I like skinny arms."

"My arms are not skinny."

"What makes you think I like you?"

"You're here. When I get you home, you're going to like me even better."

"I sincerely hope that you are not constructing some lurid fantasy. I find verbal commands distasteful." One of those whose tasks seemed to be to roam without ceasing stopped in front of them. His glance did not include Claiborne.

"Chuck, lookin' good."

"Thanks, Jimbo. This is Claiborne."

He forced himself to acknowledge Claiborne, who smiled in a simple-minded fashion. "Hello, Jim Bo." He forced himself to say these words, which sounded remarkably as if it were his first sentence in English.

"You're new here, aren't you?" His glance included every portion of Claiborne's anatomy with an obvious disinterest.

"Yes, how could you tell? Please don't mention the shirt, it was not my idea."

"See you later, Chuck." He disappeared.

This pattern was repeated many times throughout the evening. The only man who approached him was considerably older, whose ample frame was barely contained in near-to-bursting leather.

Following the briefest of conversations, he too wandered off.

"My popularity is overwhelming. Why is it that only the old and jaded are attracted to me?"

"I'm beginning to think you're a fifties queen."

"No, I think I'm a twenties queen. Is it advisable to dance?"

"Can you dance?"

"Please allow me the nasty asides, you'll confuse me."

Claiborne learned to dance in tiny, overheated black clubs in and around the Desire projects, where he was at first ignored, then accepted as just another eccentric white boy. The music played there and throughout most of New Orleans was more African than European. Accustomed to polyrhythms, he was unable to find his place in the steady thud of gay bar music.

He moved twice as slowly as those other dancers, concentrating the motion in the hips. Those around him were content to simply bounce up and down after snorting from their tiny little bottles, or move their feet back and forth in a manner that could only be described as shiftless.

After a brief time, he was the only man on the dance floor whose chest was covered. He was often splashed by the sweat that flew off of their bodies. He retaliated by spitting. After many a violent nudge into the midsections of the men surrounding him, he found himself lifted off of the floor and spun around to encounter a very indignant face. "Listen buddy, I don't know what you're doing here, but you'd better get hot or get out."

"I don't know how it works." Claiborne answered.

This man was confused enough by his remark to set him down and allow Chuck the opportunity to forcibly remove him from the throng.

A compromise was necessary for the continuation of their encounter. Claiborne wished to return uptown, Chuck insisted they remain downtown. Their desires were complicated by Claiborne's insistence on a cab, which Chuck thought ridiculous. He acknowledged its inevitability and Claiborne accepted the necessity of remaining downtown but refused to patronize any bistro within sight of Sheridan Square. The cab took them to the Peacock Cafe, a monument securely held in the downtown firmament.

The cappuccino maker thumped and hissed while an exceedingly aged soprano attempted Tosca on what sounded like an Edison-era phonograph.

Claiborne looked even more ridiculous when surrounded by old Marxists and NYU film students, while Chuck looked the perfect image of a gay man who lives in Chelsea.

Claiborne pouted.

Chuck responded. "If you'd just make an effort to be nice you'd have a better time."

Claiborne grinned across the table in a horrible fashion. "You're absolutely right. That was more fun. And to think I've only now learned that if I make an effort to be nice," the horrible grin reappeared, "I'd have a better time. Thank you for that illuminating tidbit."

"Why are you so hostile?"

"I hate gay bars."

"You seemed to like them in New Orleans."

"It was not the bars, per se, that I enjoyed. I hated them just as much there where it was still possible to have sex with another man as just another man and not some slimy facsimile of masculinity. What I most enjoyed in New Orleans was the opportunity to disgrace my family. That was a delicious power, walking into a ball, reeking of sex and alcohol, with a disreputable companion I'd picked up on the street."

"Do you have any happy childhood memories?" Chuck asked.

"I loved waking up in the morning in May, before it got too hot to breathe. The city was so preposterously overripe, the passion flowers had just bloomed and weren't yet overwhelming. I would dress myself and walk to Cafe DuMonde for café au lait and beignets and pretend to be a tourist."

"How old were you?"

"Six or seven."

"You drank coffee at seven years old?"

"A few years later I discovered cognac."

"I meant, don't you have any innocent childhood memories?"

"I used to love driving back from the summer house in Pass Christian. My grandmother kept an old Packard and someone would drive us back on I-ten late at night. I would pretend to fall asleep with my head in my grandmother's lap and watch the stars, smell the mud in the bayou, and listen to millions of crickets and the crazy prophets on the radio."

"That sounds fairly innocent. When did you lose your virginity?"

"My cousin Stephan moved to New Orleans when I was ten. He was the first person my age I knew. He was a year older than me and seemed to understand everything in the world. I taught him how to get along in New Orleans and a few years later he taught me what my body could do."

"Do you think that's the cause of your problems with your sexuality?"

"I don't have problems with my sexuality. You have problems with my sexuality."

"But you'd rather not be gay."

"I am not gay. I'm perfectly content, outside the ghetto, although at one time I was delighted at the prospect of belonging to a secret society founded on the pleasure of perversion. Instead, I found a carnal frat party of goons, with no more interest in intellect or grace than a VFW lodge in Little Rock."

"How much money do you have?"

He was appalled, first, by such a bad-taste question. Then he remembered he wasn't in the South, and that good taste was never an issue when money was involved. "I don't have any money." He began waving his arms around as if plagued by gnats. "I live only to send checks to my profligate cousins, aunts, great-aunts, and anyone else who ever had the good fortune to marry into my family. Bloodsuckers, every last one of them. What I get to keep goes into our maid's pocket. I'll probably be forced to move to the YMCA."

"We have nothing in common."

"I have nothing in common with anyone. Except my cousins, who are even sillier than I am."

"That's a thought to send me screaming in the night."

"Fear not, you'll never meet them."

"Did you have any friends?"

"Only one. My cousin Stephan."

"What happened to him?"

"Nothing. He lives in the Pontchartrain. At least I think he lives in the Pontchartrain. He cashes the check I send there every month."

"Have you ever had a lover?"

"Yes. My cousin, Stephan."

"For how long?"

"Forever. He is connected, somehow, to the café au lait, the passion flowers, the crickets, and the mud. Especially the mud."

Stephan slouched in a wrought-iron chair at a wrought-iron table, in a courtyard surrounded by a wrought-iron fence and tropical plants.

His black, shoulder-length hair was pulled back and contained in a black silk ribbon. His nose was long and thin, his face lacked pigment, the eyes were pale green.

He was clad in the requisite white linen trousers, crumpled and disgraceful. His white cotton shirt was starched into stronger stuff than he, his red bow tie held on by propriety alone.

He wore a too-small seersucker jacket with a red stain on the lapel which was either blood or barbecue sauce. He had a hazy recollection of an encounter with each the evening prior. He withdrew a tattered letter from his inside pocket. It was crumpled and yellowed by the humidity. He read it again, squinting against the sunlight. He had donated his sunglasses to some delta sub-deb the previous evening after she squealed into his ear once too often.

Dear Heart:

You see, I've met this man. He is forthright and upstanding. He does not celebrate my passion for dishonor. He labors to make me a BETTER PERSON. He is, thus, perpetually disappointed. He escorts me to lugubrious gay bars, drags me to hideous cocktail parties, and wishes me to accompany him to some dungeon-like hellhole in the meat packing district.

I no longer have the wardrobe for these adventures. Nothing is tight enough.

Why don't you and I get married? I feel certain Mirielle would have approved. We could kidnap little tourist children, raise them properly, teach them to tap dance, and work them on Bourbon.

If this is not to A. J. and Betty's taste, won't you at least marry someone? I should like to be an overindulgent godfather. You could wed my own Miss Nancellen Peasley. She would outlive you by many decades. We will decorate your tomb, tell the children the truth about you, then we'll make something up.

You have my heart. My soul arrives under separate cover. Place it under your pillow before you sleep and dream dreams of vengeance.

Your Partner, your victim,

Claiborne M. B. LeMoyne

"What are you reading so intently?"

He looked too closely at the woman now seated opposite him. He opened his pale eyes too wide.

"Letter."

"Who's it from?" she asked.

"From the loneliest gentleman in New York City."

Ice Cream

DAVID A. NEWMAN

He was thirty feet above Sanford Lake the first time I saw him.
Doing a handstand. His palms were pressed flat against the deserted bridge everybody used to jump from, including a drunk kid
from the township who died on senior night. I was on my bike,
leaning against the boarded-up snack bar, trying not to watch.
Don't puss out one of his friends yelled. Car doors slammed. Sandals crunched across the gravel parking lot. I was afraid of roller
coasters and glass elevators. When trapeze artists performed I
closed my eyes. But I watched as he pushed off, tucked into a back
flip, straightened his body out, squeezed his arms tight at his
sides, slipped into the dark water, and disappeared.

I scooped ice cream and got frozen knuckles. One day I came in
and he was there. Wearing the same red and white striped shirt as
me, scooping the same cherry vanilla and chocolate mint chip.
Up close he was older and better looking. Girls liked him. They
left him twenty-five cent tips and wrote *Got a girlfriend? Want two
more?* on napkins they left for him. His name was Julian. Some
girls called him Jewel but he didn't like it. He shoved their phone
number napkins in his back pocket and arched his black eyebrows
whenever he looked at me.

Hey Danny he said to me, you don't have to say you're sorry
every time you spill the coffee. Hey Danny, he said, you're not really sixteen are you why don't you drive, you're too skinny to be
sixteen. You're a renegade aren't you Danny show me how to make

a Reuben, I won't tell them you're underage I think you're cool Danny, not as cool as me. Check it out and he flicked a fly onto the grill. We watched it burn next to the burgers. See that girl over there, she comes in every day now. Because I fucked her once, she fucks. Trust me Danny, you know I don't lie when it comes to pie.

He lived in the township. He had cooler friends, better clothes, a car. I lived in the city, two small blocks from the Dairy. He had a face that stopped your hand from turning the page of a yearbook: shiny jet-black hair, deep black-brown eyes. When he caught his reflection in the chrome of the malt machine he paused for a second and smiled as if thrilled, like I was, by what he saw.

My mother said that Julian you work with is striking do you like him Danny? He's okay, I shrugged my shoulders and tried not to turn red. I threw a quart of rum raisin in the freezer, ran upstairs and rubbed myself against my mattress, leaving on my jeans and underwear. My mom had noticed him like I noticed him like he noticed himself and I rubbed and rubbed and held my breath. It all came out inside my underwear and I kept them on during dinner.

When little kids asked for a single chocolate chip Julian dug one individual chip out and placed it in their hand until they looked like they would cry. When fat people said they needed a double chocolate mint he said do you *need* it or do you *want* it? Guys said hey man my cone is too small and Julian said sounds like a personal problem. He got dish duty. He smoked. His soccer team won state.

My eyes shone. My lashes clumped together when freezer flakes fell on them. Lines were long: the ice cream was homemade at a plant near Sanford Lake. Hi Danny, Tally Hoffman smiled as she waited with her dad who was a fireman. I'll have a small Smurfette sundae and a single maple nut. They watched me scooping through the freezer glass that looked too thick to hear through but wasn't. Julian drummed dishwater with his fingers keeping time with the radio. That's Danny, Tally said as I spooned marshmallow on top of bubble-gum ice cream and added a cherry, the only difference between a Smurfette and a Smurf. He's cousins with Sheila Marsden, she said.

Mr. Hoffman narrowed his eyes, scanning me as if I were a flavor. He's prettier than Sheila is, he said, raising his voice on the word *prettier* so it sounded like I was guilty of something terrible. I rinsed off my scoop and handed him his cone, pretending I didn't hear him say I was pretty. A pretty boy. Pretending it didn't make me sad for Sheila and happy for me.

Hey Danny, Julian yelled, changing the station with soapy fingers. Do you like Todd Rundgren? I blinked and said yeah. Then I waited a second and asked, what grade is he in? Everyone in line laughed. I didn't know he was a singer. I thought he was this burnout Todd kid from my school. I felt hot and almost wanted to cry. It's no big deal Danny, Julian said and he touched me. On the back. He left his hand there for a second.

I walked home, my sticky right forearm covered in melted ice cream, thinking about Julian's thick wrists and soccer calves. I ran upstairs and took off all my clothes. I was naked and skinny and not fifteen and I thrust against my mattress again, this time with no clothes on. I pictured that spot on his neck right below his hairline as he bent over the freezer, pulling out empty ice-cream containers. I held my breath so no one would hear me listening to my heartbeat or see me depositing the evidence and rubbing it into the sheet and into the mattress. A thin gel covered my palm which I smelled. I stuck out my tongue—which a communion wafer was laid on every week—but was too afraid to let myself taste it.

I stained mattresses and smiled at girls. I read and reread the dirty parts of *Jaws* and *Once Is Not Enough*. I laid in the basement on warm summer days, the only place besides the lake to get cool. To get away. To touch myself and think of soccer jerseys and Julian's cologne and the way he squeezed my shoulder when I did the dishes for him. The way he touched me on the back, the way he opened the door of his Monte Carlo for me the first time we went out drinking after work.

Here you go Danny, Julian opened a Coors and handed it to me. The bottle felt cool, water beads fell over my index finger and thumb. I stared at the top of the bottle for a second. I had opened a beer bottle when I was ten. My mom caught me sipping and made me drink the whole thing, hoping I would hate it and never drink again. I did hate it. I never tried again. Wind blew through Julian's hair. I knew I would drink the beer in my hand, would drink as many he handed me. Julian kept his headlights off, everyone else's were on. We drank and drove on, speeding toward wherever we'd been heading since the first time Julian noticed me staring.

I took a big sip and swallowed, trying to keep my eyes from watering. I drank again, fast, blocking out the vinegar taste, covering the bottle top with my lips. When I pulled the bottle away, beer bubbled over, foaming into my lap, my jeans, and all over the ripped vinyl seat. Virgin, Julian said, smiling at me. I grabbed his soccer jersey from the floorboard and mopped up. I looked out the window, caught my loose smile and clear blue eyes in the side mirror and hoped I looked as good to him as I did to me.

Julian talked about his new girlfriend Tracy, she was a cheerleader, they did cocaine, they liked Billy Joel, they did sex, he told me about it. He told me what she smelled like down there: cantaloupe. He rubbed two fingers under his nose and then he sniffed then licked them and laughed and so did I. Beer came out my nose. He patted my back. I couldn't take my eyes off those fingers when he put them on the steering wheel.

I rode to Sanford Lake, pedaling quietly because it was still early. I passed a faded billboard with our state tourism slogan—*Say Yes! To Michigan!*—on it and said yes quietly to myself, pretending it was an order. The beach was empty, the water dark, the wind on the bridge cold. I set my bike down carefully and took off my sweatshirt. Goose bumps covered my arms, thin blond hairs stood on end. The lake seemed closer than I thought it would, but the drop deepened as I moved toward the railing.

I kicked off my flip-flops, climbed over the railing and stood, my bare feet pressing the same spot his hands had. It was too early to yell, to hear my voice, to hear it echo. I closed my eyes and pictured Julian surfacing, slicking back his hair with a flick of his head. Water fell down his neck and shoulders, returning to the lake like ink to a well. I kept my eyes closed. Held my arms out to my side. And then I jumped.

We went to township parties where he knew everyone and all the girls stared at him. I turned red and stood by the bushes until this junior named Christy who was pretty and chunky and pink came over. Julian patted me on the shoulder and said when you see a chance take it.

I ended up upstairs with Christy in her bra on top of me, trying to pull my pants down but I wouldn't let her. What is wrong with you shy boy? Most guys beg for it. I'm not like most guys I said and she laughed and said no you are not you little cutie! So innocent, she whispered. I like you which is why, she stopped talking for a second, unbuttoning my jeans with her teeth, I'm gonna treat you extra special. I said no I'm Catholic and she said perfect so am I, don't worry baby we can go to confession tomorrow and I pushed her off and said no! don't! I wanted Julian to do it. Only Julian. My mom is sick, I sniffed, I'm sorry. She said oh baby no I'm sorry and she hugged me when I cried because I was scared that I liked him and not her, she smelled good and kissed me and I let her. Christy slipped her tongue in my mouth and darted it around. It felt warm. I pushed my tongue into her mouth. Traced her front teeth. That feels good she smiled and said I had braces can you tell?

I sat next to her at Bob's Big Boy. She held my hand and giggled with Tracy. I traced Big Boy's hair on the placemat with my index finger. Julian got the all-you-can-eat breakfast. We ate off his plate and decided to go to the beach just stay out and drive to the beach and not go home. I have to shave my legs Christy whispered to Tracy. Julian said hang with me Danny come back to my place, you can borrow my shorts. Tracy said we'll pick you up. She grabbed her purse and said behave yourself boys.

He lit a cigarette and steered with his knees. I flicked the ashtray lid. I studied his moves, the way he smoked. He wanted to move to Hollywood and become a stunt man. You could do it, I said, wanting to say you're so beautiful more than anyone I've ever seen you'll never be a stunt man, you'll probably have your own. I'll tell people I knew you when, that you used to touch me on the back and didn't notice me staring at your legs and underneath your shorts. I'll tell people you were the one who made me notice sex on a person. On a boy. I'll tell people before you boys were just haircuts and jeans to me, boys were tennis shoes under altar boy robes. Boys were basketball teammates and kids who picked their noses, made armpit farts, and called Linda Weinstock "Moose."

I'll tell people you were a drip of smooth, cool, dark ink in the lake running down into the water, spilling all over my chest and my legs, staining my T-shirt until I have to take it off, I'm sitting in a puddle of you, soggy like in a canoe. I scoop up the ink, this time I put my tongue to it, I'm not afraid, I taste it, it's bitter and bad and delicious. I scoop up handfuls, drinking you in, black covering my lips and my teeth. You run inside me, changing me

forever, the way I think and talk and look and smile, the way I
smell and hide and look down and you'll be gone, the ink will dry
and all that will be left is a dark crisp T-shirt looking more like I
burned it than dipped it in you.

I'm still buzzing are you, Danny Boy? Julian fuzzed my hair
then motioned me to follow him inside the house, down the hall
and into the bathroom. Sit here while I shower, he said and
turned the water on. I sat on the toilet. I could tell without looking that my underwear had those clear spots on them, those excitement spots.

I had pictured him naked when I closed my eyes at night and
now he was naked for real and I closed them again, I couldn't
look. I heard him pull the clear, wavy shower door in front of him.
I opened my eyes, his body was blurred behind the door: tan
arms, white chest, hair pressed back flat, dark hair between his
legs. He soaped himself. Tracy was ragging on me so bad last night
he said. She kept saying it seemed like I was in love with someone
else. He turned around, yelling over the water as he continued. So
I go who? Christy? Beth? Michelle? Jenny? I'm naming all the girls
I've been with and all the girls on her squad and everything and
she's laughing and saying no, no, no. So finally I go Trace, what
would you say if I told you it was Danny?

Water kept running. It felt like someone had punched me in
the chest. Julian rinsed off. I didn't want to blink, didn't want to
move didn't want him to move or turn off the water. I glanced
at the foggy mirror, at the flip-flops hanging loosely onto my feet.
Julian turned off the water.

He slid back the shower door and stepped toward me. I was
frozen, my hands beneath my legs suddenly asleep. Water dripped
off his body and hit the white tiles below our feet. He moved
closer, his feet were pink from the hot water. He slicked back his
hair and leaned over me, water drops hitting my shirt and jeans. I
closed my eyes and arched my neck up. He grabbed the towel
from the rack behind me and backed away. I opened my eyes.

Julian was at the sink. Not looking at me. He threw me a clean
towel. Shower if you want to Danny Boy but hurry up, those guys
are gonna be here any minute. He left, towel around his waist,
dirty clothes in one hand. I sat for a while until I finally kicked off
my flip-flops and pushed my toes across the tile into a spot of

water that had rolled off his body. The puddle met my toe and circled around it. It felt cold.

Tracy's car was jammed with kids I didn't know. Julian jumped in
the back. I stood on the curb. There wasn't any room and I
thought about backing away, shutting the car door and watching
them drive away. Thought about quitting the Dairy and never
going in for cones when Julian's car was in the parking lot.
Thought about not scanning the soccer column in the paper to
see if he'd scored. Thought about pulling Christy out and burying
my head in her soft chest, her nail-polished hands running over
my head.

Get in Danny, Julian grabbed my hand in his and pulled me
into the car, on top of him. He was wearing his white T-shirt and
cutoffs, a pack of cigarettes in the back pocket. I was wearing his
thin red nylon running shorts. He shifted and I settled on top of
his lap. I hadn't said a word since he said what he said in the bathroom. His bare legs beneath his cutoffs pressed against my legs
and my skin. No one in the car said anything, not Tracy, not
Christy or the other girls.

We drove down the highway to the beach, Styrofoam containers and burger wrappers strewn around our feet, a cooler under
mine, a beer in Julian's hand. He leaned up to get to his cigarettes, pushing me gently forward, his chest on my back. Music
played. Stores flashed past. Telephone lines. When we passed the
fading tourism billboard he yelled Say *Sex!* To Michigan! Christy
and Tracy screamed SEX! Julian laughed, his stomach pressing
against the small off my back.

I headed out for the water the minute we got to the beach. I had
seen, had touched, had felt too much skin. My body ached with
having taken so much in with nothing, no words or sounds coming out. With no one for them to come out to.

The clay beneath my feet turned into clouds as I made my way
into waist-high water. I dove under. Julian's shorts slipped from
my waist to my crotch, there was no drawstring. The thin material
billowed around my legs. I kicked a little, staying under, almost
freeing myself from the suit. I wanted to be free from everything,
the beach, the girls, and Julian, free of anything he thought he
knew about me because he knew nothing. No one had any proof.

I'd kissed Christy. I felt her tongue. It was my first kiss and it was a girl.

I stopped swimming and pulled my suit up. My legs tread muddy water. The sun was blocked by clouds, the lake was cold. Hey Danny wait up I heard Julian behind me but I didn't turn around. Julian swam on top of me, pressing his body against mine, pulling down my shorts as he passed over me. The weight of his body pushed me down in the water toward the bottom. It was awkward and forceful and then he was gone. I came up gasping for air and saw him, dark hair flung back, white teeth smiling at me.

I don't know what your problem is I said and he said what, I'm just screwing with ya. I noticed a raft, wooden planks floating atop rusty barrels and moved toward it. C'mon, Danny, I'll race you in, Julian started swimming toward the shore. I saw his tan arms, his strong legs kicking awkwardly, his black hair thrashing back and forth as he moved his head. Saw the bridge and people on the shore. I sunk beneath the the water wanting to follow but only floated. He was further away, halfway to the beach when I came up.

I disappeared below the water and turned around, swimming away from Julian, away from Tracy and her suntan lotion and Christy and her purple bikini. I stayed underneath, getting used to the darkness and the seaweed running through my hands as I pulled myself faster and faster away from the shore and toward the raft.

I swam in a frenzy, my arms and legs moving as fast as they could, the water rushing past my ears, nearly blocking out a sound I almost heard. It was muffled and distorted, a cry that was strange and free, a noise that grew louder, full of pain and feelings I didn't know how to feel. It was a scream I kept in as I flew for three and half seconds off a deserted bridge through the cool morning air, falling toward water dark as ink, toward winter and a closed Dairy and the next summer when he didn't come back and the summer after that. It was a scream no one heard but me.

Storm

G. WINSTON JAMES

The windows and house are hysterical. Shaking so much in their frames, I'm afraid they will break. Wind. So strong. The first loud crash, the sound of shattering, the tear and gnaw of splintering tell me that my fears are justified. The second floor, where my bedroom was, is ripping away. My balls and wickets are there. Out there. In here. Somewhere. I am fifteen years old. We are gathered in the living room. In the center of our house. On an island where a hurricane has come and stayed. Raining. In the dark, the ceiling has become our sky. Lightning flashes across the plaster. Thunder booms in our missing rooms. And our rug has become our life raft. My sick brother thinks this room will be his tomb. Apart from the sickness in his body, he is going crazy.

"No. No. Mámau!" he screams, clutching Mámau. Trying to put her arms around his shoulders as if she could preserve his life. "Don't let the waterman take me!" he pleads. She holds on. Whispering consolation. Her eyes closed tightly. I know that if she cries, her tears will wash him away because he is as weightless as his mind. My brother is a rake. It is as if he has never eaten.

"I'm afraid, Mámau!" he thrashes, beating Mámau about the face. She will not let go, though. Not again. Not this time. Part of him came home from America two weeks ago. He has been losing parts of himself ever since. We are not sure how much is left. Mámau never shifts her attention. Even in the storm.

The wind beats like fists. I am angry. Not just because I am wet or because there is nowhere that I can stand where water does not drip onto my head. I am mad. Not simply because they told Mámau in the calm that all this would be was a tropical storm. Nothing more. No need to go to a shelter. I am haunted. Not solely because the last thing I saw from my bedroom—when I had one—was my girlfriend Neva's house falling down the hill like a shanty on a pushcart. Not stopping for my screaming. My reaching. I am furious mostly because I am supposed to be the child. The youngest and deserving of comfort. I should not be the one trying to keep the candles and lamps lighted while my older brother turns, flails, and whimpers. He even speaks to God, though I know he never knew Him. My father is no comfort. He has been dead for months now.

"Ralph," Mámau calls, "do you know where's the Bible?" She knows I do not know. There is only one. As far as I am concerned, Mámau keeps it hidden. She has been my Bible.

"Ralph," my brother calls—an echo, "don't you know where's the Bible?" He does not know where he is. Has not known for days who I am. I doubt he knows what is a Bible.

"Shhh." my mother calms him, though the thunder shouts her words silent. "It's upstairs, Ralph," she says. "Go. Get it for Mámau." She expects the Bible will bring peace in the storm.

"I can't, Mámau," I say. "Your Bible must be in heaven because there is no upstairs anymore."

All Mámau can say is, "Oh." She wipes the rain from my brother's face. Runs her hand down his narrow chest. His ribs are like handles. Mámau sighs. "He should have long since been in a hospital, you know?"

"Yes," I say. My last match has fallen. There will be no more light today.

Minute by minute, we all know that we are going to die. My brother's madness might just have been reason. The walls of our house strain to keep us safe. They moan. More than once I've felt the house being lifted. Mámau moans. Her spirits are quickly falling. My brother's fever only rises. He no longer moans. A tree has crashed through our remaining shuttered window.

"Very sick, Mámau," he says clearly.

"I know," she says, crying. She has tied her sundress to him. Our back wall has come crashing down.

"Very sorry," he says.

"I know," she says, crying. She has reached out her other hand to me. I am touched.

"Don't die," I say truly.

"Ralph," he says, crying. He has finally tied a memory to me. "I missed you." I see how much he loves me. Then the lucidness is gone. I am forgotten. Again. It helps me to think that my brother is just crazy.

There are duppies outside. Ghosts. And they are tearing away at our house. Clawing through our walls. Threatening to pull the rest down. The rain beats invisible drums and the wind chants. Spirited. There are mothers screaming in the streets, pinned beneath banana trees. Holding their chickens still. But what of their children? The keening of the storm slowly becomes a hum.

Leaves fill our house. What is left as the storm passes. Dead birds litter the settee. Dying ones chirp meekly as they pass. The darkness is lifting. The rain slows to a summer shower. Outside a dog runs with a baby doll dangling from its jaws.

Inside, though, my brother does not move. I think Father came down the stairs to greet him. They have left with the wind. My brother's eyes are closed. At twenty-seven he looks like father. He is not suffering anymore. My last match has fallen. There will be no more cricket with my teacher. My brother is no longer crazy.

Mámau, though, seems content to hold me in our living room. It is now open to the arriving sun. We are still tied to my brother. There is so much work to be done. We rise together.

A Handbook
for the
Castaway

ALEX JEFFERS

By noon o' the 3rd day, as being convinced both I were alive and
would survive, I looked 'round about myself. I took stock. This was
my position: I was utterly alone. The *Golden Panther* foundered
and all hands lost. Myself was lost, if living; and tho' regretting not
my survival could not doubt as my fine captain and fond ship-
mates all were drowned, a very famous feast for the fishes of this
perverse warm sea. Sweet Tom, indeed, my especial camarado,
often boasted he couldn't swim a stroke. "Hot bath water," he
would say, "ashore in port, with a pretty man to bring me tabaccie
and rum and kisses, is all the water I wish ever to become intimate
with. Altho'," he'd say, "pretty men are still rarer'n hot water or
ports of call, my dear, and myself would gladly settle for *your* attendance. Say you, hey, Robin? Would attend me at bath in Freetown
or Port o' Spain and we return to the Caribees?" And I: "Who to
attend on Robert?" My camarado: "Why, Tom himself. Who other?"
Tom was drowned, I could not doubt it. Sweet Tom was surely
drowned.

I was not a man to thank the Lord for His mercies, precious few
as they were; nor call on Him in my distress. I knew not why myself
of all the company should be spared. The tempest blew up in the
night, whistling away the unfamiliar stars, whilst all lay unawares. I
ought to say: we lay insensible; for Captain Jack had ordered out
an extra portion of rum after our relieving the Spanish galleon of
its ballast of Mexico silver and Peruvian gold; and generous he
was with it whilst himself and his new boy enjoyed the same ship's

Canary wine. His intent being of following the lightened Spaniard to Manila, a place we had never any of us seen, to find what answer that port might make either to our guns or its own strayed coin; but that plan went gone for nought when the storm discovered us and capriciously threw the *Panther* upon the reef. Did that sportive tempest too, I have occasioned to wonder, find out the Spaniards? In the infinite mercy of the papists' God, no doubt it played a gentle zephyr across their canvas and guided them easy to port. Their treasure, at the least, gone to the devil with all my friends.

This all by the way. We'd our rum or Canary; Captain and boy went to the cabin; some of us sailors below to hammocks in the hold; others—myself and my dear camarado among 'em—remaining on deck, the night being hot and heavy and still. Said Sweet Tom with a rummy breath: "I mislike these seas where the stars are strange and no ports civil or not for our landing. God's will, Cap'n'll bring us soon home." And thereupon fell sweetly asleep in my arms; and I followed after.

And then discovered myself coughing the very ocean from my lungs and nothing in my arms but sea and night and a mighty wind. Somehow a broken spar came to hand and supported me up. Waves tossed me as I were a morsel of straw. The *Panther* too they tossed, for I saw her away but saw no-one in the rigging for masts and yards all were gone; saw no-one at the crazily spinning wheel; saw—oh, bleeding Christ Jesus!—saw her heel about and strike broadside some obstruction as halted her career, as stove her in completely. Cried I out in horror and despair; swallowing more ocean as doing it. And then my friendly spar and myself go rushing past wrack and wreck; and next I knew was new morning as if the storm had never been. I lay full stretch on sand, my feet in water that lapped as it were a warm bath, one hand in water that purled like a freshening stream, if it too was warm.

It was a stream. It was fresh. Plunged my face into it and drank, sweet water being a commodity rarer'n silver in southern seas, then spewed up all my refreshment and half the ocean besides. Then wondering, sat up and gazed about, bemused.

'Twas a shore much alike many another in those latitudes, saving the lucky stream. Twice lucky, as water one might healthfully drink, and I had little expectation of discovering rum or Canary wine soon; and for this fact as I had otherwhere observed: that

where fresh water flowed always lay a passage thro' the reef. I
should have been smashed like the *Panther*, and my ribs the easier
stove in than stout British timber, otherwise.

Along on either hand ran a broad strand of tawny sands; before, the placid waters that Spaniards would call lagoona and, not
so far out, white surf on the disastrous reef; and beyond all the
ocean. My spar lay bobbing but I saw no other evidence of the
Panther; I waded out and brought in the spar, planting it upright
in the sand where its height was no taller than my own head, and
tied to it my scarlet kerchief as were a flag and I claiming the
shore for no sovereign saving it be myself.

Inland, a hill or mountain at a little distance, and barbarous
forest; coconut palms on the verge being all I recognized.

There is no profit in saying how I fared nor how I employed
the 1st day in my island, nor indeed the 2nd. Suffice it as was
water to drink; I not without matter to eat; —if the nature of it
would quail the Britishman, well, I had ate worse and it not fresh
but rotted when a child in that green and pleasant land: after
months out of port, too, fresh meats were meat, and fresh, if not
off Christian sheep or cattle. I slept in shelter, tho' I need not, and
tolerable comfort. The air being warm and breeze calm and myself alonesome, I had no requirement of all the clothing I owned:
viz, a very raggety shirt or chemise which as it would not any
longer serve to cover my shoulders I pressed it into service to
shade my head against the sun-stroke; torn canvas breeks drying
so stiff with salt as I took 'em off for comfort then found little occasion to don again when washed and soft but walked about
proud as Adam in Paradise; a stout leather belt, it also stiff and un-
gainly after its bathe but useful for the carrying of my knife, —the
which I should have been unhappy without, —and a purse of
Spanish eights and doubloons: no use in all the world to me but
pretty enough and of no such weight as I felt encumbered. I had
no boots. I required none. I had no handsome periwig or cravat
or frock coat, no fine high hat with a plume to say *milord* to: these
had never owned. Had rings of excellent gold thro' both my ears;
another on my hand that Sweet Tom gave me in earnest; saving its
ruby gone a-down a-side him in the wreck to the bottom of the
sea; it having come from its seat some days previous and he carrying it for me against a goldsmith. Where such to be encountered
in these unwholesome latitudes a question never answered.

I find myself now in the 3rd day. Have proved to myself it were an island by way of walking all 'round it, an ambulation of I know not how many hours; excepting 'twas past dawn when I set out and scarce afternoon on my return. The hours of the day in this latitude I could not measure; nor at night discover any stars I knew. —Finding no fresh water elsewhere, then determined to make my unhappy landfall the seat of my solitary kingdom, and sat me down to survey the realm and take stock. Imprimis, there is myself and my poor equipage; secundo, a splintered spar of good cedar with red Chinee silk fluttering bravely. There is a good stream of sweet water. In rocks along about the lagoona, mussels, winkles, and crabs of various sorts; a-swim in lagoona itself, many handsome fishes whether or no I own hook or net to catch 'em. I might eat gull or cormorant, tho' the meat's not tasty, can I contrive to knock one down. I have knocked down nor scrupled to eat a lizard which it was the size of a fox but slow as a tortoise and sweet to the tooth, if I should rather have it cooked. The discovery of fire for another day. In fine, I shall not starve, for have also found fruits and salads which I know to eat, including the estimable coconut; I shall not parch; of a night may sleep in a handsome bower fragrant of leaves and blossoms, not rum and sweat and sick and the hard tarry planks of the deck beneath me.

I wept as I were a babe in arms. "Tom!" I cried aloud; "Sweet Tom! Brave Cap'n Jack!" My eyes streaming and salt, I drew from my purse a piece on which I marked stamped the head of the Spanish king; and be he king in America so well as in Spain, so here in my island were I sovereign of all I surveyed and this stiff golden fellow and his companions all my subjects and all my friends. "Oh, Tommy!" cried I again; "and my merry camaradoes! All drowned!"; and I hurled His Spanish Majesty far off across the lagoona.

This is how it stood with Captain Jack and Sweet Tom and myself: I was the elder to Tommy by a few years tho' neither knew how many, for if ever told I had forgot the year of my birth. A lad was I of no family; and with no family unless it be the band in which I travelled by the English roads, stealing and scraping and often chased and often beaten; whereof our General might have treated me kindly for he thought me pretty but as often as might be he was drunken. His Lieutenant did not like me, neither. One or t'other would like have killed me, one day, I've no doubt, in drink or in malice, and felt no more remorse than who kicks a dog or drowns a cat.

Was a port on the coast we came upon in our rambles, I asked not county or town; but I was asking a pretty man (a gentleman, as I thought), of a loaf or a pasty or a tuppenny to buy such for I was famished; and he saying: "A strong, handsome lad ought not to beggary or brigandage. Happen I'm seeking a boy, in very truth. Would take ship with me, eh, lad, across the sea to Jamaica and be my boy?"

This gentleman (and I'll not name him and him no gentleman, in truth), he thereupon took me along to a doss house by the docks, where the whores for two groats fed me and washed me and shaved my head against the lice, all the while chucking and petting and fooling me, which I did not like; and calling me: "Pretty boy; Pretty; Oh, but Mr _____ did find himself a pretty." For why I knew what it was my gentleman wanted of me when they put me in a closet with only a shirt to cover me, an apple to munch, and a bed—well, I knew the bed weren't for slumber. Well howsomever, my Mr _____ had fed me and I now so little hungry as I had never been; had made me clean which was a wonder; and General and Lieutenant and Corporals (for our band was an army in small) all had had me, in the ditch and by the roadside and never offered a cup of Porter to make me merry. In short, I thought I liked him well enough tho' his member stood up bigger than my General's, —the one being a man and t'other not yet, — and hurt me something fierce when he introduced him to my arse; but he did not hit me when I cried. Poured more Porter for me instead, saying: "This to comfort you." In fine, he took me for his boy, he being captain of a Jamaica merchant; and that is the way of my going to sea.

At sea he was not so kind. I will not say so much for I do not like to remember it, but there was, in the one instance, a matter of tall boots wanting polished and myself sincerely puzzled as to why there was no rag and blacking to do it; and after, a whip. No more o' that.

In Kingston in Jamaica I crept away without no more'n my clothing that I admired for had never had so fine; and scarce thinking of the coin he'd promised for faithful service. I misdoubt he didn't find another boy to polish his boots and warm his bunk and please his prick as he called: "Mr Handsome-Does," for the voyage back to England. It never suited him to call me by my proper name; not Robert nor Bobby nor Fine Robin, but always Boy and Lad when it wasn't Puppy.

Having reached this point in my reflections, the which both happy for saying fare-thee-well to Mr _____ and unhappy being alone and friendless in Kingston Port, a rough place; —I hardly knew what it meant also to be penniless for had never been otherwise; —having, I say, come upon this 1st landfall in the Caribees in my recollection; I discovered myself hungering and a little faint, having lain a-stretch in the sun, being, as I have said, naked as a babe. Now, and I yet his boy, Captain Jack was in the sometime habit of calling me his fine Portugee, tho' as much English as he and born in Britain as he was not, or his Romany lad, for my being of dark complexion, not fair going ruddy like himself. Notwithstanding, my limbs as had before been clothed now were stinging red; and in especial my prick. And so then before going to seek out sustenance I took down the kerchief of scarlet Chinee silk that Captain Jack gave me one time and fashioned a kind of clout of it with my belt, to guard my privities against the burning of the sun. —So must I look a proper savage now! Thinking it nearly gave me to laugh; thinking too that to cover my nakedness if even in suchwise were the earliest proper British and Christian act I had performed in my island. The next I would be raising a manor house to myself and riding to hounds after lizards, crying: "Tally-ho!" Captain Jack it was told me of manors and hunts, myself having no experience in that kind. Captain Jack who gave me the kerchief and was so fond with my parts, privy to him and not private; he would never mislike seeing his gift used to bag them up. Thinking which there was no help for it but to open up the silken bag again, there standing on the strand by the spar that was all remained of Captain Jack's *Panther*, take him out as was within, play with him as the Captain might like to do again were he not drowned for all I were no boy no more, he always loving me well and his proper boy drowned as much as himself; but tho' I wept for him as I did so, and for myself, and got it over quick and fierce as could be; then licking the stuff off my hand; then making up the clout again; then going by the rocks in the lagoona where I harvested winkles; the which I ate 'em as I gathered 'em, slippery and salt, until sated.

Whereupon meant to retreat out of the sun to the shade of my

bower but, imprimis, knocking down a coconut and cracking it
open, I drank the liquid within, cooler than the water of the
stream. I contemplated the spar that saved my life, it looking the
less fine for the loss of its gay, fluttering, red pennon; thinking:
"Should build it into any house I might raise; or leave it stand a
memorial of my fellows?" With my knife prised out bits of the coconut's sweet meat and chewed on 'em. Thus came to fall asleep
there in the full heat of the afternoon, and woke me not till night
when I felt cold; and hot too, in my skin, as 'twere a fever; and my
head aching worser'n after a night o' drinking all the grog in Port
o' Spain with Sweet Tom, the Captain, and our camaradoes.

Surely I was very ill, quaking with fever and spewing up winkles
and coconut meat; —for as I truly believed myself back aboard
the *Golden Panther* with Tom wanting to comfort my distress and I
fending off his hands as wished to caress, crying: "No! For God's
mercy, don't touch me. I burn. I burn!" So he was sluicing me with
cool water—(I had got somehow into the stream, was flopping
about in the shallows like the very ugly mermaid we saw once at
the mouths of the Oroonoko), —calling me a foolish lad for stopping in the sun without a hat, and then I: "But Tommy! You're
dead. You're drowned." And he: "As will you be, Robin, if you
don't take care." Whereupon I sat up in the stream, knowing
where I was tho' still ill; shaking the water out of my ears tho' I
seemed yet to hear his voice and know him near-by.

I continued ill for some period, I know not how many days; nor
how nor what I fed myself; seeing Tom again from time to time
who railed away with me but did not deign again to offer advice;
until I woke and knew myself well again; and famished; and knew
I must change my habitation, as the pleasant bower was foul with
sick and shit and stank of piss. Indeed, I found I had never removed my fine silk clout but shat and pissed into it. So then went
down again by the stream, keeping as much as might out of the
sun; bathed; washed out the kerchief and hung it on a bush to dry.
Then, a-sitting naked on the bank, I thought me how, were
Tommy or the Captain to see me, they should call me a sad and
sorry fellow, all my burned skin flaking off me in tatters; and I re-
solved to better myself.

So then in Jamaica's Kingston had lived some while on the street
corner and near the docks, filching my victuals and sleeping raw,

my fine clothes growing filthy and raggety. "At the least," says I to myself, "here's no General nor Mr _____ who'd treat me cruelly"; altho', in very truth, I wanted companionship; and gazed with envy on other boys as had their fine captains to cuff 'em and call 'em Puppy and give 'em sugar-cane to chew. "Why," thought I, remembering what the whores in that English port said; and Mr _____ himself, likewise: "I'm prettier than the last one of 'em." —And that were a strange thing about Kingston and, so to speak, all those other ports in the Caribees as weren't Spanish, whether British, Dutch, or French: no fancy-houses by the docks and no whores for the sailors but nobody minding the lack. Even in my old band, the General had his woman, a sorry wench and he preferred my arse to her quint, when he weren't too drunken for his prick to stand; so shared her out, often as not, among the Corporals. Lieutenant as well (who were an older fellow than the General, tho' nobody liked him nor would have him for their master), kept company with a slangy tart that sometimes gave me a morsel if I were specially famished, being her own babe had died a-borning; whereupon Lieutenant'd thrash her and myself both. But I never saw a woman near the wharves at Kingston. Only brave captains with their boys and sailors with their camaradoes; and I thought how fine they looked and desperately wished to be of their company. The Navy men who might have taken me on (for they never did have sufficient sailors in His Majesty's Navy), frightened me, for all they were rumbustious and wild as any seamen; Mr _____ had turned me against honest merchants; nothing would do but I should go for a pirate's boy.

Came a day and a bold ship into port they called the *Golden Panther*; —I had no letters then so couldn't parse her name but I liked the fierce, snarling yellow cat carved under the bowsprit. I liked, too, the look of the captain, he being handsome and tall, with hair under his grand hat that was as golden as the carved and painted cat, with great red mustachios and blue eyes at once merry and sad. As grubby as I was, I liked that *his* linen were clean and white, his britches and waistcoat simple and black, his boots not so well polished as might be. Was a stout youth by him on whom his regard was fond, tho' not fond in the way as tho' were camaradoes; but no boy; and I liked that, too. When he came down onto the dock I ran to him, stumbling at his feet, crying:

"Cap'n! Cap'n! You're needing a boy? I'll shine your boots up proper, I will!"

Glancing down on me as I were a stinking turd in the street, Captain Jack nodded once; then turning to the youth said: "Clean this, will you, Josiah." He nudged me with his boot. "I'll take a better look at it after."

So the youth Josiah took me by the collar and led me into the inn Captain Jack favored, crying for hot water and soap. Making a nicer job of it than the whores had, he bathed me, saying: I was a little starved but ought plump out well given proper victual; and saying: I had the right of it; Captain Jack had no boy, —he, Josiah, having grown so the Captain liked him not so much, not to bed him; and I did know as that was what was wanted? Yes, I said: 'twas what I expected and I brave enough to bear it so only I might go once more to sea. For a fact, was a little scared, for the Captain's britches were snug and I had seen what he owned stuffed down the right leg; I thought, soft as it was, as big as Mr _____'s, hard. But I thought: "This Josiah was his boy and still loves him, so he's not cruel." Then Josiah took my chin in hand, saying: "I'll have my eye on you, so watch how you treat my Captain, boy, if he take you on." Then shook his head and with his hand shook mine, saying: "It's a proper puppy after all, under the muck." Then smiled. "You'll do. He'll like you. What's your name?"

So I told him: Robert.

"Well, my Robin," said he: "my name you know already and I'm pleased to make your acquaintance." Here, his other hand with the soap came upon my privities and introduced him to them specially. "Mind you keep all this clean," he warned, "or Cap'n won't like you."

"But it's my arse he'd be wanting, innit, sir?" I protested. I had never thought about washing those parts specially, being as the rest o' me were dirty and no help for it. "I'm not to bugger him, am I? I couldn't!"

"Bugger the Captain?" Josiah laughed merrily. "With what? This little morsel? I'll wager you can't do more'n piddle with it yet. Bide a bit, we'll see." So saying, he leaned o'er the tub where I sat and fiddled my little member till he stood up proud; then washed him all without; then peeled back the skin and washed beneath. I liked it tho' it scared me more'n the thought of the Captain's prick. A little soap got in his one eye and stung. Then Josiah had me stand in the bath and drenched me clean. Then, he kneeling by the side of the tub, beckoned me nearer, smiling, put his hands on my fundament, and put his mouth on my parts.

"Oh!" said I, but he made no reply, being as his mouth was full. I wanted him never to stop but after a time he did, releasing me from the happy ministrations of his tongue and warm comfort of his lips; leaning back smiling, saying: "You see why it wants to be clean."

But what I was seeing was how his own prick had got stiff in his britches, not so big as the Captain's, —nor Mr _____'s Handsome-Does; —but big enough, and bulging, and making a blot of wet thro' the cloth. Josiah laughed again. —He was a merry youth was poor Josiah, who always treated me kind; I loved him near as dear as the Captain only he perished not long after of a Spanish musket ball thro' the eye and into the brain; and weren't we all over sorrowful then? My Captain, he wept. —So grabbed me under the arms, lifting me from the bath and towelling me dry; and then standing before me, his legs spread, said: "Unbutton him out, Robin. Show me how you'll do for my Cap'n. I swear 'tis clean as his and near as clean as yours."

Well, and after, when Josiah took me in to Captain Jack's chamber and Captain had give me a look of guarded approbation, I clothed in cast-offs of Josiah's that were clean and fitted me nicely, Josiah said: "You'll find an apt pupil, Cap'n Jack." And the Captain smiled very nicely for Josiah and very sweetly for me, called me: lovely child; and bade me come to him.

So went I to sea again, aboard the *Golden Panther*, sure hunter of the Caribees; I being no less than Captain Jack the Pirate's boy.

1st item on my new program which I would perform as best I might for love of Captain Jack and Sweet Tom, was the making of fire. And so I found out a pleasant place deeper into the forest and a step from the stream for my new dwelling; there excavating a little pit and lining it 'round with stones; then laying a bed of dry tinder for the which I used the husks of coconuts. Laid by, too, a ready supply of fallen timber of which was plenty in the forest, I only wishing an axe to break some of 'em up convenient. Tho', wishes being granted, I had rather my camaradoes preserved and the *Panther* not sunk—in that case wanting no axe; else, having one ready to hand.

For steel I had the edge of my trusty knife. For flint I searched some, the rock in my island being mainly coral and no use for the purpose. And yet, in fine, I had a comfortable little smolder going and feeling a proper Englishman at his hearth for tho' dressed (or undressed, like) as a savage in nought save clout and shady hat which, I forgot to say, I had plaited together out of palm fronds against the sun as had made me ill. Lacking only pipe and Porter, was I. There being no remedy I forbore to regret; but went out to knock down another of the sluggish lizards, the which I butchered him nicely and skewered him in pieces and cooked him and ate him. He lacked savor, lacking salt. Now, after my illness, I made myself a new man. The tale o' my doings were tedious, being I became a man of business, always doing, or about to do, or just having done and ready for a new employment; — always to some purpose, lest I stop to think. Too, every task I purposed to attempt required all the time in the world, there being no chandler's near-by to provide such as an axe; or rope; fish-hooks or line or needles; or a measure of canvas to make me an awning for my new-built house or a sail for the canoa I made from a tree which I felled it by fire and then hollowed it out by fire as well. Once, I broke the handy sharp point off my knife; then were more careful with it, having no other and being it had served me nicely all along. Fish-hooks I tried to fashion from bones, both lizard and gull (for had made a sling of lizard gut with which to hurl stones and knock 'em from the air), neither serving; finally took a one o' my ear-rings and beat the soft gold to shape, grinding the point till sharp; the line, of threads drawn from my old canvas breeks. I went fearful of losing it and for that, maybe, never did; tho' never snaring many fishes neither till making a net of coconut fiber and going out in my canoa into the lagoona to cast it. All o' this taking up, as I said, all the time in the world. I kept no count of the days, nor the seasons such as there were; but I'm thinking 'twere some several many years. I know that my scarlet Chinee-silk clout which had been the kerchief given me by Captain Jack wore thro' in holes and my privities peeking out thro' 'em; so then must put it aside, placing it as a treasure with Tommy's finger-ring in a pretty shell on a shelf in my little house; and went about naked again being now black as a savage and proof against the sun. Howsomever, I forever kept certain of being busy all the day so to sleep in the night. Only then at evening, after supper, sitting at my fire with a coconut to hand for liquor, then had time in the world for thinking and remembering.

I began to tell of Tommy but never encountered him, being occupied with myself's misadventures and taking service with Captain Jack. Notwithstanding, 'twas Sweet Tom as I thought most on those evenings by my fire; being it was he was my companion and my friend and my camarado all those years until he was lost. I mind me, both loved the Captain, and he ourselves still, as we were sons or younger brothers, after no longer pleasing him as beddable; time to time, one or t'other of us played a game or two with another sailor or a jolly landsman in port; —I'm meaning to say: was more to it 'tween Tom and myself, than my liking his prick and the clever things he did with him, and he contrariwise mine. Those clevernesses I remembered when I lay abed, or mornings when I woke, myself a man whose member never fails but to stand to attention of a morning before I piss. Tom liked that. In fine, I was fond and loving of Tommy and he of myself.

So, then, I might rouse of a morning early, meaning to plan what I would purpose to do that day; let it be fishing from my canoa in the lagoona or gathering in fruits or harvesting salt from my pans; attempting once again to make from clay a proper vessel as would hold water and not burst in the fire (a task I never yet succeeded in); or whatsomever; but all my *intentions* and *meanings to* distracted by the eager sailor—(I called my prick: "my sailor")—demanding attention. Now, I might simply grab him and roughly stroke him till he were satisfied; I might ignore him and go by the water to piss out his stiffness, my own water spraying about and wetting me, whereupon I would bathe. More like, I would lie back in my bed, by now somewhat of a proper couch and comfortable enough, remembering my Tommy till it nearly seemed he were there near-by; and he told me how to go about it.

That was what we used to like, Sweet Tom and myself. Oh, when I discovered him for Captain Jack and he a lad, I taught him a pretty way with his mouth; and then the Captain bettered my lessons; and Tommy as apt a student as ever I was. We did not cease from pleasing one another thuswise, both grown to men; tho', be it said, was none of our fellows willing to try the endeavor excepting he'd prenticed with the Captain; nor none kept himself clean enough so I'd wish it of him. They were all for buggery, our company. Tom and I both liked a little buggering and being bug-

gered; whether properly, up the arse, or just introducing one's
member between t'other's thighs. Captain Jack told me the name
for that practice in scholar's Latin, once, but I misremember now.
Howsomever, what specially pleased us, myself and Tom, was to be
near one to t'other, gazing on him fondly, watching his handsome
sailor wake up and make his salute. Sometimes were cannon or
muskets as would shoot; sometimes old salts as chewed their tabaccie, not smoked it nicely in a pipe, and spat.

I discovered Tom for Captain Jack, I said. For myself, I think it
was, in fine. That being in Port o' Spain, that's not a Spanish town
for all its name, but British. I was not so grown as the Captain
would have me away from his bunk, no hair about my privities yet
nor yet a beard. What he used say was: I was to eat his spunk, he
liked it, and eating it would make me strong; he liked too my little
privates as fitted all in his mouth, prick and ballocks alike together, even the former being stiff; but whensoever it came about
I might produce my own emission, he, Captain Jack, would not
eat it nor would not like it, tho' myself would continue to cherish.
This said with kind pets and caresses; and true, in the event.

So, I weren't grown but had killed my 1st man: who was a
Spaniard with black eyes and handsome black beard that tried to
climb aboard the *Panther* when we grappled onto his fine ship,
whereupon I came up on him, he unprepared to see a little lad, as
he thought, with a sharp blade as might skewer him up under the
jaw. He looked to be surprised when I took the knife away and
blood jetted out of his throat, crying out—what I remembered
after, as having killed him:—"*Madre de dios! Muerto por no más que
niñito.*" Then, his blood having spoiled my chemise new-given by
the Captain, I shoved him o'er the rail he'd tried to mount, he
falling between the two ships and being properly drowned or
crushed. Then went to find the Captain to show how my shirt was
spoiled, who promised me another and said what it was the
Spaniard meant: *Mother of God! Murdered by no better than a little
child.* So I was pleased by that and it was the only Spanish I ever
learned the meaning of. Captain wrote it down for me in ink. Too,
tho' not yet capable of emission, I knew the day were coming; and
Captain Jack knew it too, marking how my trembles and judders
when he'd played me well were like his own in small, and gazed
on me strangely then; so that when recovered from my fit I would

wish to take his big, handsome prick again in my mouth, biggest and handsomest I ever met notwithstanding I'd like Tom's as well, later; and make my Captain forget. Or might cajole him, which he seldom did, to bugger me. He never liked to cause me pain. So when Captain Jack's *Golden Panther* sailed bravely into Port o' Spain to spend our new-gained Spanish doubloons and quarter-pieces and eights, I knew it time to look out for a new boy, myself to become no more'n a common pirate-sailor tho' the Captain's fond friend still. Was no lad on the docks as rushed up on him babbling as myself had done at Kingston; but I minded to watch out.

Was also that time in port a brave ship which her name were French, Captain said; but I'll use the English of it: *Lily-flower*; and her captain a buccaneer called Monsieur, which is just to say Mr as they do in France. Monsieur came from Haiti but *Lily-flower* sailed out of Martinique against the Spanish from Cartagena and Panama; and, truth to tell, against British ships too; tho' no-one said a word about that at Port o' Spain, her crew being a merry lot of French cut-throats free with their blades and having gold to spend, —Spanish or British or Dutch or French making no never mind; —and Monsieur himself as fierce a man as I ever did have the advantage of meeting. For I did meet him; himself and Captain Jack encountering one another at a tavern where one rushed on t'other as it were—(thought I, afraid)—to slay him. Only 'twas for embracing and shouting for joy and kisses on the cheeks. Now, I think I said, Captain Jack weren't born in Britain, but in France. His papa was an Englishman but his mama French, she being of a family having connections to the plantations in Haiti. So when it became time my Captain might no longer stay in England, he scarcely more than a wicked lad, to Haiti he came; where he met Monsieur, not yet having gone to sea for a pirate either of 'em. I learned all this after.

So one's calling t'other: "*Mon frère*" or "*Mon chéri,*" that is, *My brother* and *My dear,* or Captain calling Monsieur: François, his proper name. And Monsieur asks: "Josiah?" My Captain: "Dead, poor fellow, shot thro' the head. But here's Robin." So I shook the hand offered me, which 'twas almost hidden in the lace off his shirt-sleeve and owning a pretty ring as had a nice jewel for every finger on it; Monsieur looking me up and down, nodding his chin and saying, —what it meant: "A likely lad." (The French I misremember.) By which I knew he knew when 'twas sorrowful enough as I knew it myself; and I ready for a proper fit of sulking, the which Captain Jack would mislike; when the Captain: "Killed himself a Spaniard just t'other day."

Thereupon Monsieur called for grog and nothing would have it, but should drink my health and proceed to make me very merry; then very drunken; then sick. Went I 'round back of the tavern meaning to sick up in private in the alley behind. The which I commenced to do, feeling very miserable and fine and manly.

Having completed this employment, I turned away from the gutter, wiping at my mouth with my hand; when I observed some-body watching who was a mite of a scrawny lad. As I was minding to round on him for watching what it wasn't his business; and making me ashamed when I thought I might be proud; he said: "Will you help me, please?" I shouted nevertheless: "Get away with you, puppy!"; for not understanding him as he had said it in French; but then he said the English. And a proper dignified little man he wanted to be; and seemed; only for the tears as glittered at his eye-lashes. "Please," said he again; "will you help me?" "What's your trouble, then, laddy?" said I, as it were, uncaring.

Now, this was a handsome pretty boy, of black hair and green eyes and pouting red lips; clothed as fine as Monsieur, as well, with lace at neck and wrist, a gold ring at one ear where it was bloodied, being new; dressed fine and French-wise, then, except-ing no shoes and the little feet grubby. And stinking badly of piss, the which I did not like at all. His French I had not understood but knew 'twere French; so thought he came off the *Lily-flower*, being perhaps Monsieur's boy. Happened I was right imprimis, tho' not secundo. Seemed Monsieur were a man for men, as would I come to be, Sweet Tom also; liking not young boys spe-cially as seeming, to him, much alike women. —Captain Jack'd have two words to say to that, I dare say, who liked women still less than grown men. —Tho' I wasn't thinking of the Captain that mo-ment, I admit.

The boy was Tom, an English lad. His tears being about to flood, I made to comfort him, saying: "Come along with me." But he startled: "I daren't, lest my master see me with you." I: "How may I help you and I mayn't be seen? What's the trouble, then, Sweet Tom?" The 1st time I called him that, his favorite name ever after, what no man save my Captain cared to say lest he discover my fist in his ear, two or four of his teeth like dice thrown on the deck as a game.

Happen he'd been with his papa, the mother being perished, aboard a British merchant for Jamaica; the father having indentured himself to a sugar plantation in that island; when the ship was set upon by buccaneers. These no less than Monsieur and his French bully-boys aboard the *Lily-flower*; and one of 'em a surly bad man by name Pierre as said, upon setting eyes on little Tom: he'd forfeit all his share of the plunder, he would, in exchange for the boy. Which he ripped crying from his poor papa's arms; and stuck the man as continued to protest. Then taking Tom aboard the *Lily-flower*, set to treating him worser'n Mr _____ ever thought to treat me. Not by buggery, the which a boy can withstand and come to like, even. By such as shaving his head when he had no lice, none too careful with the razor neither; or making him caper about naked whilst crying: what a pretty-pretty fellow he was!; or putting him in fine clothing and pissing on him where all his camaradoes watched to laugh at the fun. Was worse as well, I imagine, what Tommy never cared to tell me; or happily forgot. I neglected to say: Pierre was a famously ugly fellow whom you'd shudder to look at as you saw him, as I did when I did; who wanted always to spoil what was fine, such as my Tom; and who owned a mislike of Englishmen as gnawed at his temper like poison. All of which to say: he took after Tom not because he liked him but the contrary.

So some of this story told, I was as near to tears as Tom and angry as I think I had never been; but petted and kissed the sad, stinking lad, saying: "Don't fear, don't cry." He: "They say *your* master is a good man, tho' a pirate." I, agreeing: "That he is, is Captain Jack, the finest man and bravest captain ever sailed the Spanish Main." Tom: "And English. Will you tell him? Will he help an English boy?"

To this made I no reply, having come over crazy-mad as has happened since; and leading him into the back of the tavern said: "Show me this Pierre." Whereupon Tom pointed the man out at table with his mates, drunken and foolish and ugly as I cannot say. Whereupon said I: "Stay here quiet, Sweet Tom"; and proceeding across the chamber to face Monsieur where he sat drinking with my Captain, the both of 'em merry. Said I to Monsieur: "Your man

Pierre has mistreated my friend." The Captain: "Your friend?"
And Monsieur, surprised: "Pierre? A very bad dangerous man. Not
a one you ought want for an enemy, chéri." And I, being as I said
crazy-mad: "Cannot be my enemy and he's dead, can he?" Then
Monsieur laughed aloud, then narrowed his eyes at me, then held
back Captain Jack who would cuff me and send me scurrying to
the *Panther*; said simply: "Attempt it, chéri," sitting back with his
mouth cruel and eyes hard.

In short, I went to Pierre as it were a servant lad with a jug
of grog for him and stuck him with my nice knife that had killed
the Spaniard. The new mouth in his throat bloodied a 2nd shirt
for me.

Then brazen as you please led Tom over to Captain Jack and
Monsieur; said to Monsieur: "My friend will depart your company
to-day." And to the Captain: "We wish to bathe now, Cap'n."

Tom being very quiet and still-like, tho' trembling. Had flinched
when I took his hand in mine, the which being bloodied and
slimy; and he, as later said: afraid more of me than my handsome
Captain, who regarded him as to speculate or judge; or of fierce
Monsieur as laughed, calling: "*Mon dieu! Quel enfant!*," —that is,
My God, such a boy, —and calling to Pierre's camaradoes: that they
should carry away the corpse and think themselves happy the ferocious lad didn't do for them as well; and calling: "More liquor!"
But I: "We wish to bathe now, Cap'n and Monsieur, if it please
you."

In the Captain's chamber up-stairs o' the inn was a fine tub;
was hot water and soap. Tom, poor lad, had not been bathed since
a year and half a year when torn from his papa's arms; was afraid
so as not able even to weep; but I stripped him naked and bun-
dled him and myself into the tub, the which being large and ourselves small handily sufficed to contain the both; whereupon I
tended him very gently until at last he wept on my breast; then
washed of his face again, and dried him, and took him with me
into Captain's bed. I like to say I made my 1st emission that night,
into Sweet Tom's hands; myself telling him how to help me and
himself licking my spunk into his little mouth and eating it. So
then slept we very sweetly, tumbled together like puppies, and
soundly; till Captain very kindly woke us in the morning.

So then my shipmate camaradoes made much of their Fine
Robin, the which I liked; saying: I was a proper little pirate now

and had have a golden ear-ring thro' my ear. And another: "Two ear-rings! For has murdered two men; isn't it a brave tiny cut-throat!" And Tommy saying, quiet and small: that he did not like the ear-ring Pierre had put on him employing no rum for the nee-dle so it festered and would not heal till the ring be taken out and put thro' mine own ear; its brother ear on t'other side owning a ring the Captain give me. I ever after the only sailor of the *Golden Panther* as had 'em in either ear. But to Tom the Captain gave a fine gold finger-ring with a handsome ruby; it being too big for Tommy's hand, strung it on a ribbon 'round his neck under his chemise; until such time as my hand grew large whereupon he gave it me. And back to the beginning o' my tale.

For Sweet Tom joined the *Golden Panther*'s company; being cap-tain's boy as it were I had planned it. But Captain Jack had changed his practice; loving me well, as he said, and keeping me with Tommy by his side and in his bunk for some little time to come. Tommy being fearful of a grown man, I might comfort him; and teach him how to please our Captain. And the Captain, tho' misliking any longer to sport with me, being I might now spot him with my spunk or mistake to put it in his mouth, said: he liked to watch myself's and Tommy's play; and have his two bold boys by him as he slept. So remained very happily together we three; until I became a great hairy youth as needing to shave and owning a proper prick; which, the Captain sadly said: it sickened him to look upon without clothes; when I moved my slumbers to a ham-mock among the other sailors in the hold or a pallet on the deck where Tommy joined me as he was able. 'Twere not so long after, neither, as Tommy learned to make his own spunk shoot; and Captain Jack must needs acquire himself a new boy; and Sweet Tom came a-looking for me. And kept by me, and myself by him, very many years and excellent adventures on the Spanish Main, till Captain Jack purposed to venture the southern seas.

Oh, 'twere very nearly happier I should be drowned with my Tom than have lost him. So, it being deep night with bright moon and myself unaccountably unable to sleep, tho' tired of a day's labors, am standing a-side my spar which it still stand on the shore mark-ing my landfall and memorializing my friends. My hand on it, as 'twere a comfort. The waters of the lagoona calm; and white surf crashing out against the reef. Myself watching; watching where the surf break and where it don't, that being the passage thro' as my spar brought me when my ship were foundered in the storm. Then comes a brave little jolly-boat thro' the passage, which it's marked by moonlight; and the boat being rowed by a single man which, his back turned, I cannot make him out; and I, afraid, step closer on the spar.

Then grounds ashore and ships his oars proper; and stands; and steps out the boat; and turns. "Has grown very hairy and black and wild," says he; "and naked as a savage besides. Has become a cannibal, my Bobby, as would cook me and eat me?"

And I: "Oh, Tom, Tommy, it's you?" My voice all chokey and hoarse, it being I know not how many years since I spoke aloud, there being no purpose of it.

"'Tis I," says he: "Your only Tom. Who other? And the *Panther* anchored safe off-shore, and our Cap'n Jack and camaradoes awaiting you fondly, Robert. Devil of a task it's been, finding you again," he says. "Shall we back to the Caribees?"

'Tis Tom, a proper fine youth as newly come a man, nicely shaved and barbered for Captain Jack mislikes his sailors slovenly; with cap and blouse and breeks, cutlass at his side and musket in his belt; and I ashamed for being naked and wild and hairy and black, tho' clean for have always kept so; and says he: "Oh, Robin, and there's your sailor. But haven't I missed the sight o' him and longed to find him again."

But I still afraid to approach and never so as to touch him. Whereupon throws him down his cap, unstraps his belt and allows cutlass fall; takes him off his shirt; and off his breeks; and says: "Here's mine," holding him in his hand stiff and pretty as ever was.

Here's my sailor, him being hard; of length maybe seven inches on the foot; of girth so my hand scarce compass him; being red and hot and veiny; having a hood of skin on him as slips o'er his head to hide him, or draws down to show his face. He likes my hand as makes him laugh with tickling, or beats him proper so he weep salt tears of his single eye. And here's his ballocks as hang loose underneath and like my hand likewise, tho' gentler; or creep up close one on t'other and on him, as two happy lads a-bed with their captain. And captain roars, shooting his spunk as spurts out on my belly and breast, myself roaring likewise; and little boys

chortle being happy for making us happy; and so to lick the bitter
stuff into my mouth, and so to swallow, and so to sleep.

So then wake me in my lonesome bed of a morning, my heartless
little sailor stiff; and take him in hand to pleasure him and him
me; and so to labor and it another day.

Birth

GIL CUADROS

*I conjure you, Armisael, angel who governs the womb, that you help
this woman and the child in her body.*
Rf. Trachenberg, *Jewish Magic and Superstition*

I feel it well up inside of me. It grows with every pass of the sun,
steals what little energy is left in my beleaguered body. The lesions
that spread daily across my testicles and legs now cease to multi-
ply. I sense the formation of an umbilical cord connecting me to
another. I am nervous of what it will become and how it will deci-
mate the remnants of my strength. I tell my lover I am carrying a
child inside me, demonlike, it drags embryonic nails slowly down
my internal organs. Marcus looks skeptical, eyes squint as if thinking, what next, commit me to a home, send me to a spiritual
healer. He smolders sage and copal, washes me in their cleansing
smoke. He strikes bells to startle me out of my stupefaction but re-
alizes the presence inside me, glides his hand across my stomach,
enjoys electricity. With a fit of anger he yells, "How selfish can you
be? What if you die before the child is raised?" The neighbors
bring sprigs of baby's breath, castor-bean stems, and nail them to
our door. The air smells rancid and cloying.

I will name the creature Armisael. The growing fetus confines
me on my balcony all hours reciting Psalms. I burn news articles
one at a time on the hibachi: the volcanic eruption on modern
Pompeii, a killer virus emerging from the rain forest, the increase
of rabid coyotes filtering into the hillside communities, feasting

on small children. The strips of newsprint writhe in my hand as they approach the fire like Swedish fortune fish curling inside a palm's heat. I see an indigo gleam radiating from my fingertips; it garners tear-shaped flames, encapsulating the ardor like the many pills I take. They float away into the atmosphere the way soap bubbles defy gravity, lyrical as Ptolemy's music of spheres.

Walking down the boulevards near my home, I expect the community to revere me, to step aside out of deference. Rather, lips snarl, hands move to strike, filthy looks, the kind I imagine Jesus encountered on his trek to Calvary. The women are the harshest, spitting before me, hacking their phlegm deeply and loudly from inside their corpulent bodies. They turn in disgust as if to deny my existence and my child's potential. It is hard to ignore my aspect, my withered limbs seem to negate any fruitfulness. Still the jacaranda trees blanket the sidewalks with their purple flowers for me; the elms canopy the sun's glare, limbs low enough to grab and even cradle me when I tire.

Returning home, I must lie down. Nausea overwhelms me throughout the day. The only thing that helps is placing ice packs underneath my arms and on the back of my neck. My head swims with sounds: the buzz of EMF high-tension lines. Marcus hangs crystal prisms in the bedroom windows and lights cinnamon candles around our bed. He touches me too gently, nuzzling my side. He licks the well of my ear, says I taste bitter. He wants to gather me up tighter, his arm a vice around my waist. He is afraid he will hurt me, cause some deformation to the child.

The child becomes apparent through translucent skin, jade eyes seem conscious, pierce the iridescence of the amniotic sac. My lover thinks he is a lowly Joseph, not important in the scheme of this miracle. I watch him stare off into the horizon, the sunset nearly blinding. In his hand a cigarette burns, smoke coils from his fingers. He worries what kind of parent would he be and sees all his flaws magnified, especially his lack of patience. I desire to comfort him, go down on my knees and press my face next to his crotch. Strongly, he pulls me up, tells me it's a piece of immortality, a part of us will survive after we're gone. I warn him not to become too attached, that there might be a chance the child will catch my disease and die early too. Marcus refuses to hear, says he can already see the changes in the world: the sky becoming gentian, the foliage smaragdine, the land ginger. From where I stand,

I see darkness drain the landscape's hue, leave somber details, an industrial fog, thick and noxious.

In my dream, I place the child in a basket and float it down a mighty river. Marcus rages at heaven for what I have done, curses me till the day of his death. The child shall never know his real fathers, or have comfort with the toys we would have made, our faces appearing godlike over his crib. How can an infected man like me be worthy of this blessing?

I do not know if the little one will appear launched from my head, or emerge from the muscles of my legs. But when the moment happens it will be as if a part of me dies. When I release him to the river I will surely crumble to the ground, crying out for Marcus, my body disintegrating into the stuff of protons, neutrons, quarks, shattering back into the dark matter of an unforgiving universe.

Drinking
Water Lilies

JAY RUBEN DAYRIT

Paul's last day on the job seems like any other at the country club. Nothing special. No banner saying, *Good Luck in Africa, Paul. Don't Fall off That Mountain* . . . some mountain in Tanzania he wants to climb while the rest of us battle the ragweed of August before the start of our senior year. Paul has already graduated, allowing himself time to do things that only happen in Patagonia ads.

Paul Hamilton van Horn III, a name that gets me wondering why he needs a summer job at all. He has cleaned the pool for only a month this summer, while A.J. and I watched from the shade of big yellow umbrellas, wanting to swim in the cool blue water rather than mix icy drinks behind the bar. We in our pressed linen jackets and bow ties, Paul in striped shorts and bare feet.

Perhaps it's best that we wear the jackets, though. The heat would probably kill Paul. Seems like a thin layer of red hair covers every inch of his body, except for the palms of his hands, the bottoms of his feet, and the half of his neck he quickly shaves in the washroom each morning. Once, as I knotted my tie, stealing sidelong glances at Paul shaving in the mirror, he told me, Ya know, Harris, I've heard every hairy butt joke in the world, and I'd be surprised if you guys come up with anything new. I never try though, because I've never heard a hairy butt joke. And A.J. never says much to Paul.

The day passes with the usual martinis as Illiam carries them to the rich fat people unfolding into plastic chaise lounges around the pool. On her way back, she always tilts her head and says something that makes Paul smile or splash pool water at her skimpy uniform with an easy flick of his foot. Though I watch her lips, I can never figure out what it is she says. Something sexy maybe. Something only the two of them share. I don't care much really, because in Illiam I haven't any interest, although she's nice. And with Paul, I've even less of a chance than A.J. has with Illiam. But A.J. cares about what they say to each other by the pool. I can tell by the way he eats the Melba toast in those little plastic wrappers, nibbling without tasting, watching Illiam's thighs slip past each other, thighs that tell A.J., Oh you're so nice, but Paul's so much better looking.

Paul *is* handsome, despite all that hair, a face that says more about him than his words ever could. Guilt-free is what A.J. calls it, with an edge of envy in his voice. A guilt-free face.

After the end of his last day, the four of us hang out by the bar; Illiam dividing tips, Paul poking at the ice in his screwdriver, A.J. and I wiping down the counter with white cotton rags. Paul suggests we go swimming since it's so hot. In the reservoir, he adds. A.J. hesitates, but only because he wants Illiam to say, Oh come on, A.J. It'll be fun. After some prodding, we finally convince him we ought to do something different before Paul leaves. A kind of farewell, we tell A.J., rather than the usual beer and pizza at Poor Penny's.

We meet in the dark of the parking lot after closing time. Two cars for four people. Paul knows where to sneak into the reservoir so A.J. follows. Riding with A.J., I watch Paul's car ahead of us, at the way Illiam rests her head against the back of her seat.

A.J. sings quietly with the radio. *Blinded by the light, wrapped up like a douche in the middle of the. . . .* Douche or deuce? Either way it makes no sense. A.J. jokes about vinegar and water, and we laugh like boys in high school. Seems like Illiam is laughing too.

I imagine what it's like to be her, to have Paul tell me, It's just sex, as I lie tangled in the rumpled sheets of his bed, smelling salty and clean. To have him reason away togetherness in a rustling voice like windy grass, sleepy and detached, not at all comforting like he intends. I don't think we even know what love is, he says when I tell him, I think I'm falling in love with you. How can we really know? he continues. We're too young. Which sounds more like, You're too young. And I imagine hearing his warm breath wrap around me, spoon feeding me those words across the whisper of space between us, a space much greater than the distance his plane will carry him the very next day. So uncomfortably easy it is for me to imagine the collapse of heart and hope Illiam will feel this night after swimming and before Paul crawls out of bed to double-check his carbon-copy ticket.

Leaving the cars at a dead end of a residential area, we walk single file through the woods, arms extended, pushing aside branches that bend away with sapling ease. We speak in hushed voices, as if people can hear us, as if people care.

The moon wiggles quietly on the surface of the water and breaks as we enter; Paul the first to step in, A.J. the last, trailing behind and balancing against the whispering current. Skinny dipping in drinking water feels strange, as if it would have been different wearing the underwear we left behind on the banks. Surrounded by lily pads and huge floating flowers, we stand waist deep with our hands in our armpits and wonder whether or not we are cold. I keep my eyes on the dark trees across the reservoir, trying not to look at the water beads on Paul's stomach or on Illiam's breasts. I try not to think about what A.J. might be thinking. I pretend what we are doing is normal.

We don't swim much. The pads are too slimy and startling, brushing up against us with dead stillness as we dog paddle past them. So we only stand, avoiding the stems, and throw small stones gathered from the bottom with our toes. We listen and see who can throw the farthest, create the longest stretch of silence before our ears catch the tiny *plink* somewhere ahead of us, so faint we must lean forward and squint our eyes as if to sharpen our hearing.

Paul says, Okay, watch this, and pitches with a vigorous *Hmmph!* We all wait, as silent ripples spread from his naked waist, passing through each one of us before disappearing into the lily pads. And still we wait . . . but nothing happens. For a second, we are all impressed, even A.J., who whispers an airy Wow, until Paul holds out his palm, and in the moonlight, we can see the pebble has never left his hand. We laugh and strike up a fountain of splashes at him, calling him Bastard and You motherfucker!

Later, we swim to the deep end near the pumps and dare each other down to where the algae grows fuzzy and black, diving down into what it must feel like to be dead. It's morbid, almost terrifying but such a relief to resurface and see their excited faces ask-

ing, Wasn't it weird? Fuckin' weird, huh? And for a moment, it
seems like there's more history between us than just the country
club. Not real memories like photographs, but an intangible feeling of friendship as sweet and strong as the water lilies around us.

After a while, we decide we are cold and wade back to the bank
under the trees dipping their leaves to the water. Still wet and trying not to muddy the insides of our jeans, we point our toes and
slip into our clothes. On the way back through the woods, we slap
at mosquitoes biting our sweet skin. We walk quietly and say nothing. There seem to be fewer branches to push out of the way.

Paul opens his car door and presses in the lighter. Waiting for
it to glow red hot in the dashboard, he holds a cigarette loosely
between his lips. A.J. leans on the hood of his own car, washed
honey yellow under the streetlight. Illiam climbs into Paul's car
and shuts the door.

Well . . . good-bye, Harris, Paul says and throws out his arms
overstatedly. I hug him awkwardly with the car door between us.
See ya, I say, feeling the asphalt scrape the soles of my shoes. Looking to A.J., Paul calls him over. A.J. does nothing more than shake
hands and step back so Paul can close the door when he sits down.

As A.J. and I get into his car and pull out of the dead end, I can
already feel Paul's absence, although I know I won't miss him. I
haven't known him long enough for that. I do, however, feel all
the sorrow and anger that comes when someone goes away. Sorrow for A.J., as lonely as I, I'm sure, but we will not talk about loneliness on the way home. Sorrow for Illiam, about to be told all the
tender meaningless things that supposedly cushion the fear that
he'll never write to her from Africa, not even so much as a post-
card. Anger at myself for wanting to be told the very same things,
not just a simple Well . . . good-bye, Harris. And most of all, a kind
of quiet anger at Paul for bringing us here to the reservoir, for
making us do what best friends, perhaps even lovers, do, only to
show us in the end, the inevitable loss of this one month in just
one summer.

They drive behind us this time. A.J. watches the bright head-
lights in the rearview mirror, while I pretend not to notice the
silence between us. The headlights take a final turn away. Paul
honks his horn. A.J. honks back.

JOE RESJAN

for Larry

His name was A-Tone. Like that. As a small boy he was called Anton, of course, because that was what his mother Molly called him. In high school, living over in Ludington, he renamed himself Anthony. He wanted to be different. In his senior year his mother died from booze and sadness, and Mavis gave him papers she'd kept. One of them, his birth certificate, gave his legal name as Aton. His mother, he knew, couldn't read or write, and this was probably the best she could do, at least that was what Mavis said. So for a while after he moved down to Detroit he played with Antoine while he took classes at Macomb Community College. He wanted the white kids to think he was foreign. When he dropped out to go into the "world of entertainment," as he always called it, even way back then, he had an inspiration: Atone, which soon metamorphosed into A-Tone. He loved the sound of it. Yes, a musical tone, an individuality. One tone. His tone. The one he was in his showbiz life.

Of course, everyone in Detroit knew him as Dyanna Ross.

Jamie, his only friend and only real competition at the Wild Blue Yonder, was watching him get dressed. Was helping him get dressed. It was Friday night, and they were at A-Tone's apartment. Tall, slender as a pencil, with pink palms and long, delicate fingers dark as charcoal, Jamie finished powdering A-Tone's face. A-Tone was nearly as dark as Jamie, but just a few shades lighter: sepia was the word he liked to use. Like Diana herself, he always said, smiling, as though he had something to do with it. A-Tone knew it bothered Jamie—his being a tad lighter. Shades meant so much, although when they were both standing in front of mirrors, decked out in gowns and jewels and hair, it didn't matter: Jamie could be a long-legged ebony Tina Turner, precarious on those high, high two-story heels, and A-Tone, ever the lithe, slinky diva, would peer out from inch-long lashes and a basket of hair that demanded its own room. They loved each other, the two men. At least they said they did. As friends, really, as far as A-Tone was concerned.

A-Tone knew Jamie wanted him, but A-Tone wanted no one these days. Jamie was getting worse about it: the fighting, the jealousies, the moodiness. The touching. A-Tone lived for his art. He was twenty-four and had never had a real boyfriend. There was that redheaded white kid in high school but he was trailer-park stuff, and he liked to hit A-Tone between the thighs so that it didn't show. A-Tone didn't want to play plantation games. That seemed a real long time ago. There had been one other boy, but he drank. Now A-Tone didn't want a lover. He had enough to worry about. But Jamie would touch him, pleading in his puppy-love eyes, but A-Tone discouraged that: he had all he could do now to be Dyanna Ross, quintessential impersonator of the world's greatest female star. Ain't No Mountain High Enough.

And besides, he knew he was dying.

"You think she'll come?" Jamie said.

"Of course," A-Tone said, smiling. He was trying on a red feathery dress similar to the one Diana wore when she played the Royal Albert Hall in London, just like in the bootleg videotape he owned of the performance. Tonight Jamie helped him adjust the flyaway weave, the hair spilling out into the air like nighttime static. A-Tone's oversized eyes, never so large as Diana's midnight ones, were accented by heavy kohl. Bright carmine lipstick, sparkles in the hair.

Jamie looked annoyed. "You're so sure?"

A-Tone wasn't sure, but he wouldn't let Jamie get the better of him. Once, a year or so back, when Jamie had his Tina Turner revue, Tina herself showed up, flattered, sang with him, camped it

up, the audience of half-drunk men and women screaming and
hooting. Now the photographs of that evening hung on his walls
like trophies. It was his happiest moment, and he referred to it all
the time. His duet with Tina. A-Tone hated him then.

"If she can make it," A-Tone said. He'd sent the note to the Fox
Theatre where Diana was playing for two nights, that night and
Saturday. He couldn't see her shows, but he let her know about
his own show on Sunday. In the note he told her he would lip-sync
her latest songs from the *Take Me Higher* album. He had a whole
new routine.

"She'll never come," Jamie said, pushing in a bobby pin a little
too fiercely. A-Tone winced.

"Don't be a bitch," A-Tone said.

He watched Jamie in the mirror: the other man raised his eyebrows in mock surprise and smiled thinly.

"I don't think she'd appreciate two Dianas playing Detroit." He
smiled.

A-Tone thought to himself: Sunday night. Why not? She'd still
be in Detroit, most likely visiting family. Catching up with old
friends. No performance. She could catch my late show. She
could visit her father and her brothers and sisters. The ones still
in Detroit. They could get Chinese food at the restaurant they always ate at—he'd followed her there three times over the many
years. Then she could come to the Wild Blue Yonder. She would
see A-Tone's special tribute.

In fact, at the Sunday show he would have a surprise, even for
Jamie, who wanted to know everything about A-Tone's life and career. It was hard keeping anything from Jamie. A-Tone stood up,
tossed his head back and the hair swirled around him. He stepped
into the sequined pumps. His ankles ached now. No: they hurt.
For a second, his eyes closed tightly, he saw colliding stars and
stark lightning flashes. There was pain deep in his throat, a
scratchiness that made swallowing difficult. Thank God he only
had to mouth Diana's lyrics. I'm twenty-four, he thought: I'm
going to be a beautiful corpse. I should be Liza Minnelli doing
Cabaret. Sally Bowles. Dying like Elsie. Laid out in beauty. Diana
only died in one of her movies, when she was Billie. Not the one
he loved, although he cried the many times he saw it. He loved all
those wonderful clothes. All that perfume. All that European runway action. Race cars and handsome Billy Dee Williams. All that

melodramatic emoting. Diana with drug-slit eyes, with candle wax dripping on her decadent Eurotrash body. Lord, that was fun.

He didn't tell Jamie how he'd waited for Diana at the stage door that very afternoon. At noon he'd left his clerk's job at the Harmony House music store, telling the manager he was ill. That was true, because he would never lie. Never. Lying diminished people, he knew. He could hear Mavis telling him that. So did jealousy, but he couldn't help that. In the world of entertainment, jealousy was, well, part of the job description. So he waited outside by the municipal parking lot, at the Fox Theatre's stage door, knowing Diana usually came early for a sound check. No one else was around. But she was late today, probably lunching with old Motown cronies, and she rushed by him, fleeing the limo. "Miss Ross," he said, and she glanced over at the skinny man with the big eyes and the shaved head. The four earrings running up his left ear. The T-shirt that wore her picture from a different tour. The baggy khaki slacks hanging off him. "May I please speak to you?" He was always courteous—he called her Miss Ross and stood way back, never pushing like other fans. She looked at him and she said, "Sorry, but I'm late," rushing by. He didn't mind. He understood the demands of royalty.

Two years ago, standing in the same place behind the Fox, he had waited there patiently, but that time in bitter winter, the snow swirling around him, piling up around his ankles, and she saw him standing there alone, an autograph book stretched out. She had the limo stop. Nothing came from his cold numb mouth. But she smiled and said, "Come over here." He stumbled over to her. Touching his cold face, she said, "You crazy boy. Walk me to my dressing room." He did, meeting her at the stage door, but he was too dumbfounded to talk to her—to tell her that he was Dyanna Ross, the most famous impersonator of her music and style in the whole Midwest. That he loved her to death. That he thought of her every day. That he lived for her. She found his silence amusing, took the book from him, and signed her name. He mumbled his name. She wrote: "To Anton"—that's how she heard it, or maybe that was how he said it—"with love to a cold friend with a warm heart. Love, Diana Ross." She kissed his icy cheek, then sent him out into the snow.

For him, that was his defining moment.

Jamie could keep his Tina Turner duet.

But he wouldn't tell Jamie about that afternoon. They would fight about it. Largely because they had both agreed to go Saturday afternoon, and wait for Diana. Lately Jamie wanted to spend all his free time with A-Tone. "Work my way into your loving," he said. A-Tone went cold at the thought. Jamie scared him. That was why he'd jumped the gun: he'd wanted to meet Diana alone on Friday.

Jamie was talking now: "I think you should retire 'Touch Me in the Morning.'"

A-Tone frowned. "But that's my favorite song," he said.

"You're in danger of becoming a lounge act," his friend said. "Bitch."

Earlier that week, on Monday, he'd driven to visit his grandmother, who still lived on the outskirts of Idlewild, deep in the woods five hours north of Detroit. A-Tone, who loved the ninety-five-year-old woman, the only relative he remembered now, faithfully visited every month, pushing his old, creaky Nova beyond its limitations, chugging the last sputtering miles until he turned down the narrow dirt road, sheltered under towering pines and sagging white birch, until the car rested, steam spewing from the radiator, in the ill-kept yard filled with automobile parts and old house fixtures. No one ever took them away. Mavis, who was expecting him, sat by the front window with the cracked panes of glass, waiting. He was the only grandchild who still visited her. She sat there, the pale face against glass, unmoving.

Inside he kissed her, telling her not to get up. She was all bone now, like sticks wrapped in pale charcoal skin, her snow white hair spotty and strawlike. "Mavis," he said. "My baby." He'd always called her by her first name, ever since he was a tiny boy trailing after her in the overgrown summer gardens. After his mother Molly died, she sheltered him. There was no one else: his father was a sometime hardware salesman in Reed City, a man crazy with girl hunger, but he never talked to anyone any more. He'd been beat up in a bar. A-Tone's older brothers and sisters—a bunch of them—were married, distant from him, and had their own miserable lives in trailers and cabins and jails. He, the latecomer, the last born, was Mavis's sweet darling. A fragile, lonely boy, dancing in her shoes and hats. She protected him, hiding him in that ramshackle house, half mobile home, half shanty, with corrugated metal plates serving as roof, with the outhouse in the back, with the generator supplying the tiny house with electricity during the cold months. Last year A-Tone used all his savings, putting in oil heat for her, and she stopped getting sick. In winter she still burned wood, lugging bulky firewood into the house, the old, old woman maneuvering the logs with difficulty. She never complained. She'd lived alone for years. Now A-Tone was a performer in Detroit. She was proud of him and saved the clippings he sent her from the Michigan gay-bar guides. He told her he lip-synced Diana in a club, and he promised to bring her to a Diana concert someday. He meant it: he'd be proud. She'd nod her head back and forth: no, baby, she couldn't go to no rock-and-roll show, she said.

"I brought you some stuff, Mavis," he said.

She nodded. He placed a bag of groceries on the table. Bread, crackers, milk, coffee. She ate so little and he knew most would be strewn in the back yard, feeding the rabbits and squirrels that came from the dark woods that stretched miles beyond the yard. Each day she fed them. Hummingbirds flitted by the kitchen window on the Japanese quince bush. Woodpeckers clamored on dead oak trunks. They were her life now. That and the scratchy phonograph records she played at night on a sputtering turntable: Louis Armstrong, Count Basie, Ella, Billie, Sarah. She called them by first names. She had a right to.

"How's my baby?" she asked, as she always did, shoulders touching. They sat with tea she brewed, hard and powerful, from roots she gathered herself.

"Fine," he said.

"Skinny," she said, touching his dusky cheek.

He grinned. "Always skinny, Mavis," he said. "Since a little boy."

But he couldn't fool her. Her eyes never moved from his, the light in them murky and dull. She has wisdom, he knew. She let her fingers linger against his cheek, and he saw her start to cry.

She knows, he thought. She knows that I will die before she will. So the patterns break, out of sync. Rhythms smashed. Unnatural order. His mother had died so many years back, a howling death. And now his, the whimpering kind. So she held her hand there, too long, and he got nervous.

"I'm fine, Mavis," he said.

"You my beautiful boy," she said.

He squirmed. "I'm working too hard," he said.

But they were just idle words tossed her way: she wasn't listening. It was never the words they used anyway. She always knew him, deep in his dark blood marrow. When he was ten, he remembered, she told him she didn't understand how her beloved Jesus worked, but He would give her no child who could do mean to others. Who would do wrong things, ugly things. It was impossible. "You are a different child," she said, "and it ain't no business of mine to question the workings of my Jesus."

He hadn't understood, but waited.

She had her eye on him for days, he knew. He'd catch her watching him throughout the long days of that hot summer. He was always alone—there was no one his age in the hidden woods they lived in. No one. When she sewed her dresses, he held the cloth smooth for her on the kitchen table. So one night she drew him close to her, pulling him onto her lap, and he smelled old lavender and dried perspiration: the smells he always loved in his grandmother. "It ain't no business of mine, but I know I don't understand His ways."

"What, Mavis?" he asked. He had just turned ten years old the day before. A skinny brown boy, a doll's face, with wide eyes and long arms that fluttered in the air.

"It be all right with Jesus for you to love other boys," she said.

And at that moment—though he tried to squirm out of her hold—he understood the confusion he'd had inside him for years: the rapid beating of his heart, the sweating around older boys, the razor pain in his gut, the choking of his voice. He thought he would suffocate, she was holding him so tightly.

"Is all right, baby," she said. "It's what Jesus said you got to do. He gives everyone a different kind of love, and that's yours. It's a hurtful love—my brother Lyle had it and he kills hisself—but Jesus don't do nothing without a purpose. Don't use it to be mean, Anton."

So now she understood that he was dying. When she held him, she felt the weakness in the bones, the wispiness of the blood, the thinning of the muscles, the cavernous eyes, the dying of the spirit. She held onto him now like she did when he was ten and she told him what he needed to hear but until then had no words for.

"It's all right, Mavis," he said.

"Course it is," she said, simply. She spooned homemade jelly

onto a biscuit, shoved it at him. "Course it is, baby. We will be together, you and me."

Then it was twilight, A-Tone's most hated time of day up here
on the dark road. When he was a boy, he ached then: then the
gnawing loneliness raced through him and strangled him. The
coming of that ink-black darkness up here in the woods, heavy
as a curtain, the stony silence of the dirt road, the awful smell of
isolation.

At night they lingered in the hard-swept parlor and listened to
music. There was nothing else to do up there. He hated it, especially after living in hip-hop lively Detroit since he left home and
high school at seventeen. Back then he didn't mind it: the isolation was temporary, he knew, because one day he'd be in New
York or Los Angeles or Chicago. The lonely high-school years in
Ludington, living with Molly and her last boyfriend, those melancholy nights alone with Diana Ross lulling him to sleep or to feverish dance, were testing days: rehearsal days. Somehow he never
thought of Detroit as the final stopping point. Now, of course, he
knew it would be. So be it.

Mavis played only Ella Fitzgerald that night. She shut her eyes,
unmoving in the rocker, and let A-Tone turn the albums over.
They were scratchy and staticky, but Ella's music was emphatically
there. It settled in the corners of the room like a welcome rain.
The night was quiet—there was no sound on the dead dirt road,
no sound in the dark forest beyond. And only the night wind
would occasionally rattle the metal sheets that served as a roof.
Otherwise, it was quiet. An owl hooted. A fierce night animal bellowed. Nature closed down. But Ella sang. Mavis, her eyes closed,
was smiling, her mouth a thin parched line, like a crack in hard,
water-starved dirt. She was happy. With Ella.

A-Tone watched her. Gripping the arms of the chair, he was
starting to panic. Feeling lightheaded, with a rapid quickening in
the heart, he felt suffocated here, hidden in the little house. A
shack, he thought, a little shack. Worse, he felt his warm head: a
low-grade fever. No, he didn't want to get sick up here, miles from
anything. They knew him at the Henry Ford Hospital in Detroit—
he'd been there once, for a week, when he had pneumonia. One
more bout with pneumonia would do him in. He felt that in his
heart. He'd never even told Jamie about the week there. No one
knew. That was the way it had to be. Every so often, surreptitiously,

he'd touch his forehead, hoping Mavis wouldn't open her eyes and see him feel his brow, sense the warmth. See the fear settle into his eyes.

Mavis nodded off in her chair, and he finally nudged her to bed.

Later, dozing off and on while lying on the cot in the hallway, the chill of August night in the woods seeping through the boards and windowsills, he played Diana though his headphones—low, so that the thumping bass line and buzzing treble wouldn't disturb Mavis. A song about old friends talking, about one of those friends blurting out a love she never stopped having. "I Thought That We Were Still in Love." Diana's reedy, pretty voice, delicate as mosquito wings, laced through the emotions, hugged him, found the soul of the lyrics and made the song echo in his heart. Only Diana could make him get that lonely. Lying on the cot, sweating with a feverish brow, his heart pounding, and the bitter taste of ashes on his tongue and in his throat, he cried. He hadn't cried in Mavis's home since he was a boy.

When he woke in the morning, coming out of a nightmare about broken tree limbs and fierce wind, Mavis was sitting over him, a chair pulled up, patting his head with a cool, damp cloth. She said nothing, but when he opened his eyes, she stood, walked away. In minutes he smelled bacon and biscuits and gravy and eggs. For the first time in days he was hungry. Mavis only cooked when A-Tone came for the overnight visit. They would have one breakfast together. By nightfall he'd be gone.

In the afternoon, he drove her around lazily—bills to pay, light shopping, short sentimental visits to other old women whose homes she couldn't walk to. He'd linger in the yards while the old women talked on yard chairs or front porches. They had their own language, which excluded him. Friends dead so many years were gossiped about. A-Tone would nod at them from where he sat, on the car hood or under a willow, nursing a lemonade. Mrs. Ryers, his old choir teacher, now over one hundred, squeaked like a trapped mouse, laughing at something Mavis whispered. Nothing had changed since he was there as a boy.

This was the dead part of Michigan, he knew: the poorest landscape of the state. Late afternoon, the roads were deserted. He drove her to Evart, through Baldwin, to the outskirts of Ludington on the lake. No one was out except for vagrant children playing in long yards where sinking tables of rain-damaged garage-sale goods lingered week after week. Battered cars and pickups rusted beside leaning sheds. Old washing machines sat immobile by over-grown forsythia bushes. Here and there, though, a satellite dish was tucked into a garden: the shiny alabaster surface stark against a landscape of decay and darkness. Driving through it all, A-Tone was starting to choke on it all: out of here. Get me out of here.

"Time you brought me home," Mavis said at last. She'd been watching him.

"You sure, Mavis? You wanna visit Leona?"

Mavis chuckled. "Boy, I dislike that woman more'n you. Child, take me home." She smiled. "You got that long ride home, and I don't like you driving on the dark roads."

Back at her place he stuffed the few clothes he brought with him into his overnight bag, making room for the vegetables she packed for him: overripe tomatoes, lush green peppers, cucumbers fat as missiles, and eggplant the color of dark blood. "Fatten you up, baby," she said. And there was fried chicken, cold from the refrigerator, wrapped in dishtowels that smelled of lye soap and many scrubbings. "Go home, baby," she said.

Whenever he visited, she said the same thing, always at mid-afternoon. She saw the impatience, the drying up inside him. No place for an entertainer, these dead woods.

But today she made him wait. "Hold on," she said, smiling. She returned from a closet in her bedroom with a faded rectangular box, tied up with old red twine. "This be for you," she said.

He smiled. "A gift?"

"I vowed never to give this up, but it's time," she said. "Open it."

He opened it up, slipping the twine off carefully. Inside was a gown, a long, slinky, blue sequined gown, with black fur at the collar and cuffs, with glittering faux pearls hanging off the midriff, bugle beads running down the back. Gold thread was woven in wavy falling lines, a waterfall of sun against the cobalt blue. He lifted up the gown, and the cloying smell of mothballs flooded the room. He brought it into the light, swirled around with it, ran his fingers over the careful, deliberate stitching, the pristine fabric, and somewhere deep in the lining of the dress there still lingered the trace of long-ago perfume, a faint gardenia hint. He buried his face in the aroma. He heard music now.

He looked at Mavis, and she was smiling.

"Ella's dress," she said simply.

"You're kidding."

"She done give it to me in nineteen forty-five. Just after the war that took your uncle Raymond."

Again A-Tone buried his face in the fabric, got fizzy from the mothball scent. "Why?" he said.

"I done admired it one night, and she was a good, caring woman. I made her some of my fried chicken, the smothered chicken you loves, and we gots to talking. That's all." She sat back.

Back then, A-Tone knew, so many black people—the rich ones from down state and Chicago, those middle-class doctors and lawyers and successful businessmen—vacationed at Idlewild. Then it had been the premier resort area for black folk, who had no-where else to go to party on the high road. Elegant lake houses and resplendent cabarets circled the water at Idlewild. In those postwar days the area attracted the big-band sound, done black-style, the jazz combos, the Count Basies, the Ellas, the Cab Callo-ways, the Louis Armstrongs. Mavis worked the resort, backstage in the dressing rooms. She cleaned and ironed the stage costumes. One night, chatty with Ella, she admired the dress hanging off a hook. It was a fine piece of glitter and light. When Ella left, there was this very box, with this very red twine, and a note. The dress was a gift. "Remember me," the note said.

"You never told me," A-Tone said.

"I ain't never told anybody. It's my story, and Ella's. And now yours. You take it."

"Mavis. No."

Mavis was already repacking the dress. "I ain't got the note. Your grandfather was a man who carried it around, like it was his'n. It got the woman up against him, I guess. And so he lost it on the road. But I still got hold of the dress."

"Mavis," he said.

"It's all right, boy. Get moving on."

When he was small, she had talked of the marvelous feast days of Idlewild, the fancy nightclubs on the lake, the ballroom danc-ing, the celebrities dining in the halls, the black doctors from Detroit or Chicago pulling up in red convertibles and those long white silky Cadillacs. He loved the stories because Mavis got glassy-eyed and lively, but whenever he asked what happened to that world, Mavis would close up. "Things changed," she said. And that was that.

"What things?"

"Never you mind, baby." But sometimes, walking with her through the roads, she'd point out a ramshackle house or a rusting mobile home. Or an abandoned house, the roof caving in. "That's where Charlie lives—he worked with Lena Horne when she was here. Them is his grandkids playing there." He'd see a bunch of poor kids hiding in the shell of an old car. So he realized that so many of the black folk populating the dark dirt roads, the clusters of families struggling under the weight of no money in their pockets, had come upstate to work the bourgeois black resort. Maybe that's how it was. So long ago. Now the bloodline had nothing to do because the jobs were gone but not the babies being born. The clock had stopped way back when.

Suddenly A-Tone realized why Mavis always referred to performers like Ella by their first names: to her they were old friends from another period of her life.

Mavis tied the box with the aging twine. It was fragile and snapped. Carefully she stretched the twine until it circled the box.

"But why give it to me, Mavis?" he said. "You kept it so long."

" 'Cause it's time," she said.

"Time?"

" 'Cause you and me, baby, ain't got no more time."

On Wednesday, back in Detroit, he took it to be dry cleaned at the shop where he always brought his gowns. Monty, the owner, an old customer and friend from the drag-bar scene, got rhapsodic about it, because Harry knew a class-act costume when he touched it. He promised it back by nighttime. But A-Tone didn't tell him it had belonged to Ella Fitzgerald. He and Mavis had their privacies. This would be one more. For a short while. Of course, eventually everyone would know. He decided he might—maybe—tell only one person—his friend Jamie—and then, thinking about the dress as he clerked at the music store, ignoring the heavy-metal white kids from Dearborn who imitated his soft velvet voice back at him and made their wrists go limp, he had an inspiration: Sunday's drag show. He stopped moving.

He would wear the dress.

On Friday he would send a note to Diana at the Fox Theatre,

and he'd mention the show on Sunday. That show was the one people waited for: the new routines, the special guest stars—last week was Miss Chicago, some tired obese queen who did a wonderful Peggy Lee—but the spotlight would be on him. The headliner. Dyanna Ross. Because Diana herself was in town that weekend. He would be the star. He would wear Ella's dress, and the night would be his: brown sugar of one generation becoming brown sugar of another. The line of royal descent. His heart pounded. It was, for him, a staggering concept, and he could think of nothing else after he conceived the idea. His eyes closed, he saw himself in the blue sequins. It took his breath away.

That night he altered the dress, sewing into the morning hours until his eyes became blurry. And the wet coughing began. He skipped a doctor's appointment the next morning, telling himself the fever had gone. He slept in, so he was late for work that afternoon. Waking up late in the morning, he dreamed his teeth were all pulled out. Then, at last, the pain in his head might stop. But when he sat up in bed, the throbbing was still there.

On Saturday he met Jamie for a late lunch across from the Fox Theatre, at the Metro. They had planned to wait for Diana at the stage door, but A-Tone knew he couldn't stand in the growing heat. The day was too hot. He was edgy and nervous: he didn't mention to Jamie how he'd waited the day before, watching Diana run into the building.

"But you wanted to come here," Jamie said.

"I'm tired from sewing," he said. Last night, long after Jamie left his apartment, he'd finished altering Ella's gown.

Jamie's eyes got wide: "You got something new?" An edge to his voice.

A-Tone smiled. He played with French fries on his platter, pushing them here and there. He couldn't eat. Then he decided to tell Jamie about Ella's dress and his plans to wear it in his Dyanna Ross show on Sunday. He never could keep a secret from Jamie. And this was the biggest secret of all. He blurted out the story of Mavis and the gown.

"Imagine if Diana shows up. I'll tell her afterwards it is Ella's. When she comes to the dressing room."

He talked on and on, suddenly happy to share the news of the gown with Jamie, but he noticed Jamie got too quiet. He waited for his friend to say something funny or clever, but Jamie's face looked tight and flushed. A-Tone had been talking too fast, rushing out the words, hardly waiting for Jamie to respond, but his friend now was frowning. His eyes burned with anger. He hadn't touched his hamburger, but he'd squashed the fries into oozing pulp.

"What's the matter?" A-Tone asked him. "You look angry like a hornet."

"Ain't mad at anything," Jamie said.

"I know you, girlfriend."

He waited. Finally Jamie drew his lips into a tight line. "Just a little tired of your selfishness."

A-Tone frowned. "Meaning?"

"You done nothing but talk about that goddamn dress since you sat down."

"But—"

"It's a dress, damn it."

A-Tone was getting another headache. Maybe it was just one long headache, he thought: it ebbed and flowed. It was always worse when he argued with Jamie, he knew. For years they had argued about stupid things, mainly other guys, other performers, makeup, song selections, stuff like that. Bar and club spats. Dumb stuff. Sometimes they were serious spitfire fights but those were about A-Tone ignoring Jamie's loving attention. Jamie was older, maybe thirty, and sometimes he talked about the fact that he'd never had a lover. Neither had A-Tone but he was twenty-four. That wasn't unusual, especially among performers. But Jamie had been his friend for four years now, maybe five, and most of that time he refused to accept the friendship A-Tone offered: periodically he'd "get at it," to use A-Tone's words—that is, professed love, infatuation, feelings that went beyond. It came in waves, these avowals of love. The touching. He wanted more. Lately he'd been waiting for A-Tone to come around. "We got each other," he'd say.

A-Tone called it Jamie's period. That time of the month.

But A-Tone was weary now: he was nauseous. There was no time to begin such romances, especially with Jamie, who was not attractive to him and whose mercurial moods sometimes alarmed him. One time, in anger, Jamie slapped him. He apologized right away, but the deed was done. Jamie had cried after that incident, begging forgiveness, which of course A-Tone gave him. A-Tone believed no woman should be slapped.

"You're not talking about no dress," A-Tone said, sharply.

The eyebrows went up. "And what might I be talking about, Miss Thing?"

A-Tone whispered. "You just jealous. One jealous queen. Sunday is my night to shine with Ella and Diana and—"

Sarcastic: "And Mr. Potbelly White Folk."

"What that mean?"

"You know what it means."

"Jealousy. It's a horrible thing."

Jamie knew how to get to him. For the past few weeks A-Tone had been getting outrageous tips from some portly white guy, an older guy, who always came early and seated himself in front on the side. A massive man, with a bald flaking scalp, with lumpy business suits, he laughed uproariously at the performers, enjoying the comedy, and applauded wildly anything A-Tone did. One night he gave A-Tone three twenty-dollar bills, the stuff of legends. That was the night A-Tone did his comedic Dyanna—he came out with two wobbling puppets on either side. He was all the Supremes that night. As he mouthed the words to "Someday We'll Be Together," he gently lay down the Cindy Birdsong puppet—because she was a good perfect Supreme—and then shoved Mary Wilson away from him, ending by hurling her tell-all tabloid bio on top of her. Mary Wilson, whose book had sullied Diana. Mary Wilson, so hungry for attention she'd go to the opening of a drain, as Jamie always put it. The audience loved the routine, and Mr. White Man laughed so hard he spit his drink across a table. After the intermission, when Diana returned as a solo, twirling and dipping to "Reach Out and Touch," sequins popping off her gown like spray from a wave, he bowed to her. He came back every weekend. He was obnoxious.

He ignored Tina Turner.

"Just what is your problem?" A-Tone said.

Jamie stood up. "You are embarrassing yourself. And Sunday you'll run around in a mothball smelly dress. Even Diana don't wear clothes that old, although"—he grinned—"the diva do like to recycle some old tattered dresses."

He left A-Tone alone in the restaurant, storming out with shoulders high and eyes wide. They'd been too loud, both of them elevating their voices, singing out the words over the nosy heads. People were still staring at him. "What are you looking at?" he said to no one, and people busied themselves in their food.

He'd make up with Jamie late that night, go clubbing with him.

Suddenly he felt faint: his stomach dropped. Everything went black for a second, his head swimming. He reached for the water glass and knocked it off the table. Its contents splashed on a woman passing by. She started to say something as the waitress hurried over, but when she saw A-Tone slumping in the chair, his body limp and crumbling, she stopped. She screamed. A-Tone slipped away. Later, coming to in the ambulance, he remembered only the shimmering blue of a dress, the bright yellow of spotlight spreading on him, the sound of applause. He wanted to stay in that moment forever. He was dreaming that he was in love.

On Sunday night Jamie didn't show up at the club. A-Tone figured he was doing it for spite, but it didn't matter. Actually it did matter, but A-Tone refused to think about it. Everyone knew Jamie could be unreliable; that's why, at thirty, he was still second-string drag. But there was just too much to do. A-Tone had got a headache early in the afternoon, a tension headache, he told himself, and nothing could relieve it. The afternoon was chaos. His car broke down, so one of the bartenders, Billy, gave him a ride to the club. The long haul back from Idlewild and Mavis's world on Tuesday night had exhausted the water pump, and right now he had no money for a new one. So he rode the ten blocks to the club in drag, his usual street drag of cocktail dress and modest heels that were only so high. Just a little makeup. It got him into the mood. He liked being driven to the theatre, and Billy was an old friend who loved him. When A-Tone drove his own car, he did so carefully so the cops wouldn't pull him over. That was a fear he had. Not that it was any of their goddamn business how he dressed. He smiled: once, in fact, he'd dated a Detroit cop, a beefy black guy named Ted who was married and lived by Greek Town.

But as the evening moved on, as he sat there in the dressing room and watched the other performers move on and offstage— all the Chers and Bettes and Madonnas with their screaming fans and over-the-shoulder flirtations—he grew impatient. He wasn't feeling well, and he needed Jamie. He started to dial his home number, but stopped: no, he thought, let him pout. Jamie, he figured, just couldn't deal with A-Tone's triumph. Let him not be here for the glorious night. He rubbed his temples, and for a moment the dull, deep pain seemed to ease.

Dressing up relaxed him a bit. It always did, even when he was a small boy up north. Suddenly, in the mirror, there would be an entirely new person, a beautiful woman. It was the perfect place to hide.

In the cramped dressing room, tucked into a shadowy corner so he wouldn't have to talk to the other performers who were yelling and laughing, sitting there, he smiled. He got happy. He was wearing the gown. He'd put it on early, just so the others could see. They oohed and aahed, of course—any new gown was cause for fluttering—but they didn't understand. He knew they didn't like him much of the time—he headlined and let them know it. He was Dyanna Ross. He kept to himself, preferring to create an aura, a mystery. He didn't like their catty conversations. And he didn't tell them whose dress it was. None of their damn business. One thirtyish white guy, Jonnie Cokes, aka Cher, touched the bugle beads running up and down the back. "My, my," he said. "The Pointer Sisters ain't got nothing on you."

A-Tone ignored him, but, looking in the full-length mirror, he realized what Jonnie meant—and it was something he'd sensed when he'd played with the dress at home. It had a used look about it: it looked years old, out of fashion, despite A-Tone's careful alterations to make it fit. He looked a little dumpy in it, he admitted, because the hemline dragged a bit, one arm looked uneven. That was his fault. He'd got tired sewing late at night, and he should have stopped; no, he went on until he got dizzy. He'd even blacked out for a few minutes. But it was all right, he told himself. It was elegant, it would catch the light and no one would notice the slight imperfections. Show business was all that, he knew— grand illusion, the spotlight masking the rips and stains and faded material.

Jamie would have reassured him, and he kept watching the door, expecting Jamie to appear. Hoping. To hug him, to say— Girl, you got to tone down that eyeliner. You look like a Valley girl on a Halloween date. To say something like that. Jamie loved him. They were friends.

And he waited for the stir that would rise from the audience when Diana herself sauntered in with her entourage, her bodyguards hovering near. He'd hear the roar from inside the dressing room, and understand she was there for him. Then he would be ready to perform. He'd lead off with the slow, hypnotic ballad—"I Thought That We Were Still in Love"—and then he'd finish with a rousing, frenetic "I Will Survive," Diana's sultry cover of Gloria Gaynor's anthem for drag queens everywhere. That should bring down the house. Perhaps she would even perform with him— he'd heard she danced on stage with RuPaul—but at that vagrant thought his heart fluttered, the sweating began, and the palms got cold. Stop it, he thought: you'll ruin the makeup. It took so much time to put himself together as Diana. As Dyanna. He smiled: it took Diana hours to put herself together as Diana. Such artistry took time. You couldn't rush things.

At ten o'clock, fixing a nail, he got ready to go on, but he had lost heart. Jamie hadn't showed, and, worse, one of the bartenders, Rich, the one who wore his pants so tight and was sleeping with the owner, volunteered the news that Diana was performing that very night in Cleveland. He'd brought A-Tone a Diet Coke and mentioned how he'd seen Diana at the Fox the night before. "It's a shame she's in Cleveland tonight," was how he put it.

"What do you mean?"

"She mentioned last night she'd be in Cleveland tonight." Then he left. A-Tone closed his eyes: how had he missed that news? He hadn't seen the two shows at the Fox—he had no money for the good seats up front, the ones the scalpers charged a fortune for—and he just refused to sit in the balcony for Diana. He'd never drop that low. He went to her shows as, well, Dyanna. Looking like her. He could hardly sit in the balcony in drag. He always waited for someone to buy him a ticket—Jamie usually did—but this time nothing happened. He refused to let himself think about it—a bizarre turn of events, how she had come to town and he had had to miss her. But he didn't want to be greedy. He'd had his private moment with her. That was okay for him. He was okay with it.

So he performed, and the audience loved him. But he didn't care any more. Sometimes he believed most of the applause was for Diana's signature songs—for her remote diva image he had momentarily stepped into. A borrowed life. Stealing her applause because he had none for himself. But he refused to think about that idea now because it always brought him crashing down. During the second and final show, he lost all his energy, going through the emotions and waiting for the applause. He just wanted to go home. To sleep now. To take his medications. The dress was too heavy and he felt he couldn't raise his arms. Afraid he'd topple over the small elevated stage, he held back, denied himself some classic Diana movements—sweeping her head back and thrusting her arms to the sky, as she always did in "Ain't No Mountain High Enough"—and the audience who knew him and her forgot to applaud. He didn't care. I want the night to be over. The dress weighed him down, and he felt rooted to the stage, he thought. The ankles ached, the legs were wooden. He tasted vomit high in his throat. He wanted to go home. I'm sick, he thought.

The fat white man was again in the front row for both shows, and he laughed and hooted and carried on. A-Tone found his attention unnerving, throwing off his moves. The man applauded in the wrong places. When he clapped his hands, he made a thunderous sound, pulling the beefy palms together so that the noise rang throughout the house like a quarry blast. He scared people. He did it for no other performer, A-Tone noticed. He was Dyanna's biggest fan, stuffing five-dollar bills—everyone else got one-dollar bills—into A-Tone's hands. During the intermission the man sent a drink backstage, but A-Tone refused to come out, sending thanks by the bartender. The other performers would mingle in their street drag during the intermissions. Not so A-Tone: he was Dyanna Ross. The aura. The mystery.

During the second show, A-Tone watched him closely. There was no way he could ever like such a man—florid, beet red face, wisps of thinning gray hair flying over his shiny scalp, the suit he wore misshapen and tired. The belly that went on forever, bursting the buttons of the limp white shirt. He always wore the same businessman's uniform. He drank scotch, neat, buying two at once, so glasses always cluttered his table. He wouldn't let the waiter clear the table. The empty glasses sat there like trophies or notches on Billy the Kid's belt. A-Tone always thought that pretty stupid. He hated drinkers: his mother Molly had died from drink, just thirty-seven years old. His father lived with wine and loneliness. The only time A-Tone came close to having a real lover since moving to Detroit was a boy name Louis, a white boy from Farmington Hills, whose alcoholic breath finally made A-Tone say no.

He'd been there. A-Tone had a drink once a month—if that. Drinking aged you. Like cigarettes.

When the last show ended, he bowed and the man slipped a bill into his palm. He heard the man mumble: "My name is Harry." Backstage, A-Tone realized it was a hundred-dollar bill. He'd never gotten one—never seen one. He grinned. This was real money. Not the forty or fifty dollars he usually made. His first thought: I can buy a water pump for the Chevy. I can get back up to Mavis next week. Then he smiled: if I'd got it two days ago, I could have seen Diana at the Fox. And had money for dinner afterward.

He went to thank the man, who suddenly seemed flustered by A-Tone's coming to him. They'd never spoken. "Let me buy you a drink," Harry said.

"No, thanks," A-Tone said, but the man waved over the waiter. A-Tone ordered a gin and tonic. His late-night drink. Then the man began to talk, slurring his words because he was drunk, running his mouth about A-Tone's grace and interpretation and how this song or that reminded him of his grandchildren. He went on and on, and A-Tone, eyes closing and the acrid taste still back in his throat, tried to listen. And then tried to leave. But the man ordered him another drink, which A-Tone refused to touch because he never drank more than one drink, but Harry didn't seem to notice. So A-Tone sat there, weighed down by the blue sequins and the runaway bugle beads, his shoulders sagging under the weight, and he realized he was still smelling mothballs. Did he imagine it? Goddamn that dry cleaner. For a second he thought he'd shock Harry by telling him he was really Ella and not Diana, but he saved that little joke for himself. Harry was still running his mouth, and letting his chubby fingers touch A-Tone's pencil-thin fingers. It made A-Tone nervous. Harry's skin was pasty white, and he thought of Mavis serving him Wonder Bread as a boy. This man was the whitest man he'd ever seen.

Finally, he got away, forcing Harry to let go of his hand. Smiling himself away. Bowing graciously. Diana nodding to reporters. The place had thinned out after the shows—it always did—but A-Tone now realized how desolate the place looked. It was last call. Chairs were already up on the tables at the back, the waiters nudging the customers out the door.

"Where's Billy?" he asked the manager.

"He's gone. Why?"

A-Tone frowned. "He's my ride."

"If you wait, I'll drop you off."

A-Tone shook his head. That would be another hour or so. He had to get home. He had pills to take.

Harry, of course, was listening. "I'll drop you off."

"Oh, no," A-Tone said. "Thank you, no." He had a policy about riding off with customers. "I——" He was going to be sick.

"You live far away?"

"South of Eight Mile, ten blocks away."

"Close. On my way. Come on. I'll wait for you to change."

A-Tone debated. But it would take him too long to change, to get back into street drag. He wouldn't make it: already his eyes were tearing, his stomach was heaving. He was going to get sick now. He feared he'd black out like yesterday at the Metro, and end up in the ER of Henry Ford. Home. Get me home. "Okay," he said. "We gotta go now."

In the car the man was nervous, and A-Tone realized how it looked: this pasty white man, sixty-five years old if a day, and a young black guy dressed like Diana/Ella in a blue sequined dress. The matching blue pumps. Diana's awesome tornado weave. The heavy scent of lavender in the car.

A-Tone even smiled, enjoying the image.

"Turn here," A-Tone said, and the car pulled down his street. "By the mailbox," he added. The car pulled to a stop.

A-Tone started to thank him, gathering up the folds of the gown, when Harry reached out and touched his cheek, letting his fingers rest there. A-Tone jumped back, as though he'd touched live wire. "Come on," Harry said.

"What?"

"I wanna do it."

"Please."

"I'll pay you."

A-Tone swung his head back and forth, dizzy now. "No," he said. "No."

Harry reached out again, and A-Tone pushed his hand away. He glanced up at his dark apartment building, toward the cheap studio he rented on the tenth floor. No lights. Nothing. No one on the street.

Suddenly Harry threw the car into gear and sped off, leaving a strip of rubber. For a second, before the car went too fast, A-Tone tried to get out, but Harry had locked the door. A-Tone, nervous, fumbled, uncertain which lock was which. The window went up and down. "Stop this," he said.

"I just don't want you mad at me," Harry said.

"I'm not. Really. Please. Now drive me home." His stomach fell.

"I wanna talk," the man mumbled, but the words were said through his teeth.

"No, please. Turn around."

But Harry was sweating now, and angry. He drove faster, wildly, and he turned onto the entrance ramp to a highway. A-Tone sat there, facing forward, his arms wrapped around his chest, begging Harry to turn back. "Where are we going?" But Harry, out of control, it seemed, had no direction. He wouldn't speak and he just drove and drove. Staring straight ahead. Speeding. The veins on his temples bulged. Every so often he mumbled to himself. The car swerved and A-Tone remembered the table littered with empty drink glasses. Now I will die, he thought. Now it will happen. Harry was breathing hard now, and when he turned to look at A-Tone there was nothing in the face but raw confusion: he didn't know what he was doing. The car had all the energy.

Mothballs, A-Tone thought, almost giddy. Mothballs.

At one point the car careened off an exit, almost smashing into a guard railing, and then it sped up. Looking out the window, A-Tone read a sign that said Warren, and he'd never heard of that town. He wanted to be in Detroit, where it was safe. People knew him there. Dyanna.

The car stopped, suddenly, alongside a clump of trees, and A-Tone fell forward. Harry, shaking now and with his eyes half-closed, reached out blindly and cupped his hand around A-Tone's neck, trying to pull him forward. A-Tone fought him, and for a minute he slapped at Harry. But the man didn't say anything, just held A-Tone off with that large extended hand. Sweat poured off the man's face. Finally, A-Tone heard a click, and Harry reached over him, opened the car door. A-Tone stopped struggling, alarmed. With that same arm he shoved A-Tone until he toppled out of the car, into the dirt. And then the car sped off, with dust flying and brakes squealing, the passenger door still wide open. Stunned, A-Tone lay there on his side, the taste of dirt and vomit in his mouth, watching the red taillights flicker and disappear.

Everything got quiet then, and dark. He didn't know where the hell he was.

There was nowhere to walk to. He saw house lights through some trees, but he couldn't go there. Not at three in the morning. Not dressed like that. Not in those runway heels. Dyanna in the suburbs. He stood, hobbled in the heels—one was broken off— and the weave of gigantic hair hung in his eyes. Everything on his body hurt. He heard a late-night car and ducked—staggered— into the clump of trees. For a second he thought the car's head-lights had caught the blue of the dress, the sequins, but the car disappeared. I'll sit in this spot until morning, he told himself. Hidden in the bushes. I'll wait for the local police to drive by: they'll make fun of me, they'll laugh, but they won't hurt me. Then, peering through the darkness, he saw a string of stores, a strip mall, a gas station. There would be a pay phone. This could be over soon. He had no money but he could call 911: tell them he was kidnapped. They would come get him. Make it melodramatic.

He heard another car and he ducked back into the trees, but the car slowed. He realized, with a sunken feeling, that it was the same car that had just passed by. He hid behind a tree. The car stopped up ahead, backed up, stopped again, and a bunch of teenaged boys jumped out. They were howling and laughing, car-rying on. They were drunk. A-Tone listened as one bellowed: "Man, I seen a black chick in a prom dress. I ain't seeing things." The others howled.

They found him. They circled him, staring with wonder, and when he tried to move away from them, they tightened the circle, pulling in close. One of them reached out and touched his breast, and giggled. A-Tone tried to get away. "I'm first," one said, "I'm first. Senior privilege." He grabbed his crotch and gyrated. They all laughed. One of them was standing behind him now, his hand on A-Tone's ass.

"Stop it," he said. He tried to use his woman's voice, but the words squeaked. The boys looked confused. They were hayseeds, he saw, dressed alike in T-shirts and jeans. One smoked a ciga-rette. One smelled of oil.

By the time they'd ripped the dress off and discovered A-Tone was a male, it didn't matter: he was too sick to care. They slapped him, angry now, knocked him to the ground, kicked him in the head and chest, all over, spit on him, went wild with lightning fury and hatred and teeth-clenched curses. One of them couldn't stop laughing, the high-pitched, rolling sounds spilling out of him. Blindly, eyes vacant with fear, A-Tone thought for a minute one of the boys was his first boyfriend, that redheaded freckled boy from Ludington. He remembered the same twisted mouth, the broken teeth. The hitting on the thighs. He got confused. He couldn't even cry out now because the welling vomit choked him, gurgled deep in his throat. At last they got tired of kicking him. Bored, a pudgy dark boy urinated on his face, which made them laugh. They walked away. One came back, turned A-Tone over with his boot-clad foot and, like driving a stake into a heart, pushed a broken tree limb into him. It was then, the pain so ferocious and fiery he lost his breath, A-Tone went unconscious.

When he came to, it was morning. Groggy, eyes tight with blood and pain, he couldn't stop his mind from reeling. Sitting up, he remembered nothing of last night. Vaguely, numbly, he pulled the shredded gown around him, covering his nakedness, but it hurt to move now. He felt like his insides were ripped apart: he was hollowed out. He'd lost his center. The dress hung over him like a cloak, held against him by his own trembling hands. He tried to remember what happened but nothing worked. When he opened his mouth, he tasted dry vomit. So he spat. Blood covered his hand and he got dizzier. Somewhere there was the clanging of metal against metal and he headed toward it, stumbling on the path through the park, banging off trees. The dress kept slipping off him and he had to hold it tighter. His hands kept giving out. At one point he was crawling.

When he got near the garage, he fell into some bushes, lying there until the pain made him kneel. He threw up on the lawn. There were voices in the garage, some laughter. Men laughing. He smelled hot coffee. When he closed his eyes they burned. When he opened them, the light was too bright. I need a doctor, he thought. A doctor. I am dying. But he couldn't move now. He listened to the sounds of the garage—the whir of the generator, the pluck-pluck-pluck of a power tool sucking bolts off a tire, the clanging and the scraping. There was a radio on, low and staticky. It was tuned to a oldies station, so A-Tone lay there, going in and out of consciousness, while Neil Diamond and Paul Anka and Connie Francis and Patti Labelle sang to him. He'd wake to hear the tail end of Whitney Houston. He was going out, he knew. It was over. Once, coming to, momentarily lucid, he thought he heard Diana singing on the radio. It was "Reach Out and Touch." He tried to get up. After all, Diana was singing. In the past she'd always saved him. Told him what to do.

Just before he fell onto the floor of the garage, startling the mechanics whose mouths dropped open, standing there with wrenches and screwdrivers suspended in air, A-Tone realized that it wasn't Diana. It was a different show he'd walked into. It wasn't his cue. Or was it Diana? No: some godawful singer like Olivia Newton-John. He waited for his cue. He was ready. Play the song now. The last thing he remembered was Diana singing in his ear: she was telling him it was all right. He could have peace now. He could go on.

***

Lionel isn't home when Mavis returns from work at one in the morning. He's out with friends, drinking maybe. She sighs. She will not fight him any longer. No matter: nothing can ruin this night for her. One of the older girls has gone to sleep and forgotten to change Molly's diapers. The baby is hiccoughing and sobbing. Mavis holds her, hums in her ear as she changes her, and Molly drifts to sleep. The house quiet now, Mavis stands near the kitchen table. The oblong white box rests there, where she placed it, the thin red twine still keeping it sealed. Smiling, she brews herself a cup of root tea. It relaxes her. In the night window over the sink she sees her reflection: a young, good-looking woman, firm, black skin tight over high Indian cheekbones, her eyes bright with cold fire and determination. The kids are sleeping, and that is all right. She nods to her reflection, almost ritualistically. Finally, seated, she unties the package, bunching the twine and slipping off the cover, and the blue sequined gown suddenly shines before her, sparkles like fireworks as it reflects the overhead light of the kitchen. It's a smooth pile of splendid color and exquisite sparkle. For a minute it reminds her of candy. She rests her hand on the fabric, enjoying the metallic feel of the clustered sequins. There is a slip of paper on top, no bigger than a torn note to the milkman, but the few lines thanking her fill her with rapture, choke her, and she starts to sob. When Lionel wanders in later, bumping into the door frame and swearing loudly, he finds her there, half-asleep, her hand resting on the blue gown, her eyes half-closed, and a smile on her face she'd never used before, at least not with him. He starts to say something because it makes him angry, but he doesn't. Switching off the kitchen light, he tip-toes by her quickly. She doesn't move. In the dark of the kitchen the metallic blue sequins shine.

Weightlines

DREW LIMSKY

Denny was in bed with Alex, thinking about light bulbs and his problem with milk. Since Alex had driven up from Washington and Denny liked being with Alex, their sex should have commanded his attention, particularly because they weren't just fooling around and were about to go for the money: Alex was hanging over the edge of the mattress—weighing it down with his heavy shoulders—and lifting the bed skirts impatiently, in search of a rubber. Denny was surprised when Alex actually produced one, since they'd packed up and moved most of Denny's things to his new apartment that afternoon.

In the last Woody Allen movie Denny had seen, a woman who was in bed with her lover suddenly found herself thinking about foxes and hedgehogs—while the man was screwing her, she categorized the people she knew as either one or the other. But Denny wasn't involved in anything so structured; he was just preoccupied with his headache and what had caused it.

That night, Denny had eaten a hot-fudge sundae for the first time in two years. He had trouble digesting dairy, but that day he'd tried some pills to temporarily correct the chemical imbalance in his stomach, and so far his bowels were holding steady. But the sundae had given him an ice-cream headache, and the bright apartment was making it worse.

Denny looked over Alex's shoulder, and the room was so bright he almost had to squint. Since he didn't want to interrupt things to kill the lights, he said a silent prayer that they would expire on their own. Then Denny became anxious that they really would burn out all at once—he'd been in the apartment for six months and had yet to change a bulb—and that he wouldn't have the money for new ones.

He was having money problems, and worried about paying for everything. He didn't feel he could afford to live alone anymore, so he'd decided to move from his studio in Chelsea to a place below West Twelfth, on Seventh Avenue. He would be sharing an apartment with an older man named Ned who hadn't looked well when Denny had interviewed to be his roommate; he'd seemed involuntarily thin and hadn't been capable of deep breaths. Ned wouldn't be Denny's first sick roommate, though, and the move south would cut a couple hundred off his rent.

Alex figured things out and slid inside him. Alex was two inches taller and about twenty pounds heavier than Denny, and Denny was impressed by his size and weight, was drawn to his substance: he liked that Alex could pin him to the planet so he wouldn't float away like a stray hair or one of those silvery helium balloons people send to their friends in hospitals.

They had met at a bar two months before—Alex had been in town with friends. When Alex had driven up from Washington the following weekend, Denny had the flu, and Alex had taken such good care of him, waking him every four hours with aspirin. Denny's last boyfriend, Samuel, hadn't been much of a nurse, promising to bring Denny orange juice when Denny was sick and then forgetting it on his way over from work.

Alex's eyes were closed so tightly while they made love; he looked like he had a headache, too. Denny reached up and held Alex's head between his palms. He put his thumbs on Alex's eyebrows and gently opened his eyes; Alex blinked at him. Alex's eyes were so dark—even in this light it was hard to tell where his pupils ended and his irises began. Liquid eyes, that was the expression. Because of his strong features, he could carry that severe military haircut; it didn't seem like a punishment, as it invariably did on other enlisted men Denny had seen, their hillbilly pug noses and narrow eyes surrounded by blemished skin. No, Alex was a handsome man. Great profile. Latin lover. Denny liked when Alex spoke to him in Spanish, and he tried to recall a few words of his own from high school.

"*Aqui*," Denny said. "Can you look at me? I like it when you look at me."

"Sorry," Alex said, and arched his back, dipping into Denny, making the hair on their chests touch. Denny felt so present, so here when Alex did that. "I was thinking," Alex said, "that this is the last time this year."

Alex had just gotten the word about his transfer to a base in Hawaii and they probably wouldn't be seeing each other for a long time. The comment was very characteristic of Alex, who had the habit of noting first things and last things. This is the first time we had pizza together, Alex had said that afternoon. Denny liked Alex's conscientious way of marking time: it proved he was on top of things, grounded. Denny would try harder to keep track like that.

Alex continued to talk to Denny as they made love; he praised Denny's body, complimented his muscular arms. That was another good thing about Alex, that he made Denny feel healthy and strong.

Alex made Denny flex his biceps. "How do I get guns like that?" Alex asked, even though he'd played football for the Navy and his own muscles were nothing to sneeze at. Denny was about to suggest that Alex do more squats, which supposedly released lactose into the system and promoted all-over muscle growth, but he kept his mouth shut because it was a rhetorical question. Lactose was also the chemical in milk that Denny had trouble digesting. But no more: tomorrow he would eat dairy at every meal until he got to his new apartment. As Alex fucked him, Denny reminded himself to ask someone at the gym about lactose and also to go to the clinic for his test results.

Alex helped Denny move the bed before Denny went to work. It was so early, still dark. Before he headed back to Washington, Alex made Denny get back in the car. He drove to the East Side, to the river; they parked near one of the bridges and stared at the purple bruised sky.

"Our first sunrise," Denny said, beating Alex to the punch, and Alex laughed.

Denny leaned over and sort of fell into Alex's lap. He was comforted by the warm odors there—both the lingering soap smell on Alex's thigh and the stale scent of gasoline in the air under the dashboard. Alex was in shorts and Denny liked the feel of Alex's hairy leg against his cheek. He was so thick, had a man's sturdiness though he was only twenty-two, five years younger than Denny.

The night before, they had taken a bath together—their last bath and all that. Denny had gotten out first to let Alex finish. Seeing Alex's tan knees and calves emerge from the bubbles, and the black hair on Alex's chest getting wet with bath water as he slid deeper into the tub, Denny had savored a pleasing, appreciative thought: who is this man in my bath? Alex looked so good, like something expensive in a store that you couldn't help but pick up and hold in your hands for a while. Still wet and hugging a towel, Denny had locked his eyes on Alex and leaned against the sink; safe and good inside the moment, all he could hear were his own sated breaths and the sounds of the beautiful man in the tub pouring water over himself with his large, cupped hands.

Sometimes in bed Alex would reach for Denny's face, spreading his fingers over Denny's eyes and forehead, letting the weight of his smooth, finely shaped hand rest there. Actually, Denny wanted Alex to do it now, in the car, but he didn't ask—he didn't want to start crying into Alex's big hand, couldn't afford that kind of scene. Alex was leaving and wouldn't be able to take care of him that way anymore. Denny knew he shouldn't be thinking these things about someone he had known only a few months—it wasn't healthy.

He sat back up. "You should get on the road."

Alex winked at him—he looked as if he were about to say something comforting, something in Spanish, didn't, and drove Denny back to the Village.

Denny worked the early shift at the gym, checking membership cards at the desk unless he had to train someone—that was where he made his money. Things had been slow, this being summertime—people were still in Europe and on Fire Island, and a few of his male clients had moved away, one to San Francisco, another to Key West. The lesbian couple he'd trained for six months had decided to relocate to Vermont to breed Dalmatians, not that they'd been serious about the program, actually managing to gain weight on Denny's plan.

The morning crowd was steady but light, which gave Denny time to watch people's bodies as he ate his bodybuilder food—mostly tuna and rice; today he added a hunk of Swiss cheese—from plastic containers. At ten he would get a break and go across the street to the diner. The day before, the girl behind the counter had offered him a free milkshake, and now he would be able to take her up on it.

There was a man who came to the gym every morning like clockwork, a man too thin not to have it. He always did a full two-hour workout even though he probably couldn't keep much food down. Maybe he used one of those nutritional formulas advertised in the gay magazines between ads for mesh underwear. He looked too fragile for daylight; his workout clothes were embarrassingly brief on his frail body and the skin on his face had such an odd waxiness, a translucence, to it. He wore his blond hair in a blunt ponytail that didn't help matters, but Denny guessed that the man was vain about his hair, which had no gray in it.

Denny grabbed the edge of the desk and flexed the muscles of his chest in an isometric exercise. He was itching to get to his workout and couldn't wait until his shift ended at four. It would have to be a quick one, though, so he'd be able to make it to the clinic before it closed at six, or maybe it was five, he'd have to call.

That morning, Denny had found a notice about exterminator visits under the door. *To obtain the best pest control results for you and your neighbors,* the notice had read, *please notify the front desk immediately if you see or suspect any insect activity.* Denny had shown the letter to Alex and they had laughed about it—was it possible to suspect insect activity without actually observing bugs? Since you couldn't hear them, didn't you have to see something like that in order to be convinced—wasn't that the way things usually worked?

He looked at the ponytailed man again. The man's half-shirt kept riding up on his back as he did pull-downs, exposing a column of eight vertebrae that Denny could actually count from across the room—his bones looked angry and sharp under his skin, poking out like eruptions. Denny's own back was usually so layered with muscle that you couldn't see any bones at all, not even his shoulder blades. Alex's, too. The man doing pull-downs was probably younger than forty, younger than thirty-five, but Denny couldn't be sure. The disease had made him timelessly ugly and Denny couldn't take his eyes off him.

Denny went to his friend Stephanie's for lunch; she lived just a few blocks from the gym. He peeled off his shirt for the walk over because he liked the feel of the sun on his shoulders, and even more than that, Denny enjoyed seeing his body reflected in store-fronts and car windows and other people's sunglasses—car win-dows were the best, because their slight curvature caused a distor-tion that made him look broader than he was.

Denny had well-developed abdominal muscles, but was pre-pared to lose some of their sharpness if he continued to eat fatty dairy food. It was a trade-off, but he wanted to be more beefy; now with Alex gone pretty much for good, Denny wanted some more poundage to weigh him to the earth so he wouldn't go flying off into the atmosphere like all the wispy sick men in the city.

He saw Stephanie sitting on her stoop in men's underwear; she was looking at something else, not him, so he waited before pull-ing on his shirt because he wanted her to see how fit he was. She was watching a man on the sidewalk who was moving with exag-gerated slowness; a pair of toy dogs were yapping in protest and trying to drag the man ahead with quick, pointless little steps.

"You look thin," she said, finally turning to Denny. Stephanie watched too closely for things like that; her cousin, a former roommate of Denny's, had died from it.

Denny frowned, even though he'd asked for it, taking his shirt off in the street like that. "I've gained weight since the last time you saw me."

Stephanie looked doubtful, played with the ends of her wet hair. "Since last week?"

There was always a lot of food in the apartment because Stephanie and her husband gave a lot of dinner parties. She fed Denny two different kinds of pie and offered him a third, which he gratefully accepted—even though his stomach was starting to recoil—because healthy people had good appetites. The third pie had whipped cream on top, so Denny popped some of his little pills before he dug in.

"Eat up," Stephanie said. Stephanie was a good friend. The apartment was beautiful. It had a garden. Her husband, who was overweight and made a lot of money, was at work. Stephanie was getting fat, too. Her arms and shoulders were slim and lovely—from the waist up, she looked so taut in her ribbed tank top—but her thick and dimpled legs, which emerged from two pairs of boxer shorts, looked like tubes of curdled milk, like she had given up the gym entirely. Denny didn't tell her that he intended to eat his way to his new home, preferably with milk products, but he did help himself to a second piece of the whipped-cream pie. He saw Stephanie's pretty gray eyes grow wide with approval and felt a little drunk from the sugary richness of the cream.

Not long after he'd broken up with Samuel, Denny lived for five months with Stephanie's dying cousin. Nick had been a bartender at the first gay bar Denny had ever been inside, and Denny had a huge crush on him before Nick's illness had begun to show. He'd been a beautiful man, a musclebound model for a classy male pictorial—the kind with the glossy, backlit photography that provided the men's blue eyes an unnatural glow and made the hair on their chests and legs look like it had been brushed with glitter. There were gossipy stories about Nick, that he had been a hustler, that he'd been the lover of a famous movie actor, that he'd raped someone or been raped. By the time Denny moved in with him, though, Nick's life had lost its hint of salaciousness; it wasn't even Nick that Denny had lived with—the real Nick had floated off somewhere long before Denny moved in with him. The disease had destroyed much of his brain; he had become a child again and he watched a lot of cartoons.

Nick—or the nine-year-old boy who had impersonated Nick—had slept in the outer room of their one-bedroom apartment on Bank Street. He was a good roommate: despite his mental deterioration, he wrote accurate phone messages and kept the apartment neat. It took him a long time to make his bed or handle linens, though, because he took inordinate, sensual pleasure in airing things out—he would grab the corners of towels and blankets and wave them over and over until he tired. Hanging plants rocked and strained from their hooks, and magazines would blow open, but Nick's little storms never did any real damage. They couldn't; he was too insubstantial. Denny would ask Nick what he was doing and Nick would tell him it was a code, a message to the Indians—Indians fascinated him. Sometimes he pretended he was one, fashioning a loincloth by tying a rope around his waist on which he would string two hand towels, one in the front and one in the back. He would dance around the apartment like that, almost naked.

Of course, the first time Denny had seen him, Nick was wearing a real Indian costume. He was working the bar one Halloween, seemingly oblivious to the stares and comments he drew with his bare chest, laced-up-the-sides chamois pants, and elaborate feather headdress. Someone had applied lines of red and green war paint to his face and arms. He must have been wearing baby oil that night, because his body was shiny, lacquered looking—he was working hard, but not hard enough to cause a sweat—and his smooth torso was like costly, polished armor. An Indian was a good costume for a well-built man.

Nick had lost weight after his pictorial days; shirtless, he could no longer attract that kind of admiration. The bulges of his arms were compact, and his fabled muscle definition had faded and was only detectable in the kindest light—daytime tended to wash it out entirely. At the time Denny had lived with him, Nick had the body of a light teenage wrestler—a welterweight, a featherweight—who had dieted too hard to make his class, or a high-school swimmer. A "swimmer's build": that was the way skinny guys in the Personal section described their bodies. Denny didn't know whether a welterweight was lighter than a featherweight, or if "swimmer's build" had always been a euphemism for scrawny, but he did know one thing: Nick had gotten very thin. When Denny had watched him send his smoke signals to imaginary tribes, he'd half expected the bubble of air under the comforter to lift his roommate off the ground.

He was having a shit workout. Bench pressing, Denny didn't have his usual strength, his arms buckling under only moderately heavy weight. When he got up, the bench was dark with his perspiration. His stomach started to churn when he tightened his weight belt, and he had to go to the bathroom. Maybe the milk pills weren't so effective after all.

Back on the gym floor, he stood under a light fixture, lifting his arms above his head to study his definition. He stared into the light, thinking of the clubs where he'd danced, clubs with silver disco balls and the nights, humid and golden, where he'd grabbed the bottom of his shirt and pulled it over his head, listening to throbbing music as he showed off his hard work and hard body—it had been so long since dancing had given him that kick. He was tired, drained, and still had to work on his shoulders before he went to Samuel's—his ex-boyfriend had left a message at the desk reminding Denny to stop by and see their new apartment—and there was something else he'd meant to do beforehand. But he was too spent to walk over for his appointment, and he would be able to rest at Samuel's. His ex-boyfriend had said something in the message about making dinner, and Denny didn't want to pass up a free meal. He had to eat more.

Samuel looked a bit soft because he'd thrown out his back and hadn't been to the gym in a month; his current boyfriend, a guy from Chicago who repaired clocks, was recovering from knee surgery. They had matching, caplike haircuts; their straight hair fell to about halfway down their heads where it abruptly stopped; below that, their hair was very short, short enough for Denny to make out their white scalps. The effect of their haircut was that of an inverted step, which Samuel told Denny was called a weight line.

They seemed glad to see Denny, probably because he wasn't the kind of ex-boyfriend who caused trouble by making gratuitous references to the former relationship. Still, Denny was uncomfortable listening to them talk so candidly, so safely, about their temporary medical problems. Despite their complaints, they were moving around their little apartment so briskly and talking with such unnecessary volume; the two reminded him of the toy dogs he'd seen in front of Stephanie's apartment. Denny was exhausted, feeling like he would never be able to get up from their couch. He swallowed more pills and ate some quiche and tried an interesting sort of pudding.

There were vacation pictures on the wall of Samuel and his boyfriend. "When did you go to Europe?" Denny asked, trying to be polite, but feeling as if he needed to breathe before he got to the end of the question.

"Blair, when did we go to Europe?" Samuel asked, and Denny pushed a fork around on his plate, suddenly less hungry than before. Samuel had always been lousy with dates. Blair said something, but Denny didn't listen to the month, the year, because he didn't care when they went to Europe, just wondered why Samuel couldn't seem to answer a question without consulting Blair, why he was so solicitous of him.

Denny studied Samuel's boyfriend, trying to figure out how Blair had inspired the kind of behavior from Samuel that Denny had always sought in vain. Such an odd name, Blair, a woman's name: it was, in fact, the name of the fat blonde girl on that terrible sitcom from the eighties about a female prep school. Denny stared at Blair as long as he could without giving himself away, and came up with nothing: he was just a cute, slightly rounded guy in a T-shirt. He probably kept good time, though, which made sense in light of his profession; his voice had sounded authoritative when he'd answered Samuel about when they'd gone to Europe.

Denny was woozy when he finally got up to go to the bathroom. He opened their medicine cabinet—he looked inside everyone's medicine cabinet—and read the labels on their bottles. Muscle relaxants for Samuel, Tylenol-3 for Blair's knee pain, nothing more revealing. Not that he'd expected to find anything. Samuel and Blair had just celebrated their third anniversary by getting tested. Both still negative. He wondered what time the clinic opened in the morning; the doctor was such a nice woman. Maybe tomorrow.

He went to the toilet, checked the bowl afterward for some kind of sign. He wanted a glass of water. He ran his wrists under the running faucet because it was supposed to keep you from fainting. He felt better after a minute.

He'd been surprised when Nick suffered no physical symptoms, until, of course, he stopped talking and went into the hospital to die. Up until then, it hadn't seemed such a bad way to go— become a child again, play cowboys and Indians. Denny wondered if his new roommate would die on him, too. When Denny and Alex had dropped off the bed at the new apartment, Ned had come to the door, coughing, in jeans and a bathrobe left carelessly or intentionally open at his chest; he was as bony—and as flagrant—as the thin man from the gym. Until that morning, Denny hadn't noticed that the apartment shared a block with a health club, a hotel, and a hospital (the hospital Nick had died in), which was utterly appropriate, since the tribe of gay men did three things if it did anything: pump up, move around, and become ill.

In the hall outside the bathroom Denny accidentally jostled a shelf, knocking to the floor a stack of letters and an egg-shaped brass paperweight. As he bent down to collect everything he felt sick to his stomach.

Samuel called out to him, asked if he was okay.

"He hasn't looked well since he got here," Denny heard Blair say.

Fat fuck. "Yeah, I'm fine. Can I use your phone?"

"Sure, the portable's in the bedroom."

He pocketed the paperweight and one of the letters and went into the bedroom to call Alex. He noticed things that Samuel had owned for a long time: a secondhand metal desk; the mantel; that gilt-edged mirror with the spider-web crack in the corner. There were other things he didn't recognize, ugly things Samuel had acquired while with Blair, like the odd net canopy over the bed.

Alex picked up after two rings. "I've been eating milk products all day," Denny said, because he couldn't think of anything else to tell him.

"How do you feel?"

"Not so good." He looked out the window—when had it gotten dark?—and tried to think of the Spanish word for tired. "I'm so tired, Alex."

"Me, too."

"How was the drive?"

"It would have been better with your face in my lap."

Denny sat on the bed, the same bed Samuel had always owned. "So you enjoyed that?"

"You know I did."

"Are you packed yet?"

"Almost."

"Hey, you ever think about getting one of those sailor tattoos, a ship across your chest?" Denny asked.

"Should I?"

"A tattoo would look good on you, maybe just an anchor on your arm, like Popeye."

"You should get one," Alex said. "You're the muscleman."

"Not for long, not without you to make me eat my spinach."

"Where are you?"

"At my ex-boyfriend's. Listen. Alex?"

"Yeah?"

"Listen," Denny repeated. Dead tired. "You took good care of me." Denny pressed his hand to his face and shivered a little. It was hard to swallow. "*Muy bien.*"

"*Gracias,* no problem. Will you call me when you get home and give me your new number? My phone will be disconnected in the morning."

Denny figured it had been three years and ten months since he'd last slept in this bed, the last time he and Samuel had made love. It was important to keep track of time now, to know the ends of things.

"Calls to Hawaii will get pretty expensive," Denny said, reaching to finger the paperweight in his pocket. He knew it would be the last time that they would talk.

The letter crinkled in his jeans as he walked home. He didn't care much about the letter's contents; he'd only been interested in the envelope because the sender had addressed it to both Samuel and his boyfriend. In the apartment, he'd noticed their names on the same line, joined by a flowery ampersand, and had wanted another look.

The envelope documented something Denny had missed out on: he had never shared an address with Samuel or anyone else in that way, and he knew that he never would—somehow he felt certain that he wouldn't live to see his name on an envelope with someone else's. With each of his steps, the hard little egg inside his pocket scraped his hipbone, which was sticking out too much. He was embarrassed by his sudden and futile thefts, grabbing for the egg as if it were a tiny rock of ballast in a coming storm.

He walked on subway gratings; an oncoming train roared under his feet. The upward rush of air caused discarded newspapers and fast-food containers to fly over his head and swirl all around him; he reached into his pocket and threw Samuel's letter into the air, where it joined the garbage squall. He walked home slowly, in no great rush to start living with a sick stranger, but he had so little left and it was all he could afford.

Fire

ROBERT DRAKE

6:55 p.m.

Ophelia's dark hands moved evenly over the gleaming surface, smoothing out yellow and pink copy from the TelePrompTer upon the white of the broadcast desk. From where she sat, she could feel the heat of the lights, see the one-dimensional city mural behind her, feel the worn carpeting beneath her feet. The coanchor of the Channel Seven News Team sat to her left, and he rifled through copy as well, pausing now and then to try and whistle a particle of food from between his fat white teeth, to pat his yellow hair into place, to smooth the fabric of his shirt, his jacket, his tie across his chest.

Ophelia looked to her right, into the darkness of the studio, and she saw Adam standing there, beside a camera they wouldn't be using for tonight's broadcast. He waved to her, a boyish wave that was full of enthusiasm. He'd seen her do the news a number of times and it still made him childishly excited, but then he was the same way when they sat on his sofa, in the living room of his apartment, sharing a bowl of popcorn and one of her Channel Seven promo spots would pop on. He was thrilled by her success, Ophelia thought, *he thinks I'm a star!*

She smiled at him and bowed her head back to the copy.

A grizzled stagehand thrust his arm in front of Adam, the fingers on the man's hand twisting and turning in a series of semi-elaborate, numerical motions. Adam jumped a bit, then relaxed, reaching up to run his fingers through his thick head of black hair. His hair was too long and full for this time of year; it needed to be cut, shortened, thinned, trimmed. There was a kind of frantic scurrying throughout the studio as the stagehand stepped in front of Adam, his voice booming out, "We go in five . . . four . . . three. . . ."

The last two numbers were silent; scurrying rustled away to a whisper. Adam positioned himself to watch Ophelia deliver the news. The first time he'd done this had been more than five years ago, when Matthew had taken him here to meet Ophelia on one of their earliest dates. Adam was twenty-eight then, shy and impressed by his new friend's media connections. Now, Matthew was dead, and he thought of Ophelia as his own oldest, dearest, and trusted pal.

Adam heard the tinny bleed-through of the news theme from a technician's headset. It distracted him for a moment as he looked for its source, and then he was brought back to Ophelia; her voice caught him by surprise.

"Good evening, I'm Ophelia Stern."

"And I'm Stefan Grimsby. Welcome to Channel Seven News."

"Our top stories tonight: a fifteen- and a sixteen-year-old are dead after a shootout with police . . ."

"An area preschool teacher is accused of sexual abuse . . ."

"And there's another bomb threat from the self-named Republican Remover."

As Ophelia and her cohost began their separate stories, Adam wandered back into the darkened recesses of the studio. He walked along the wall at the base of the control booth, slipping from shadow to shadow, his feet passing quietly along the cement. His hands were jammed into his pockets. He thought about Matthew, his partner for four years. He thought about the night Matthew was killed, the night of his own beating, the night his life had changed, faltered, cracked, and darkened. He thought about the next year of his life, this past year of his life. He thought of learning to walk again, training to fight, becoming something greater, something more than anything he had ever been before, something still relatively unknown to him. He thought of his capture and defeat of the man who had slaughtered his boyfriend, and he thought of the scattering of Matthew's ashes into the water of a sound beloved by them both. He thought of death, and its ongoing presence in his life, a presence he had been able to ignore before but now could not. A presence that now cut clearer and permeated deeper, into every crevasse of his existence. A presence that was with him always, slouched heavy across his shoulders.

He walked back toward the light, toward Ophelia.

"The self-dubbed Republican Remover has directed a third bomb threat against the city. The threat is inspired by the appearance of conservative Senators Roland Port and Cameron Swanson at tomorrow's fundraiser for Republican gubernatorial candidate Jackson Fordham. The terrorist has threatened to blow up the banquet hall of the Fordham Hotel, the hotel owned by the candidate's family and the site of the fundraiser. Fordham has provided no word of a relocation attempt for the fundraiser. Senator Port was quoted earlier today as saying he still planned to attend the fundraiser and that to do otherwise would be to 'knuckle under to the forces of homosexual terrorism.' In a single letter to city police, released earlier today, the Republican Remover self-identified as a person with AIDS, but did not provide information regarding sexual orientation, gender, or race. Senator Swanson could not be reached for comment. Earlier Republican Remover efforts resulted, separately, in the deaths of Republican mayoral candidate Loretta McNally at her campaign headquarters and conservative financial backer Robert Jensen in his home . . . Stefan?"

"Thank you, Ophelia. It was 'Make Way for Ducklings' time today at the city zoo when hundreds of the little fellas . . ."

8:13 p.m.

I am sick.

Edward coughed up a glob of yellow mucus into the sink. His hand reached unsteadily for the faucet, turning on the cold water to wash the phlegm away. He looked up from the sink into the mirror. He looked at the puffy sacs of flesh under his eyes, the hollowness of his cheeks, his thinning hair, his sallow complexion, a stick for a neck. A Kaposi's sarcoma bloomed in the hollow of his throat.

He coughed again, a hard cough that shook him, and he crumpled halfway to the ground, stopped by his hold on the sink. The coughing subsided, and he raised himself upright again on wob-

bly arms. He had water in the corners of his eyes from the coughing and he wiped it away, angrily. He turned and shuffled into the
apartment, toward the living room and away from his bed.

"Eddie?"

Edward turned around in the middle of the living room to see
Andrew standing in the doorway to their bedroom. Andrew.
Handsome as the day they met; young and beautiful and healthy
and here. Edward hobbled toward him. "Andy?"

Andy reached out for him. "Edward."

Edward let himself be taken in the boy's embrace, let himself
feel the strength of the man's arms about him, listened to the re-
assuring thudding of the heart beneath the muscles of this chest.
Edward's breathing was rough, ragged, rasping against the fabric
of Andrew's shirt.

"Andrew."

Andrew reached up with his hand to tilt Edward's face toward
him. Andrew bent his head to kiss Edward's opening mouth and
Edward accepted the thick flesh of Andrew's tongue against his
teeth, against his tongue, Andrew's lips kissing now his face, his
cheeks, his neck, with each kiss health returning, Edward's face
filling out, his muscles strong, his body beautiful again the way
it had been before the disease, the way it had been when he met
Andrew.

Andrew guided Edward to the bed and they fell upon it, Andrew's hands moving over the wholeness that was Edward's skin
now, the fabric of Edward's shirt falling away, Edward's belt coming undone, his jockey briefs, his pants collapsing around his ankles where Andrew, his teeth rubbing lightly against Edward's left
nipple, reached down to pull them free.

Andrew's mouth was upon Edward's stiffening cock, the thick
shaft deep in his mouth, his throat, then his lips moving about the
fleshy head, a drop of pre-cum gleaming in the slit which Andrew
lapped away with a quick stab of his tongue before taking Edward
deep within him again.

Upon the bed Edward moaned, Edward writhed, Edward sweat.
"Andrew," he said.

He felt Andrew's cock then inside his ass, its hardness hurting
him until the pain subsided toward a kind of pleasure Edward
thought he had forgotten, recently. He felt the cock inside him
dancing, moving, jabbing his prostate and sending him along

ridges of emotion that invited him to give in, to fall over, to be consumed.

Andrew fucked him, hard, and Edward fisted his own dick in a hand wet with sweat from his own body.

"Edward."

"Yes."

"Edward, do it."

"Yes."

"Oh Edward, do it. Do it for me. Do it for us."

"Yes."

"Do it now!"

"Yes!" and Andrew let out a yell and Edward felt Andrew's seed spill inside him, even as Edward's seed splattered his own hollow belly, his own emaciated chest, his own Kaposi's lesion at the sunken base of his withered throat.

"Yes," Edward said, and he was alone in the bed, damp with sweat and the acrid smell of semen. He lay there a moment until his breathing steadied, and then he sat up, reaching for his underwear, reaching for his shirt. He looked at the night table, at the picture from three years ago when he and Andrew stood together atop a Hawaiian volcano, their arms around each other, smiling and healthy in the afternoon sun.

Andrew was dead two years later.

Edward would be dead soon enough.

A coughing fit attacked his body and he sat there, succumbing to it and letting it pass. When he had steadied himself he mopped the cum up from his chest with his underwear and tossed them toward a pile of dirty laundry. He stepped into his pants and pulled them up, buckling the belt tight about his waist. He slithered into his shirt. As he buttoned it, he thought about what he knew his promise to Andrew moments ago had meant. Edward thought about what it was to be lonely, he thought about what it meant to know Death intimately, more intimately even than he had ever known Andrew. For Death was there in Edward's most private of thoughts, hiding, crowing like a perverse Peter Pan for him to come join this particular emaciated band of lost boys.

Edward had realized, not too long ago, that there was a way for him to cheat death by validating his personal existence; a way of making a difference that went beyond wearing red ribbons and sending the occasional check. He had realized, and he had acted, and Andrew had approved so he had acted again and he would act tomorrow. For himself, for Andrew, for the friends he had watched wear away and die and for the rhetoric he had heard on C-SPAN. He would act and he would do something beyond any worldly faith; he would act as his own redeemer, his personal messiah.

He got up and checked his medicines.

11:47 p.m.

"Stefan Grimsby is such a fucking asshole."

"Why?" Adam swung open the tall glass-and-metal door for Ophelia as she fumbled among her keys for the one that would open her car. They both nodded to the heavy, middle-aged security guard behind the desk as they left the Channel Seven studio. "Good night, Carl," she called over her shoulder and then they were out in the night, Ophelia with her keys clutched tightly in her right hand and a slim briefcase tucked between her left arm and body; Adam with his hands jammed into the front pockets of his pants. They stood there a moment, then she looked to Adam and smiled. He smiled back, and they started walking across the slowly sloping cement of the parking garage toward her car. A quiet breeze blew past them.

They reached her small white Corvair with the red leather interior. "Did you drive?"

"I walked." Adam's voice echoed about the empty structure.

Ophelia opened her car door and tossed in the briefcase. "You need a ride?"

"No. So why is Stefan Grimsby such a fucking asshole?" Ophelia turned from checking out the interior of her car for stowaways to look at her friend. Adam gave a small, mockingly deferential nod of his head as he said, "If I may quote you."

"You may." She leaned back against the open doorway of her car, one leg bent; an arm rested upon the top of the car window, another arm stretched out along the roof edge of the low vehicle. "I guess you missed it, hm? The dig he got into me during the first station break?"

"After his groundbreaking 'Make Way for Ducklings' story?"

She gave a wry smile. "Yes, that. Anyway, Grimsby turns to me after the clear sign and says, 'You just had to get that in, didn't you?' I said, 'What?' He said, 'That bit about the killer not being a fag.' I said, 'What!' He then went off on this diatribe: how the Republican Remover's offing the best and brightest hope for this city's future and how the killer has to be a 'faggot' because only a 'queer' could have this kind of vendetta, this kind of agenda against two upstanding, fine—" she shook her head and waved her hand in front of her face to indicate the end of that conversation. "I don't even want to get into what he said about the AIDS aspect of the whole thing." Ophelia tapped a key against the metal frame of the window. "The thing that pissed me off the most," she said, slowly, measuredly, "was that he kept talking until we were cued to come back from the break." She shook her head. "Dumb fucker."

"While we're on the topic," Adam said, his arms crossed now upon his chest and his body rocking gently, momentarily, on the balls of his feet, "have you talked at all to our buddy the police chief about this Remover guy?"

"Yates? You kidding me?" Ophelia shook her head. "Yates won't talk to me. Channel Two has him. Me he tells to go get fucked."

Adam raised his eyebrows.

"Well, not really," she said, "but the thought's there, I know it. That man hates me. Has ever since I started nailing him for all that hate-crime shit he tried to pass over last year."

"I remember."

"I know." She bit at her thumbnail for a moment, then looked at her thumb in disgust. "What am I doing?" She showed the hand to Adam. "This is a forty-five dollar manicure!"

Adam shrugged.

Ophelia looked out at the city for a moment. She asked Adam, "So what's up next?"

He shrugged. "Probably sleep. A little reading before. You?"

She shrugged. "I'd like to run but that's hardly safe so I'll probably curl up in bed with a good book—something unfinished that I'm already into and there are plenty of those—and a pint of Ben and Jerry's."

"I knew I'd forgotten something."

"Wanna join me?"

He shook his head. "Believe it or not, I've gotten over my fear of sleeping alone and in the dark."

"Good for you."

"Actually, the sleeping alone part—" he looked to her; she waited "—I kind of like it."

"That's okay."

"I know. I know it is." He looked down to scuff the right toe of his shoe against the concrete. "It's just weird though, after four, five years."

She reached out and rubbed his arm affectionately. He smiled at her. She got in the car and rolled down her driver's-side window.

"Hey, Ophelia," he leaned in through the open window to talk with her, "you think Yates will do anything about these threats tomorrow?"

Ophelia listened to her engine idle for a moment. It sounded good. "I think he takes them seriously," she said. "I think he takes them seriously enough to have a bomb sweep before the fundraiser, probably beef up security. Why?"

"Just curious."

"Hmpf." She turned on the radio. Static, and she pushed a cassette into the tape deck. "You know," Ophelia said, adjusting the volume as Jennifer Warnes began to warble about how she could "Rock You Gently," "Yates thinks that guy is behind it."

"That guy?"

"That guy, the guy in black with that pink triangle over his heart; 'The Man' guy."

Adam looked at the ground and shook his head. "Any excuse. . . ."

"Yeah, so that's what Yates is going to be looking for tomorrow: a guy in black tights and a black mask and a pro-gay emblem on his chest."

"I hear they're everywhere these days."

Ophelia laughed: "Not in my neighborhood, girl." Adam reached in and squeezed her shoulder. She continued, her laughter gone, "You know he gets fan mail?"

Adam frowned. "Who? Yates? Who from? Militiamen? The Unabomber?"

"No, no," Ophelia shook her head. "The Man. From kids, mostly. Gay teens. Thanking him for standing up for them. Dozens of letters a week, but we've nowhere to send them so they sit in my office."

Adam said nothing. After a moment's silence, he leaned in

through the window and kissed Ophelia on the cheek, "Good night. I love you."

"Good night," she said, "Thanks for coming by and keeping me sane tonight."

He was already walking away, a bounce in his step. "It was fun," he said, turning to wave back at her, "drive safe."

She beeped the horn of her car as she drove past him and was gone. He walked down the final steep incline of the parking garage, past the guard in the lighted booth that eyed him suspiciously until he nodded hello and the guard nodded back and Adam was out, into the city night.

He wouldn't go home for a while. He had work to do yet.

7:23 p.m. (the next evening)

Senator Port is a corpulent old white man sitting in the back of a rented limousine heading for a political fundraiser where he is among the featured speakers and guests of honor. His cummerbund is too tight and he shifts about in the back seat of this limousine, trying to loosen the cummerbund somehow, trying to edge it back along the border of his pants. When he breathes, there is a rasping noise that issues forth, a relic of his heaviness. One of his hands pats the flesh of his thigh to no particular beat; the other clutches an aging scotch, the glass wet with perspiration and the drink weakened by melting ice. He speaks: "You nervous 'bout tonight, son?" and the flesh of his jowls flaps about his shirt collar.

The man Senator Port speaks to sits next to him in this limousine. He is younger—thirty-six to the senator's sixty-three—and handsomer, without excess flesh on his frame, with a body well muscled from days spent running or working out with free weights. His hair is a pale brown color, and he has a full head of it. He wears it short. He is a clean-shaven young man. He is the senator's son, Roland, and he is fidgeting, rubbing his right foot against an itch on his left calf; holding but not drinking from a similarly weakened tumbler full of scotch as that of his father's. He looks out the window, at the passing streetlights, the storefronts and passing cars. "No, I'm not nervous," he says, finally taking a drink from his glass, "But I think this is a mistake."

"Why?"

"Why?" Roland rustled about in his seat to face his father better. "These bomb threats. This whole Jackson Fordham thing."

"The bomb sweep of the hotel came up clean. You don't like Jackson Fordham?"

"Like? What's to like? I don't respect him. He has to be the most self-aggrandizing politician I've met since I started trailing you around to political functions and I was what? eight then?" Roland shook his head, looked again out the window, and took a second sip from his drink. "He's evil."

"Don't talk that way about Jackson, boy. Jackson's been good to us, to our family, to our party. He's made possible the bulk of legislation that has enabled us to garner heavy public approval—"

"Legislation I think is shit."

"—and keep our positions of power well-placed, as is necessary to run a proper country." The senator drained his drink and set the empty glass within the wet bar. "You'd be well advised to be a little bit more appreciative of the hand that feeds you, especially as you're someone who so desperately needs to be fed."

"Don't start this."

"Don't give me reason to." The senator looked out his window now, the night darkened further by the tint of the limousine's glass. "Thirty-six years old and still in college—"

"I'm pursuing a Ph.D."

"—still unmarried, still fucking around like you were some twenty-year-old kid."

"At least I'm not bloated by corruption."

The senator was silent. The only sound in the car was the rasp of his breathing, the sound of his jowls edging against each other as he clenched and unclenched his jaw. "You've got a mouth on you, boy. Always have. That's your mother's fault, God rest her."

Roland finished his drink and reached out to place his empty glass next to that of his father's. He settled back in his seat and waited.

"We're here," Senator Port said, and the limousine pulled into the curving driveway of the Fordham Hotel. The senator let loose with a "Brr" and he shivered his bulk in his seat.

"What?" asked Roland.

"That man," the Senator said. "Did you see that man as we pulled in?" The senator's liver-spotted hand reached up to tap the glass of the limousine window beside him. "He was horrible, all worn away; skin and bones in a pale, thin overcoat. Like some sort of fuckin' ghost."

"Maybe he was."

"You're a bastard, son, you know that?"

"Oh, how you wish that it were true," Roland hummed quietly. "Oh, how I wish that it were true."

Edward, in his pale, thin overcoat, watched the limousine ride past him as it pulled into the driveway of the Fordham Hotel. The hotel was an old building from the turn of the century, all of its fixtures and designs carefully and expensively preserved throughout the years. Edward turned to follow the limousine toward the maw of lights that was the entranceway to the hotel. He approached and he saw the crowds thronging a cordoned-off strip of red carpet: the curious, the journalists with their notebooks and questions at the ready, the photographers and their cameras; the various local television news stations. He slipped behind them, past the crowd of fans and media attendants. He edged carefully along the back of the crowd, pressed between the living warmth of their flesh and the inanimate coolness of the hotel behind him. He waited there, on the cusp of admission, until the doorman was distracted by the passage of Senator Port into the hotel and then Edward, too, slipped inside, turning as he entered away from the main hall that would have carried him with Senator Port toward the entrance of the banquet room.

Edward headed back, into the bowels of the building. He passed closed gift shops and barbershops and jewelry boutiques. He passed the comings and goings of hotel staff from housekeeping and room service. He received a few strange looks and odd glances as he walked but Edward ignored these.

He expected to encounter policemen but he saw none; he supposed they were all tightly cordoned around Senators Port and Swanson, and Fordham.

Edward approached and entered the service stairs. He began his long climb up the stairs to a floor that would bring him level with the gallery above the banquet hall, but he had to pause for a moment on every landing to rest. He was sweating heavily now, not from a fever but from exertion. The overcoat he wore wasn't heavy by itself but he had stuffed it full before leaving and now the weight was beginning to slow him down. He stopped at the second landing and reached up to mop his brow with his right

sleeve. He hated feeling this damp. He turned and twisted a little
bit to loosen his shirt where it had stuck to the flesh of his chest
and back. He looked up. There was a window on this landing. He
looked though it, toward the night. He saw the moon, full and
ripe in the sky. He saw two stars.

He thought he heard Andrew whisper to him from the landing
above.

He stopped resting.

7:52 p.m.

Moonlight washed its way down the outside back walls of the
hotel. The Man moved from shadow to shadow, his hands and
feet moving surely upon the brick, from windowsill to windowsill
to the metal ladders of fire escapes. He was a black form upon the
building, a living shadow in the night, his body lifted to the third
floor and his fingers seeking the opening of a window. He found
one, and jostled it upward, quietly. He slipped inside and closed
the window behind him. He hadn't been surprised at the lack
of police presence along the outside back of the building; Yates
didn't want to keep him out. Yates wanted to make sure that once
he was inside, The Man would never be able to leave.

The Man turned left. His footfall was soft upon the carpeting
of the hallway, and he made his way past window after moonlit
window on his left, in a hallway all but abandoned by light. Every
several feet he ducked small portholes of brightness on his right,
shining at him from windows cut into the doorways of the banquet hall gallery.

He found what he was looking for when he turned the first
corner.

Edward stood there, peering into the banquet hall. The Man
watched him for a moment, the thin frame standing there on tip-
toes to peer in at the wealth and the power and the food, his face
lit by the yellow light pouring in through the small round window.

"So you're the Republican Remover."

Edward whirled about at the sound of the voice. "Who?" He
fumbled, he clattered, something fell to the ground that he scrambled to pick up. The Man crossed the distance between them
quickly and knelt to take the fallen object from Edward's hands.

"It's just a clock," Edward offered quietly, looking up into the blank blackness of The Man's masked face. Edward's gaze drifted to take in the broad muscles of The Man's shoulders, the power lurking behind the black fabric of his costume; the pink triangle emblem above The Man's left breast. "You? You're gay?" Edward asked, and his right hand snaked out to touch the shiny pink triangle emblem and feel its smoothness.

The Man nodded.

Edward smiled, a smile that made a death's head of his skull as his lips pulled away from his teeth. He withdrew his fingers. "Then you understand."

The Man looked down at the timer in his hand.

"They have to die," Edward said. "I have to kill them." The two men stood. "I, me, they're killing, they've killed me, they killed Andrew, and I have to kill them so that they can't kill any more people, can't help kill any more people."

The Man handed back the timepiece to Edward. It had a blank, digital face, and The Man watched as Edward tucked the mechanism deep within his coat. "Thank you," Edward said.

The Man spoke again. "I can't let you do this."

Edward's smile faded away. "What?"

"I can't let you do this. It's wrong. I have to stop you." The Man looked away for a moment, then back at Edward. "I'm sorry," he said.

Edward started backing away from him. The Man followed, keeping the distance between them from widening. "You can't," Edward said, and then he was sneering at The Man, his body coiled down and he hissed at him, spitting words. "You don't know. Wrong?" Edward laughed, a bitter, hollow sound. "You don't know what it's like. Look at you. You're well, healthy; strong and sturdy. I was that way, once, not so long ago. I was that way and I had someone but they," he jerked his head in the direction of the lighted portholes, "their machinations, their morality, their delays took him away from me and made me a condemned man and now . . ."

"Now?"

Edward straightened up. "Now it's time someone put a stop to it. Stopped them."

"Not this way."

"I've wired each of the three central speakers' chairs—the ones

Port, Swanson, and Fordham will be sitting on—with a high-level plastic explosive that resembles nothing so much as a wad of spent gum." Edward moved now to open his coat, the fabric of it spreading out like a cloak to drape his body and yet reveal, "I've packed my body with seventy-five pounds of various and sundry explosives and this—" his hands moved about the digital time-piece The Man had returned to him only moments earlier— "is the starter piece. Thank you." Edward pressed a connection from the mass of wires leading from the stuffed pockets of the overcoat into the back of the timer. The watch's face lit up to reveal a series of three red zeros. Edward's fingers played about a few of the buttons below the red numbers and he took stock of the explosives packaged against his body. He looked at The Man and grinned. "It's amazing, the things you can get your hands on when you're not afraid to take the risks."

"When I go, they all go," Edward said. "Maybe new people come in, maybe they don't." He shrugged. "The cycle, at least, if not broken—I'm not unrealistic—is weakened." Edward looked down at the timer he clutched to his chest. "And me? I get to die with some modest sense of purpose and self-control." He looked levelly back to The Man. When Edward spoke, his voice was flat, and hushed: "You should go now."

"I don't think that's possible."

"Oh, but I think you'd better." Edward's fingers moved to press the buttons beneath the numbers. The Man moved toward Edward quickly, slapping the man's hand away from the buttons before he could depress them. Edward yelped, turned about, and half dove, half fell toward the nearest set of doors opening onto the banquet-hall balcony. He fell into the light, staggered in momentary bright blindness, and fumbled his way to the guardrail of the wooden balustrade below, which he used to hold himself upright and to rest.

A collective gasp rose from the crowd, then faded away into silence as they watched him.

Edward watched the crowd. He saw the men in their tuxedos, he saw the women in their expensive evening dresses, and he saw the plates filled with food, the glasses filled with champagne and wine and everywhere, everywhere he looked was a vast sea of money and power, money and power that might have saved him, once upon a time, had he been one of the few blessed with access.

Edward looked about the banquet hall, the rich tapestry curtains running along its sides and gathered long and full at the ends. At one end of the hall the tapestries covered an otherwise un-adorned wooden wall, but at the far end of the room the fabric framed a large, perfectly circular Tiffany stained-glass window de-picting da Vinci's *Last Supper*. Edward took in the three crystal chandeliers spanning the banquet hall's center, the amber color of the walls, and the faux Sistine Chapel spattered above him on the ceiling.

"My," he mumbled, "that's a tad much."

Three policemen moved quickly up the back staircase to breach the hallway outside the balcony. They threw open the safety doorway of the staircase and lunged through. The Man's fist caught the first one in the face and sent him down, the second one tripped over his falling comrade and The Man clubbed him unconscious with a swift blow behind the neck from a hammer made of fists. The third one, seeing what had happened to the first two, turned and headed back down the stairs but The Man stepped into the staircase, leapt over the railing, and landed square on the policeman's back. A sharp *thwap!* of The Man's fist and the policeman was no longer a threat.

The Man turned back to the open doorway above him and Edward in the balcony. The Man raced the stairs and reentered the hallway, pausing only at the edge of a shadow to peer through the open gallery door. He saw Edward, standing there, staring at the crowd below him. He saw round Senator Port with a hand-some, younger fellow beside him. He saw thin Senator Swanson and suspiciously tan candidate Fordham all staring up toward Ed-ward on the balcony while they talked among themselves. He saw the drinks in their hands and upon the tables; he saw the food and expanse of finery and everywhere he looked The Man too saw money and power.

Edward addressed the crowd. "You have murdered me!" he proclaimed in a voice somehow filled with resonance and depth. "You have murdered me and those I love and it shall and will stop!" Edward was starting to sweat again, and his forehead was shiny with the wetness.

The Man saw Fordham motion to two policeman near an exit. The two cops turned and left and The Man stepped deeper into the shadows. He heard their footsteps upon the concrete of the stairs, he heard their exclamations of surprise at the sight of the fallen three officers. He heard them yelp shortly after entering the hallway when two small pink triangle throwing stars grazed their necks, supplying each man with a concentrated dose of animal tranquilizer, and their bodies collapsed slowly to the carpeting of the corridor. The Man fingered a third throwing triangle carefully as he turned back toward Edward.

A shot rang out. The Man slipped the metal triangle inside a compartment on his belt. Edward had fallen behind the wooden balustrade and his fingers fumbled with the buttons beneath the numbers on the timer.

The Man appeared in the doorway to the balcony. Women screamed and The Man could feel the fear rising in the room. Chief Yates had done his work. The image of him that had been sent out repeatedly over evening news broadcasts and in daily newspapers had trained these people to fear him.

The Man didn't mind.

He stepped quickly down to Edward. He knelt down and touched the man's right shoulder, gently. A darkening bloodstain was spreading there. "Are you all right?" The Man whispered. Edward was sweating profusely now, but he managed to nod. The Man removed the glove from his right hand and felt Edward's forehead; he was burning up. The Man placed the glove back on his hand. "You've been shot. You have a fever. We have to get you to a hospital." He moved to place his arms beneath Edward's body.

Edward shook his head no and tried to wave The Man away. "Leave me."

The Man tried harder to scoop Edward up in his arms. Edward resisted, digging his back into the wood of the floor, wedging himself against the balustrade. "No," Edward said, "Please." The Man was afraid to move roughly in lifting Edward for fear of hurting him.

"I can't leave you."

Edward nodded weakly, distracting The Man for a moment as Edward's fingers moved about to press the buttons of the clock upon his chest. The three zeros now read "0 45." Edward smiled at The Man and relaxed into his arms. "Go," he said.

The Man looked at the red numbers. He considered his options. He didn't know how to defuse a bomb. Further, the mechanism was fastened to Edward so tightly, it was as if it were flesh of Edward's flesh. There was no separating the man from the machine.

. . . "0 43" . . . The Man could escape, but that meant Edward and the people in the ballroom would die—and Edward would realize what he intended. He could escape, trying to carry Edward with him, but the bomb would probably go off before they were safe, killing them both. . . . "0 41" . . . He could try to toss Edward out of the hotel before the bomb went off but then Edward would still die, The Man then responsible for the fact that Edward's death was without the meaning Edward had sought—perhaps The Man too would die with Edward in the blast—and Jackson Fordham, Senators Port and Swanson would continue to live, and vote, and hate, supported by the moneyed people gathered around them this evening.

. . . "0 40" . . .

The Man bent and kissed Edward on the forehead. Edward murmured, "Andrew?" his eyes closing.

The Man brushed a few wisps of hair back from Edward's forehead. "Adam," he said, "what's your name?"

"Edward," Edward said. The words must've felt thick and heavy in his mouth for their sound poured out slowly.

"Edward," The Man said.

Edward said, "Andrew," and smiled. He closed his eyes.

The Man stood upright, in full view of the crowd. He looked down, briefly. The numbers on Edward's chest read "0 33." The Man turned to race up the stairs of the gallery and a phalanx of policemen met him there with weapons drawn. He turned about and saw similar squads of policemen appearing at every doorway along the balcony and so he leapt atop the railing of the balustrade and scampered along it as if it were a balance beam until he reached the far end of the room. A few shots rang out from handguns, pinging against the brass of the rail he stood upon and thudding into wood below.

"Stop shooting, you idiots!" Fordham yelled from below. "You'll kill us all!" The Man looked down to see Fordham standing still at the end of the table, a cigar clamped between his teeth and his face flushed red with rage; Port and Swanson cowered in their seats, their arms waving in futility, trying to cover their heads. The Man couldn't hear them whimper but he could sense Fordham's disdain for the two. The handsome lad The Man noticed earlier at

Port's side was, simply, gone. The waiters and servers cleared out when the shooting started.

The Man saluted Fordham. "Sayonara, old boy," The Man said. The Man leapt off the balcony railing to swing upon the heavy tapestry, crashing through the large stained-glass oval of Jesus' Tiffany head toward the night. He was gone even as one of the policemen in the balcony cried out, "There's a bomb!" and the place erupted into screaming; smoke and fire and exploded flesh.

And the light of Israel shall be for a fire, and his Holy One for a flame: and it shall burn and devour his thorns and his briers in one day.

—*Isaiah 10: 17*

PETER CASHORALI

Once, long ago, a king ascended his throne. He had waited many
years to do so, enduring much hardship and suffering. And so,
when he finally entered his kingdom, he did so in power and
glory, and established a court second to none in splendor, and his
generosity passed into proverb almost immediately. Because of all
this, men flocked to his court from even the most distant lands,
eager to enter his service. Nobles, knights, and servants all wore
his livery with great pride: flannel shirts, Levi's 501 jeans, and
work boots, with handkerchiefs of various colors but only a single
pattern—the king's!—tucked in a back pocket of their jeans to
signify rank.

One day a young man named Patrick walked over the drawbridge and into the bustling courtyard of the castle. He had heard
of the king's court since he was a boy in his parents' cottage, waiting for his own story to begin, not knowing it already had. He applied to the major-domo for a position. Because he was young,
strong, and energetic, he was taken into the king's household immediately and given a very important duty.

Every evening, at the close of dinner, the king received a private last course. The nature of the dish was a mystery, since it was
carried in on a silver tray beneath a silver cover, which the king
never lifted until everyone else had left the great dining hall.

---

[1]"The White Snake," *The Complete Fairy Tales of the Brothers Grimm,* Jack Zipes,
translator.

Then, in complete privacy, the king would enjoy whatever it was, sometimes lingering over it, sometimes finishing in a few moments, after which he would once again cover the tray and call to have it removed. The bringing in and removal of the silver tray became Patrick's work.

It was a dream job at first. Patrick's mornings, afternoons, and evenings were his own, and he got to hobnob with the best and brightest, highest and most handsome men of the kingdom. But as the months became years and the years passed by on their way to wherever it is years go, Patrick became curious about just what it was he set before the king every night. He dated the chief cook for a while, to see if he could learn anything that way. But the cook finally confessed that he didn't have a clue what was under the silver dome lid. Each evening, when the other courses were were all being carried into the dining hall, he went down a flight of stone stairs beneath the kitchens. There, on a little table at the foot of the stairs, he both found and later returned the covered tray. Nor could any of the king's many ex-lovers fill Patrick in on the secret. None of them—not even in the blissful early stages of candlelit dinners for two—had ever been invited to share the last course, or even to stick around to see what it was. Patrick's need to know what lay under the silver cover began to nibble away at him until he was completely consumed.

And so, on an evening when an unusually large number of guests feasted at the king's table, and the running and carrying from the kitchens to the dining hall made everything a little harder to keep track of, Patrick made a quick detour to his own room with the tray. Setting it down on his nightstand, he locked the door. And at last, trembling with eagerness and fear of discovery, he lifted the silver lid. There, coiled on a dish without either sauce or garnish, lay a white snake.

"What a strange thing to have for dessert," Patrick said to himself. "I wonder what it tastes like?" A drop of cloudy liquid lay beaded on the tip of the snake's mouth. Patrick touched his finger to the drop and put it to his tongue. The taste, though it sent a shiver up his spine, was gone before he could classify it. Far from satisfying his curiosity, the flavor—whether it had been salty or sweet, bitter or biting or bland—inflamed it. "I'll have a piece of this," declared Patrick. "Just a small piece, and then I'll take it to the king. I'll have a bit from the middle. That way I can push the two ends together, and he won't notice that any's gone." And so he did. But even as he ate and tried to name the taste, he heard two voices raised in argument, just outside his window.

"Yes, you did."

"Ridiculous. It flew away when you weren't looking."

"Don't call me ridiculous—you ate it. That was my moth and you just snatched it away and ate it all up yourself. You're such a glutton. I don't know why I stay with you."

Now, Patrick's room was on the third floor, and there was nothing outside his window but the top of a camphor tree. Even though he was anxious to get the tray to the king, he ran to the window to see who in the world had not only climbed the tree, but was up there eating moths. There was no one in the tree except a pair of mockingbirds. Patrick was baffled, until one of the mockingbirds said, "Because I'm the only one who's willing to put up with your paranoia, sweetheart." Then it flew away, and the other flew off after it. A large white moth crawled out from under a spray of camphor leaves, said, "Thank heavens they've finally gone," and fluttered away in the opposite direction. And that's how Patrick realized he could understand the language of animals.

But he had no time to marvel over this. Hurriedly, he picked up the tray, rushed downstairs into the hallway that was now full of servants bearing dirty plates and glasses back to the kitchens, and, as calmly as he could, bore the royal last course into the dining hall. He set the tray down before the king. Without thinking, he reached for the lid, but caught himself quickly. If the king noticed, he gave no indication. "Everyone," he said to his guests, as Patrick moved to his position at the doors. "I'll join you in the ballroom in half an hour. Remember, tonight's the white party." Everyone rose in a high state of excitement and quickly went off to their chambers to dress. Patrick closed the doors and stood outside until the king called him to take away the silver tray.

The white party was a huge success, as were all the king's white parties, black parties, beer busts, and champagne brunches. Days passed. At first Patrick waited anxiously for the king's displeasure to erupt—men had been known to disappear in the castle. But after a few days it appeared that his tampering with the tray hadn't been noticed, and he relaxed. He performed his duty for the king's table each night as he always had. Though he still enjoyed the pleasures of the court, he now spent most of his free time roaming the castle and surrounding forest, listening to the speech of the animals.

One day the king called him out to the terrace, where he was drinking margaritas with his current boyfriend, Bruno. Actually, Patrick had overheard one of the king's cats remark to the other, in the catty way cats have, that Bruno was about to be promoted to we'll-always-be-friends. But Bruno wasn't aware of this yet, and still watched the king with fierce adoration, and the rest of the world as if it were his lunch. "Patrick," said the king, detaching his gaze from his boyfriend's. "Bruno here seems to have misplaced a gold ring I've given him. I'd like you to find it for me."

"Okay," Patrick replied, which was what everyone always said to anything the king requested—he wasn't very big on "Your Majesty" but he did expect unconditional obedience. Then Patrick left the terrace, wondering how on earth he was going to locate the gold ring.

He searched through the castle diligently, looking under pillows, down drains, inside dirty-clothes hampers, but without much hope and less success. Then, passing through the yard behind the kitchens where the poultry were kept, he overheard a duck complaining to a chicken of his digestion.

"I've eaten something that doesn't agree with me," he griped.

"Really," said the hen sympathetically. "What does it feel like?"

"Small and cold and totally indigestible."

"Oh, my," clucked the hen. "That sounds like jewelry. You want to be careful about jewelry. I had a cousin once who swallowed a diamond earring, wouldn't keep still about it, and next thing you knew she'd been whisked into the kitchen for exploratory surgery. You'd better keep quiet about this."

"But my stomach hurts," grumped the duck. "Why should I be quiet?"

That was all Patrick needed to hear. He caught the duck, who was in no condition to be evasive—"Told you so," the hen called after him with a perhaps pardonable note of self-righteousness in her voice—and brought him inside to the head cook. "Here, Tony," he said, handing the unfortunate waterfowl over. "The king wants warm duck salad for lunch. And use the gold ring you'll find in its crop for his napkin ring."

When the meal was cooked, Patrick himself brought it out to the terrace and set it down on a round glass-topped table. "Lunch for two," he announced, then, realizing the king was alone, he amended it to: "Lunch for one."

"Oh, you were right the first time. Lunch for two," remarked the king thoughtfully, pulling the gold ring off of his napkin. "Though Bruno won't be joining us—he's been promoted to the Company of Perpetual Friends of the King. Patrick," he murmured, shifting his extraordinary blue eyes from the ring to Patrick's eyes as he said his name. It made Patrick's knees go loose and his breath escape in a sigh. "Only the duck and I knew where this ring was hidden, and since I haven't said anything you must have been talking with the duck. No, I'm not angry," he assured Patrick, whose face had frozen. "It only makes you more interesting to me than you already were." He smiled like the beginning of a three-day weekend, holding up the gold ring. "Let's see how well this fits your finger," he proposed.

Well, Patrick had slept with the king before—everyone had; everyone wanted to again. But the idea of actually being the royal boyfriend made the world swim before his eyes. He blinked rapidly to clear them, and suddenly Patrick noticed something very strange. There were lines in the corners of the king's eyes. Tiny lines, almost completely concealed by his perfect tan, practically unnoticeable when the king turned the light of his magnificence up all the way, but—lines. Now, many men had grown old in the service of the king; that was only to be expected, if not exactly looked forward to with great joy—it was young men who could do the most for, and expect the most from, the king. But while his subjects and servants and courtiers were expected to grow old, the king himself wasn't. Not even a little bit. Ever. That's what being king meant.

The shock of this loosened the spell Patrick had lived under so happily—because to tell the truth, the king was something of a magician. It wasn't just that the king himself now seemed less than the most desirable man in the world. Suddenly the terrace and the towers of the shining castle rising up into the blue sky and the plans that had been made for that night and next day and next week all seemed just a tiny bit tired. Patrick thought, I've stayed here too long. So he said, "Actually, I was going to ask for a leave of absence. Um, maybe do a little traveling. Visit my family."

At first, because he'd never encountered this answer before, the king couldn't understand it. But after it had been rephrased and repeated enough times, he finally understood what Patrick wanted to get across. "You've gone crazy," he said, nodding his head in complete understanding. "I've seen it happen before, though never in quite this way. It's very sad, really. Well, under the circumstances I think travel might be just the thing. And if you ever regain your senses, you're welcome to return. Though of course, not to the same exalted position you currently enjoy—certainly not to the position you were just offered!—because frankly, Patrick, you'll be too old. But we'll find you something." Patrick thanked him very much, said he'd had a lovely time, and left the castle.

Of course, he had no idea where he would go or what he would do. He had a few gold coins in his pocket, a fresh croissant stuffed with ham and brie that Tony the head cook had run out and given him as he passed the kitchens, and not much else. As he walked along the road that led away from everything he knew and toward everything he didn't, he wondered if, after all, this wasn't the stupidest thing he'd ever done in his life. The birds from their branches sang of how splendid it was to be out and about in the wide world, but Patrick knew that when the sun began to set they'd change their tune, and sing praises of going home to a cozy nest.

He walked along, and suddenly he heard three voices crying for help. Patrick followed them and came to a small pond. The heat of the sun had caused the pond to shrink, leaving a wide circle of mud around it. Three small fish lay out on the mud, panting for breath, too weak to move. Patrick quickly but gently scooped them up, carried them back to the water, and lowered them into it. The fish revived immediately and swam out to the middle of the pond, diving down and out of sight. Before he followed his brothers, the last of the little fish looked back at Patrick and called, "Thanks, mister! We owe you one." Patrick continued on his way.

After a while, he heard another voice, and this one also cried for help. He followed it and came to a pine tree, where after a moment he discovered a large honeybee. It had been investigating a stream of sap, somehow gotten turned around so its wings stuck in the resinous fluid, and was now in danger of being smothered. Patrick carefully freed the bee and set it down on a stone, where it busily began to clean itself. As he turned to walk on, the bee called after him, "Thank you, sir! Someday I'll repay you for your kindness."

It was now late in the day, and Patrick was hungry. As he thought about finding a place to settle down for the night and eat his croissant, he heard a third voice. "Is anyone gonna help you?" the voice asked, and then answered its own question: "No, no one's gonna help you. In a world like this? Are you that crazy? Who'd help anybody like you? No one, that's who. So shut up and stop complaining." Patrick followed the voice to the other side of a thick growth of brush. There he found a rat, all his ribs showing, talking to himself in the final extremes of hunger. When he saw Patrick, the rat rolled his eyes. "Oh, the end of a perfect day!" he complained bitterly. "It's too much to ask to be allowed to die in peace, with a little dignity. No, it's gotta be messy. Yeah, Jack, you got it right: it's a rat. A nasty dirty rat. Step on it! Squash it! Give it to the dog to play with!"

"It's Patrick," said Patrick. "Not Jack." He took the croissant out of his pocket, still wrapped in its white linen napkin, and put it next to the rat.

"What's this?" the rat demanded, sniffing at it. "Poison?"

"No," Patrick replied. "It's food."

"So why don't you eat it?"

"Look," Patrick said, a little impatiently. "Do you want it or not?"

"Don't be so touchy," the rat admonished him, tearing the napkin away with his sharp teeth. "Ooo, aren't we fancy! A croissant. Would Your Ladyship care for some more tea?" He ate ravenously, squeaking with pleasure.

As Patrick turned to go, the rat muttered something under his breath. "What?" Patrick asked.

"I said, 'Thanks,'" the rat snapped. "Are you deaf or what?"

"Would we be having a conversation if I were? You're welcome." Patrick continued on his way.

Night fell. "Since I don't have anything to eat," Patrick said to himself, "and I doubt if the ground is any softer to lay on than it is to walk on, I might as well keep walking. I'm sure to get somewhere sooner or later."

By morning he had—a large and prosperous-looking city, prepared for a festival. The preparations, though, all seemed to have gotten rather old, and now the banners were dingy, the bags of confetti lay unopened, and the balloons had lost most of their helium, giving them that bleak, dispiriting look balloons take on under such circumstances. The streets were all lined with people, but most of them sat glumly on the curbs, looking at their watches or napping. Patrick stepped up to a man sitting in a portable lawn chair and said, "What's happening here?"

"Nothing," replied the man.

"Well, yes," admitted Patrick. "I mean, what should be happening?"

"Oh," said the man, "we *should* be shouting and cheering and throwing colorful paper streamers over the heads of the prince and his new life companion as they parade down the boulevard. And that's certainly what we'd like to be doing. But his first companion died, and his best friend died, and his second best friend, and several aquaintances, and a lot people he'd heard of but never met, and his own health is problematic. So as you can see, we're all on hold right now."

"I see," said Patrick. "And is his new life companion comforting and sustaining him through his time of trial?"

"Now, there's the problem," replied the man. "Prince Douglas should have already chosen his companion by this time. In fact, up until a couple of days ago that's what he was doing, in the usual manner. All potential suitors had gathered up at the castle, and the prince was going to set each one a task. Whoever succeeded at his task first would be Prince Douglas's companion. I mean, there was a preliminary screening process, of course. Each suitor had to be well born, and a nice person, and know which fork to eat his salad with. But just as everything was getting started, part of the castle began to sink, and then the prince changed. He made all the tasks impossible, and everyone who failed had his head cut off—which is *not* the usual manner, at least around here. Well, after a few heads had been lost, all the other suitors ran for their lives. And here we are, with no idea what happens next."

"And what does Prince Douglas look like?" Patrick wondered.

"Here, I'll show you," said the man, taking a book of postage stamps out of his wallet.

Patrick opened the book. There, each bearing the word LOVE and boasting a self-adhesive back, lay displayed eight miniature portraits of the most beautiful man Patrick had ever seen in his life—and he'd seen quite a few. "The suitors who ran away," he declared, handing the book back to the man, "were fools. Prince Douglas is worth any risk. How do I get to the castle?" The man gave him directions, wished him luck, and Patrick was on his way.

The castle stood on a hill overlooking the city. As Patrick approached it, he felt the ground shake every few minutes, and when he began to climb the hill toward the castle's gate he saw why this was so. One of the castle's towers was sinking into the hill. Not very quickly and not all at once; not more than an inch or so at a time. But it was already very noticeable, and every time the ground—so solid underfoot—rumbled and trembled, the tower sank a little deeper.

When Patrick got to the gate, the gatekeeper wasn't inclined to let him in for an audience with the prince. This was because his 501s and flannel shirt, which had once shown him to be in the service of a powerful king, now marked him as a commoner. But Patrick still had a few gold coins in his pocket, and by the judicious use of these he gained admission. A servant showed him to the door of the prince's chamber, then left. Patrick knocked, but hearing no answer, opened the door and stepped in.

He dropped, almost spraining his ankle, because this was the sinking tower and its floor was already several feet lower than the rest of the castle. Patrick regained his balance immediately. "Hello?" he inquired, looking around. It was a spacious and rather oddly furnished room, with drapes drawn over all the windows and many end tables arranged in a circle. Each table held several silver-framed photographs, no two of the same man—some were in vibrant middle age, some in the flower of youth, some barely out of boyhood. Within every silver frame was a border of black crepe. In the middle of this circle of faces sat Prince Douglas. He was so much more beautiful in person than he was on a stamp, such a vacation for the eyes, that at first Patrick didn't catch what Douglas was repeating to himself over and over again.

"John," murmured Douglas in a sad, dull voice. "John. Bill. Terry. Lee. Tim. Carlos. Fred. Michael. Jim. Joel . . ." He murmured an entire litany of names, ending it with: "And soon, me." As he uttered these last words, the earth rumbled and the entire room sank a little further. Then he said, "John," and began his litany again.

"Hello," Patrick said quickly, not liking the sensation of the floor sinking beneath his feet.

"Who are you?" asked Douglas.

"Patrick," said Patrick. "And I'm applying for the position of suitor. Unless it's already been filled."

"Get out of here," Douglas said wearily.

"You've lost so much," Patrick observed quietly, looking around at all the portraits. "Why don't you let me bring you something?"

Douglas scowled at Patrick as if he'd like to kill him, which, as it turned out, was what he had in mind. "All right," he said, his voice suddenly like two stones grinding together. "I had something once. A pearl. The largest, most perfect pearl I had ever seen. But it fell out the window, and I could never find it again. Bring me back my pearl, or I'll have your head." Patrick walked over to one of the windows, pulled back the drape and looked out. The window had already sunk below ground level, but still commanded a breathtaking view of the ocean.

Patrick left the castle and walked around to the back. A path led down the face of a cliff to the narrow beach and Patrick descended, looking out at the ocean. He had never seen it before. It was even vaster than the forest and only slightly smaller than the sky, reaching from the east of the world to the west, coming in from over the horizon to break, and break, and break on the stones at his feet. He knew the pearl was there somewhere—"But where?" he asked out loud. "And how can I put my hand on it?"

Then, as if in answer to his question, he heard two voices far out on the water, singing over the sound of the waves:

Though it's hidden,
though it's tossed
in the ocean
never crossed,
nothing's really
ever lost.

Soon he saw, swimming in toward the shore, the three little fish he had rescued. Two of them did the singing, while the third, between them, carried a large pearl in his mouth. Patrick waded out into the water, and the third fish put the pearl into his hand. "Told you we'd do you a good turn someday, mister," said the fish. Then he and his companions dove beneath the waves and were gone.

Patrick climbed back up to the castle in great excitement, which was only slightly dampened by the periodic rumbling of the ground. When he got to the prince's door, he jumped down into the room. "I've brought you back your pearl," he cried, interrupting Douglas at his litany.

"What?" asked Douglas.

"Your pearl," Patrick repeated, holding it out to him. "See?"

Douglas took the pearl from him and looked at it. "It was a figure of speech," he said.

"Beg pardon?"

"I didn't lose an actual pearl," Douglas told him. " 'Pearl' in this sense means an experience of wholeness, of everything being connected and contained in a single, unfathomable meaning. Something that's both eternal, the way the pearl is a mineral substance, but at the same time is alive, growing, as the pearl grows in the oyster." He sighed, gazing at the pearl. "This is beautiful."

"So are you. Keep it," Patrick said. "Well, then tell me something else to do."

Douglas shook his head and let the pearl drop from his hand. "Go away."

"You're so bitter," Patrick murmured forlornly. "I could change that. I could make the sweetness of life flow again, if you'd just let me." He reached out to touch Douglas, but the prince pulled away.

"Then do that," Douglas said, withdrawing into himself again. "Make the sweetness of life flow again. Don't come back until you've performed this task."

"All right, I won't," Patrick swore, walking away from Douglas, though this seemed entirely the wrong direction for accomplishing what he had to do. He jumped, caught hold of the threshold of the door, and swung himself up and out. Behind him, the prince returned to "John. Bill. Terry . . ."

He stepped outside the castle. The sunlight blazed, a breeze played with his hair, but the ground rumbled and Douglas slid a little deeper down. Suddenly a voice said, "Busy." Patrick looked up, and the honeybee he had rescued flew by. "No time to chat just now, sir—busy," it called back. A few seconds later, a second honeybee flew past; it also said, "Busy." Then two more, no, a dozen, no, it must be hundreds of honeybees swarmed past Patrick and around the side of the castle. Patrick followed, as the hundreds of bees were joined by thousands, all remarking, "Busy. Busy. Oh, great to be busy," to one another. By the time he'd walked around to the side the castle, huge honeycombs were under con-

struction at the tops of several windows—which were the only portions of the windows still above ground—in Douglas's part of the
castle. The honeycombs grew larger as he watched, until they
joined together in a single golden mass, and though every bee
spoke in its own voice while it flew, when they were gathered together in work it was one enormous buzzing voice that sang:

> Busy through
> the world I roam,
> visit flowers,
> hurry home,
> and sweetness fills
> the honeycomb.

Soon there was a muffled cracking of glass, and as Patrick
watched the honeycomb began to collapse. The great swarm of
bees dispersed in all directions, and as the honeybee Patrick had
rescued flew past him, it said, "One good turn deserves another,
friend." Patrick hurried back inside the castle.

The prince's chamber was now so far below the threshold of
the door that Patrick, in order to enter, had to turn around, carefully lower himself until he hung from the threshold by his fingertips, and let himself drop. He landed on his feet, but lost his balance, went over backward and sat down in a pool of honey a foot
deep. The windows had broken open, the drapes come down, and
honey, its flow lessened now, still oozed down in golden sheets.
"Here it is," he declared triumphantly. "The sweetness of life,
flowing for you once more!" He stood up and walked over to
Douglas with some difficulty.

"You have a very literal turn of mind," Douglas observed. He
was still sitting in his chair, the honey up to his calves. "This is impressive, but not really what I need."

"I'm getting you what you ask for," Patrick protested, getting a
little frustrated.

"That's true," Douglas had to admit. "You are. So perhaps I
should ask you to bring me what I really need. But what would
that be?" he wondered.

"I know what you really need," Patrick began tenderly. But
Douglas froze him with a look, and he thought perhaps he was

being too literal minded again. He waited quietly while Douglas pondered the matter.

Then the prince's face brightened, which was a sight worth waiting any length of time for. "Patrick," he said. "Bring me an apple from the Tree of Life." Patrick was silent. "Can you do that?" Douglas asked.

"Maybe," said Patrick.

"Do you know where the Tree of Life is?"

"Um, not exactly."

"I hope you can find it," Douglas said quietly. "Because without an apple from the Tree of Life, I don't see how I'll ever get out of this room. And Patrick? I don't really want to sink into the ground."

"Then stop reciting those names to yourself all the time," Patrick said, a little desperately.

"But I can't help it. They're dead. All of them," Douglas replied. The light died out of his face, and he began once again, "John. Bill. Terry. Lee . . ." Patrick scrambled out of the room as quickly as he could, noticing, as he hit his head on it, that the ceiling was now below the lintel of the doorway, beginning to seal it off.

He hurried down the hill and into the streets of the city. But now the enormity of the task hit him, and he was overtaken by despair. There wasn't much time, he had no idea where to begin looking, and the only thing he knew about the Tree of Life was that it must be somewhere very far away. He sat down on the curb with his feet in the gutter, put his head in his hands, and groaned.

"Yeah, it's a rotten world, all right," a voice at his elbow remarked cheerfully. He looked up, and there sat the rat whose life he had saved. "How's it going, Jack?"

"It's Patrick," Patrick said glumly.

"Aw, jeez, buddy, I'm sorry," apologized the rat. "For a second you looked like this friend of mine who once did me an incredible favor, but I guess I made a mistake. So I hope you'll excuse me for not having been eaten by my mother at birth. What's the problem, Jack?"

"I need an apple from the Tree of Life, and I don't know where it is," Patrick said miserably.

"That's it?" asked the rat. "That's the big problem? Wait a minute." There happened to be a narrow opening to the sewers under the sidewalk where they were sitting. The rat slithered and squirmed through the opening. Shortly he was back, and in his mouth he carried an apple that glowed like the tenderest spring dawn. "Here you go, sport," said the rat, laying the apple down next to Patrick.

"Where did you get this?" Patrick asked, picking up the radiant fruit and letting its light play in his eyes.

"I've got a little place of my own down in the sewer," the rat replied with modest pride. "It's not much, I guess, but it's comfy. The Tree of Life's there."

"The Tree of Life is down in the sewer?"

"Yeah. It grows right next to my front door."

"The Tree of Life?"

"See, you got that high-school diploma and it's paying off, isn't it?" said the rat. Then suddenly he caught on. "Oh. Ohh, *I* get it. It's the Tree of Life, so it's gotta be someplace *fancy*. Someplace *far away*. Not where just anyone could get it—anyone being yours truly. You got some nerve, you know that? Have you ever been down in the sewer? No. So how do you know what's there? You don't. There's all kinds of good stuff down in that sewer, because people like you flush things without even knowing what they are. You want the apple or don't you?"

"I do," said Patrick, very humbly. "Thank you. Thank you very much."

"You waiting for something?"

"Um, the song?"

"The what?"

"The song," Patrick prompted. "You know, like the ones the fish and the bees sang."

The rat stared at him, then shook its head in disgust. "The fish and the bees," he repeated. Then he sighed wearily, stood up on his hind legs, clasped his paws in front of his chest, and sang,

You're a real pain
in the rear,
pretty songs
you want to hear,
while Doug's about
to disappear.

"Oh!" cried Patrick, and he snatched up his apple and ran back up to the castle as fast as he could. By the time he got to the prince's door, the tower had descended so far that the doorway was almost completely filled with the outer wall. But there was still a narrow opening at the very bottom. Patrick carefully put the apple into his shirt, got down on his belly, and by squirming and slithering was just able to squeeze through. He dropped down— the fall was long enough for him to realize that if this didn't work, neither he nor Douglas would see the light of day again—and landed in a heap.

"I've got it!" he cried, scrambling to his feet.

But even as he spoke, Douglas was just ending a verse of his litany. At the words "And soon, me," the earth rumbled—now a much more menacing sound, heard on all sides of the room— and the tower sank. They were now sealed in under the ground. "I hope this isn't just another figure of speech," he said, holding out the glowing apple, now the only source of light in the dark room.

"Is that the apple from the Tree of Life?" Douglas asked, his voice the faintest of monotones. "Pretty, isn't it. But it's too late."

"You're here. I'm here. The apple from the Tree of Life's here," Patrick said sternly, to cover up the fact that he was rather frightened. "How can it be too late?" He walked across the still-sticky floor to where Douglas sat. "Here," he said. Then, because it suddenly occurred to him that if this *were* just an apple, and here he was sealed forever in an underground chamber with no other food, he could certainly use the carbohydrates, he added, "Half for you and half for me." He divided the apple in two. Instead of diminishing its light, this had the effect of more than doubling it, so the room was quite well illuminated. He put half the apple into Douglas's mouth as he put the other half into his own, and together they ate.

Patrick could never later describe the taste of the fruit, though as he bit in he thought it was very like the flavor of the white snake, only more musical. But he almost immediately forgot about what he was eating, because as Douglas bit into his half of the apple his eyes suddenly lit up and looked into Patrick's eyes, and this was much more interesting to him. The two of them ate, watching each other, and the joy grew in their faces like light, until it seemed that the whole room was illumined by their delight in the sight of each other eating. Douglas rose from his chair, and as he did Patrick—his own head spinning at the sight as if it were he who had suddenly risen very quickly, not from a chair but up

into the sky—heard the song the birds sing when the day is especially beautiful and it's so wonderful to be out and about in the
wide world. And because this is a very unusual thing to hear when
you're sealed in an underground chamber, Patrick automatically
glanced at the windows.

Instead of being filled with rocks and earth, they opened once
again to the blue sky and its breezes. The pictures were all still in
place on their tables, but their black crepe borders had turned
the palest shade of lavender, and, what was more important,
Douglas was no longer seated in their midst.

"I've never heard the birds sing like this before," Douglas
laughed, turning from the window to Patrick. "It's like I can almost understand the lyrics!" Later the two of them left the tower
and went down into the city, where the prince and his new life
companion were showered with confetti and cheers by the greatly
relieved populace. But before that happened, Patrick—finally!—
took Douglas in his arms and taught him how to understand the
language of the animals.

Slender

KEVIN BENTLEY

Sixth-grade boys were uniformly shrimpy, but many of the girls had already leapt the chasm—girls like Dina Potter: tall, with hairdos and hose, go-go boots and fur coats. Giantesses armored in harlequin glasses and padded bras, they chuffed around the gravel schoolyard in cliques, posing for high-school guys who drove by honking and catcalling, and chanting quietly beside boys like me, *fairy fairy fairy*. I asked my older brother Bart what that meant. "Oh, a fairy's a male whore," he told me.

I made a serious misjudgment on Valentine's Day, when I slipped a love note wrapped around a rubbery troll doll I'd crafted in my Mattel Thingmaker into the pocket of Dina Potter's vast rabbit fur coat and sat back coolly at my desk to await her response, dreamily writing *Kevin 'n' Dina* in loopy cursive strokes across my binder.

"Eeeeeek!" Her melodramatic shriek got everyone's attention. "Oh, God—look what that *fag* put in my coat!" Mr. Striber, a mentally ill Mormon with a facial tick, made me go outside the cottage (a flimsy walled annex classroom up on cinderblocks) and stand with my nose in a circle he drew just out of reasonable reach for the rest of the afternoon. I knew then that the best I could hope for was the speedy arrival of summer and my chance to reinvent myself while everyone forgot about my humiliation.

Happily for me, a fat, dull-normal kid named Karl Brent attracted the most virulent attention. He wore a black raincoat buttoned up to his chin without regard for the weather and carried a monogrammed briefcase, which was one of the things about him that made me uncomfortable—surely it was only a matter of time before someone would point out that he and I shared the same initials? Karl entered the playground every day whistling and swinging his briefcase, his equally unpopular little sister Mona (who wore fifties-style starched petticoats that stuck out from her body and molded corkscrew curls) holding his hand, and every day he'd be tripped and jumped and kicked and punched and made to eat dirt while Mona ran for the principal, the briefcase usually ending up on the roof or thrown in front of traffic.

Then Karl Brent made his bad lot worse with one simple and fateful slip-up. He sucked Troy Sager's dick. Troy Sager was a hood who lived alone with his mother in an apartment over the Hondo Cocktail Lounge, where she worked nights. He was tall and willowy, with mean dark eyes and a long, elegant, pointy nose. He wore a ripped jean jacket and was said to carry a switchblade. He was often absent for days at a time, sent up to the D-Home. One day Troy was seen showing Karl his knife in a far corner of the playground, and for a week or so they hung out together, dumbfounding everyone. Then Karl ditched class with Troy one day and went to his apartment, and the next day Troy let it be known that Karl had sucked his dick.

When the news broke, 6-A reached a point of near hysteria. Nobody was working, notes were flying, and Mr. Striber was beside himself. A crony of Dina Potter's got up to use the pencil sharpener, stopped in front of Karl, and spit in his face. I had the bad luck to be accepting a note from someone at just the moment Mr. Striber spun around from the blackboard, and he dragged me outside the cottage by the collar, slamming me up against the flimsy metal wall.

Mr. Striber was a broad-shouldered man whose starched white shirts were always sweat-darkened in a wide circle around the armpits by second period. He was probably under thirty, and he'd have been sexy if he weren't so ill tempered and pious. Married, with several small children, he flirted all day long with Tony Buck, an up-and-coming jock. When I wore my trendy Indian moccasins to class he sent me out to run two laps backward around the track, sneering, "I'll run those squaw shoes off you!" Tony, on the other hand, was subjected to daily mock-serious corporal punishments for his antics. "Tony, my stick's just *itching* for your butt today!"

"I want to know what's going on in there," Mr. Striber said leaning over me, one arm propped on the wall beside my head, pale blue eyes bugging. "Why is everyone throwing things at Karl Brent?"

"I don't know," I said, naturally. "Something everyone says he did. . . ."

"What does everyone say Karl did?"

"He went to Troy Sager's house and—"

"What? What did he do?" He was right up in my face like a drill sergeant, and suddenly I felt like I was confessing not what Karl may or may not have done, but what I knew I secretly wanted to do so bad it made me dizzy to even think about it.

"He sucked his dick!"

Mr. Striber's eyes bulged like a cartoon character's might, and his twitch, which made it seem absurdly as if he were winking in conspiracy ("Just kiddin'!") worked spastically. He had me by the shoulders and he gave me a great teeth-rattling shake with each word: "Don't-You-Ever-Let-Me-Hear-You-Utter-Such-Filth-Again! Do-You-Understand-Me? Do-You?"

The entire cottage must have shifted as everybody sped back to their seats from the row of windows from which they'd been watching. I sat at my desk with my head throbbing where it had banged against the metal wall. As pencils scraped and my chastened classmates took down the math problems Mr. Striber reeled off, I stared at my writing hand, my lap, Karl's head buried in his arms on his desk, the sandstorm blowing against the windows. I noted all these things as if seeing them for the first time, as if I were an alien anthropologist just beamed down from Alpha Centauri. I was a stranger with a secret. I no longer recognized myself.

We didn't have to change into gym clothes yet (*dressing out,* coach called it), but we had an hour-long PE period before lunch in which all the sixth-grade boys came together to do jumping jacks and sit-ups on the sticky blacktop, and then were sent off in teams to play football, basketball, or baseball, depending on the season. We hadn't had an organized phys-ed class at my old school back in Alabama, where at recess you could throw around a ball or sit in the shade and read. Till now, barring my father's few lame attempts to make me shoot baskets in the back yard, I'd completely avoided sports. Now, PE made me hate school and hate my life. In the bullpen of that one hot and awkward hour a day, my wits counted for nothing; my ignorance of the games, and my tendency to avoid a ball in motion, were deemed pathetic.

The hours away from school were poisoned with dread of the next day's gauntlet. I read a sappy Scholastic paperback, *Craig and Joan: Two Lives for Peace*—a story about two teens who killed themselves with carbon monoxide because they were so upset about the Vietnam war and because their parents thought they were seeing too much of each other—and contemplated suicide in colored Magic-Marker block printing in my diary. "I'd rather die than wrestle tomorrow." "If I shot myself in the foot, would I still have to play basketball?" It's true that these terse entries usually perked up by the last line: "Went to K-Mart with Mom and bought the new Mama Cass album. Bye!"

El Paso is built on desert, and that inhospitable fact could never be effaced, no matter how many sickly nonbearing mulberry trees people planted, no matter how many cement and rock walls were sculpted, breaking the yards and blocks into ugly hot grids. The sand blew back in and drifted against everything in frequent sandstorms, and tumbleweeds lumbered down streets with names like Edgerock and Sandstone and lodged against dusty evergreens on front lawns. The desert was always in sight, always encroaching, ready to bury the tacky flagstone ranch houses and leave only the twin horse heads atop the Bronco Drive-In poking out of the dunes like *Ozymandias*.

The playing field was a transitory landscape of dust devils and shifting dunes, the backstop having to be dug out regularly. One scorching morning near the end of the school year, I stood daydreaming so far outfield I could barely hear the crack of the bat hitting the ball, when Mike Carson summoned me. Mike was in 6-E, a class in which I knew no one, and I was vaguely aware that he lived on the block behind mine, in a house my mother always flinched at when we drove by because it looked so trashy: rusty van on the lawn, flaking paint. I knew he was considered weird, but not like Karl Brent—he was shunned, but nobody picked on him. He was short and wiry, and was said to be a good batter when he played, but he didn't bother. He wore black T-shirts and his father's old army fatigue pants, had clear olive skin, bowl-cut, dirty-blond hair, and round wire-rimmed glasses.

On this day he was doing something typically outré: he'd buried himself, lying on his back in the sand piled against the schoolyard wall. "Hey, c'mere, help me with this. What're you waiting for, the ball to come this way?" I walked over. "C'mon—just push it up over my arms. Careful! Don't get it in my face, for fucksake!" I patted the sand down right up to his neck. "They used to bury people like this for torture, you know? I saw this movie once. They buried this guy up to his neck and put honey on his nose and then ants came and just ate his brains." I stood back. "OK, now walk over me. Go ahead."

I put a foot gingerly above where his legs should be.

"No, c'mon, walk right on me." I stepped elaborately up and down his buried torso.

"OK, that's it, just stand there." I was standing on his crotch. "See? You're standing right on my *dick* and I don't feel a thing!" I heard a chorus of angry voices yelling my last name, and turned to see the ball whizzing and skipping along the ground. I ran off after it.

After that, Mike and I seemed to happen into each other often out pedalling our Stingray bikes around the neighborhood. When school let out for the summer, he started coming over and ringing the doorbell: "Wanna come out and ride?" We'd pump our bikes down hard-packed trails into the desert in the heat of the day, sweat soaked, pulling wheelies and wiping out, exploring. We found junked cars, illicit trash dumps strewn with interesting items, caches of empty liquor bottles, and sun-warped porno magazines. Mike liked to talk about the Beatles and girls he wanted to fuck. "You ever tried that?" he asked, pointing to a wrinkled photo in one of our squirreled-away magazines. A heavily lipsticked woman in a black bra and panties was giving a blowjob to a red, disembodied penis.

"Nope," I lied, primly. Actually, I had first tried it with my friend Chuck Watts in the fourth grade; he'd been sucking off his older brothers. We did it to each other for a while during a commercial break in "The Outer Limits," without much excitement, then went into the kitchen for jelly doughnuts, to get the odd, tangy flesh taste out of our mouths. And then there was all that group activity on the army base in Alabama I'd since tried not to think about. I'd been going into the woods to smoke cigarettes and pull down my pants with a gang of neighborhood misfits from

another school for two years back at Fort Rucker. My older
brother Bart acted shocked when word reached him on the block
that I'd been seen *butt fucking* (actually a kind of noninsertive rut-
ting) with Randall Tarp in an Off-Limits Zone. "You better not let
Mom and Dad find out what you're up to," he warned darkly.

Although he was a little strange, dressing in an approximation of
hippie garb (army surplus and fringe vests) and carrying around
fake joints he rolled from pencil shavings, compared to me Mike
was a boy's boy. He cursed and spit, he could take apart his bike
and put it back together, he had a chin-up bar in the doorway of
the room he shared with two younger brothers, and noticeable biceps. It was like having the pet chimp I'd wanted ever since the TV
show "The Hathaways" (which starred Peggy Cass as the mother
of three chimpanzees): he swung from tree limbs and did hand-
stands, he shouted nonsensical sounds when he was excited, and
it seemed as if he just about always had a rigid erection jutting in
his jeans. My mother said he was crude and complained that my
room always stank after Mike had been over. It did; he carried
around matches to light his farts.

In the back corner of the Carson's unlandscaped, broken-toy,
loose-brick, and lumber-cluttered back yard, Mike had built a
roofless two-by-four and plywood fort up on stilts, and that summer between sixth and seventh grade we slept there every Saturday and as many weeknights as my parents would allow. Sleeping
out was thrilling: you were outside all night, directly under the dis-
quieting black sky and stars, away from parental hearing and the
childhood trappings of your own room, unprotected. I would an-
ticipate one of these nights in Mike's fort all day, till I was almost
sick with excitement. I might be reading one of my mother's book-
club gothics in my frigid, air-conditioned room, or window shopping at Bassett Center with her, or mowing the lawn, but all the
time I was thinking about what would happen that night.

Mike had recognized in me a fellow obsessive wanker; that was
really what we had in common. I knew it deep down from the moment I stood on his erection. We were masturbating together in
no time, squatting with our pants down in the blazing sun beside
a dune on our desert forays, or lying on our dank sleeping bags
up in the fort. At first we stared straight ahead; soon we were staring at each other's dicks and synchronizing our ejaculations.

We'd begin by playing cards or Monopoly by flashlight, stripped to our underwear half inside our sleeping bags. Then we'd tell all the dirty jokes we knew, generally the same ones. We didn't laugh at the punch lines after the first time, but raced ahead to the next. Then Mike would start talking about whatever girl he currently wanted to fuck. (At this time, it was Heidi Reichtoffer, a hard-looking German exchange student with straight brown hair, to whom he'd never spoken a word. In fact, Heidi dated GIs.) "I really got to shoot," he'd say. "Want to jack off?"

One night late in June we were winding up a marathon Monopoly game in the early hours of the morning. I was clearly losing; I almost always lost, too preoccupied with our near nakedness and Mike's warm breath in my face as we leaned across the board to pay attention to the game.

"Let's say the loser has to do something. Whatever the winner tells him to do, he has to do it."

I nodded OK. I had a pretty good idea he wasn't going to ask me to steal a car.

Several rolls later I handed over my remaining pink and yellow bills.

"You lose. Suck my dick."

"Uh-uh! I will not!" I knew I had to feign disgust. Strangely, I felt in control, as if I had plotted every step in our acquaintance up to precisely this event, as if I had *made this happen.* "I'm not putting your dick in my mouth!"

"Look, you agreed the loser has to do what the winner says. C'mon. Hey, I'll do it to you too if you'll just do it first."

I didn't answer. He threw back his unzipped sleeping bag, a sweet odor of clean sweat and damp flannel and canvas wafting upward. We were both silent. A breeze was soughing through the willow trees surrounding the fort, and his chest tightened with goosebumps as he shivered once, his penis leaping whitely in the moonlight.

"C'mon—*please*, man."

I leaned toward him as he scooted up further out of the bag, and took him in my hand. The excitement and guilt were dizzying. This wasn't like back in the woods when I was too little to reach orgasm, when I'd had no concept of *queer*, or consequences stronger than a spanking. I took the head of his dick in my mouth, shocked at the pure physical strangeness of it, certain I was making an irrevocable mistake (*Cocksucker!*), unbearably aroused. As he held my head gently and rocked in and out of my mouth, crooning, Mike was no longer the awkward, apelike, doltish bike pal I thought I knew. Who I was now I had no idea. My cowed, conforming self-image separated from me and rose into the night sky like the ghosts leaving the wrecked roadster in "Topper."

As we drove away from the officers' housing at Fort Rucker, Alabama, I'd imagined my experiments in the forest being dispersed around the globe with my army-brat accomplices like the dismembered limbs of a corpse in a *True Detective* story. Now my underground life had reclaimed me. Nights up in the creaking fort, Mike and I dispensed with time-consuming board games and drew straws. I'd stolen a copy of *Teleny, or The Reverse of the Medal* from Bart's sock drawer, and we read aloud from its flowery descriptions of male sex, and then ordered each other to act them out. I gritted my teeth when Mike carefully entered me the first time, Wilde's purple commentary ("He pushed with all his might. The Rubicon was crossed!") before me.

Mornings, I'd wake feeling foul breathed and stained, unwilling to stay for pancakes flipped by Mike's obese Jehovah's Witness mom. He bounded up cheerfully; I couldn't wait to slink home and shower, brushing my teeth rigorously and gargling with Listerine. I'd avoid Mike for several days and flinch at his salacious monologues when we next went out riding. "*Hedda* likes you!" he'd shout over his shoulder, laughing. "Heada' my *dick!*"

With the return of my double life, I began to notice myself critically in the mirror. Up till now I'd parted my hair on the side and swooped my bangs across my forehead with HisSpray, believing implicitly my mother's assurance that I was a very handsome boy. Now the taunts of Dina Potter and her crew of furies rang true. I was an ugly, spotty fairy. I walked, ran, and threw like a girl. And I was pudgy. I had round cheeks and my mother bought me husky-size jeans. If I reached for the last cinnamon roll at breakfast, my brother and father would turn and mouth, "Chipmunk cheeks!" I had seen from Karl Brooks's example that being overweight could push you over the line into public scapegoat and acknowledged queer, and I determined to shed my baby fat before September.

I accompanied my mother on her weekly visit to the commissary at Fort Bliss. As we glided down the air-conditioned aisles I looked skittishly away from the sunburnt and muscular young GIs and their childish, pregnant wives pushing carts stacked with formula and disposable diapers, six-packs of Coors, and cartons of cigarettes. I scanned the shelves anxiously till I spotted them: box upon box of powdered Carnation Slender decorated with svelte women in swimsuits and laughing athletic men in tennis shorts. On the individual packets, a torrent of pink or brown or white liquid cascaded into a tall sundae glass. You drank it, and you became slim. I reached past the tired-looking, medicinal cans of Metrecal, which my father drank from time to time, and selected several cartons of Chocolate Royale, Rich Vanilla, and Strawberry Supreme.

"Honey, you're going to starve! Just have one slice of pizza," my mom would say at dinner, shaking her head.

"I'll eat his share," said Bart, while I gurgled the chalky dregs of my Strawberry Supreme through the straw and sped out the back door.

"Why don't you just move in with Mike?" my father yelled.

I'd tell myself that each time with Mike would be the last, but a few hours later I'd be locked in the bathroom feverishly masturbating as I replayed our last encounter, or imagined what we might try next.

Like some gothic secret that wouldn't stay bricked in, smirking references to homosexuality leapt out at me from magazine covers, my mother's latest Harold Robbins potboiler, and the "Tonight Show." Every night Johnny would make a smug joke about Fire Island, in my mind a sort of Gilligan's Island where all the huts were beauty parlors, since according to Johnny the place was jammed with nothing but hairdressers. Then Truman Capote would high-step out like a trained bear cub, slapping Johnny's hand and baby talking for fifteen minutes while I squirmed with embarrassment and my father fumed, "They ought to just shoot him."

The nights I didn't spend at Mike's, I often babysat for the young couples who ran around with my Aunt Janet and her husband. All the couples but Janet and Chris had new babies, and the work was easy, since most of the time the baby was already put down when I arrived and I spent the long evenings scanning trashy novels for sex scenes and masturbating with my face in a pair of Tip's or Dave's jockey shorts fished out of the hamper. The husbands were all good looking, boyish jocks who made a point of offering me a Coors and leaving me the latest *Playboy* on the coffee table. Then they'd have to drive me home at 2:00 A.M., drunk, flushed, and horny from flirting with each other's wives.

Tip, whose tow-headed infant Shelly screamed in my face for a solid hour before collapsing with her bottle while I sang her most of *The White Album,* was a hulking twenty-four-year-old baseball jock with big white teeth, a thick reddish-blond mustache, and massive arms heavily furred with platinum hair. Six years back he'd have been beating the shit out of me, but now he was roaring down the deserted interstate with me in his white Mustang, thighs spread wide, one hand on the bottom of the steering wheel, offering me a joint.

"What are you now, thirteen? Shit, girls today, I bet you get more pussy than me."

This was so ludicrously off-base I could make no answer, but that was OK. Like Mike, Tip liked to talk about sex. It was hell in that shithole 'nam, he told me, but the hooch maids could give you a blowjob that felt like your brains were being yanked out the end of your dick. "Know what I mean?"

I knew. I glanced out of the corner of my eye at the bulge in his white jeans, and stared straight ahead.

"My you've gotten so slender," my mother said, without irony. "But honey, those bangs! You look like Veronica Lake!" She reached to smooth my hair back with a worried look. I'd starved myself slim over the summer, somehow still managing to grow taller, and I'd fought and sulked to be allowed to keep my hair longer. We drove to the PX and Sears for new school clothes, and I chose tight, flared slacks, Day-Glo socks, and paisley shirts. The signature piece of my new look was a gold Nehru shirt with a glass-jeweled medallion on a large gold chain. I thought I looked like Dickie Smothers, but my brother howled and said, "Whoa, *Sammy,* my main man!" Terry Swain, a twice-flunked eighth-grade hood who'd been in the D-home for strong-arm robbery, pushed back his greasy hair and whistled as I walked briskly across the blacktop on the first day of school, my neck chafing against the stiff Nehru collar, peace medallion banging against my chest. "She's got a new figure!" he yelled after me.

"I think Brenda Smalley wants to go steady with me." I detailed the heady first few weeks of seventh grade in my diary with determined optimism. "Mike came up to me in the hall and said something dumb. He's so immature."

My homeroom teacher, Miss Boyd, liked me, and wrote long, appreciative margin notes on the essays and stories I turned in. I was briefly celebrated for my vacation memoir, "The Dog Who Ate Beans," about a long family car trip to City of Rocks, New Mexico with a flatulent dachshund, which was read aloud to all the seventh-grade English classes. This high profile backfired when Miss Boyd read one of my Poe-inspired gothic tales to 7-C, and was interrupted by several of my PE persecutors shouting out, "He's a *fag!*" The class erupted in debate as to whether or not I truly was a fag, and Miss Boyd delivered a tearful lecture on the cruelty of adolescents, then doled out a nasty homework assignment in the hated grammar text. Gwen Hindemuth, my steady of that week, reported all this to me at lunch, promising to stand by me through the scandal, and then breaking up with me by note that afternoon. My new persona was already wearing thin.

We had to dress out now for gym, and my head would ache from the strain of staring straight at my feet or into my locker while all around me, bumping and shoving in the narrow space between the waterlogged, sticky benches, sweat-drenched boys yanked off torn blue gym shorts and clenched, shocking, eggshell white buttocks flashed dangerously at me from every direction. Bigger, more developed guys from the eighth-grade football team stalked around flipping their half-hard penises and smirking, waiting to catch you looking: *Whyn't you suck this for me?* Coach Brown, a disturbingly attractive younger man with a lean, taut body and cold gray-blue eyes, sat in his glassed-in office, hairy legs up on his desk, scowling out at us, occasionally pretending to make some marks in a grade book. If you tried to rush through or skip the tense, crowded shower enclosure, he'd be up at the window yelling, "Barkley! You call that a shower? Get those panties off and get back in there before I come out and soap your pussy myself!"

The mumbled epithets I spent my days trying to avoid operated on one level, and had to do solely with bullying and the revenge of the stupid, who I could put in their place during the other six periods of the day. It was a practical, if formidable problem, trying not to get beat up or socially ostracized; it was a kind of tag or hide and seek. My sense of injustice at being called a fag for hating sports was genuine. I went to parties and went steady and broke up with girls. For the constant, hot undercurrent of physical desire that kept me terrified lest an erection give me away in the rank, tantalizing proximity of the locker room, that drove me to my knees before the very worst of my oppressors in the secret hours of the night, I had no words.

I'd figured that the start of classes and fall weather would separate me from Mike. We didn't hang out together at school, and sleeping over was kid stuff. But two things happened that fall: My father was ordered to Germany for two years and we stayed behind, and my brother Bart had a serious motorcycle accident and was in the hospital across town for several months. My mother came home from teaching school to pick up my little brother and then rushed back out to visit Bart every night, leaving me alone in the house for hours. Mike would be at the door, or tapping at my bedroom window, moments after she backed out of the driveway.

We used the garage. One side was furnished with a rug, a TV set, and an old brown sectional couch with strings of metallic thread hanging from it like Christmas tinsel. We used the TV for light, syndicated episodes of "The Addams Family" and "The Munsters" murmuring in the background, amid the odors of car exhaust and lawn mower. Sometimes we'd play strip poker and suck each other off. Often we improvised new scenarios. One of us might be stripped, blindfolded, and tied spread-eagled against the wall with ropes looped over the open rafters, while the other remained clothed, quietly detailing how we'd reached this moment, and what was going to happen next, dry mouthed and shaking with awe at our own imaginations. I might have to stand atop an old desk for ten minutes by the clock, bent over holding my ankles, while Mike inspected my ass, spreading the cheeks, slapping the backs of my legs with a ruler. Sometimes Mike would be a burglar armed with a toy pistol who'd break in and make sexual demands at gunpoint.

Later, I'd be sitting on the orange-flowered couch in the den reading, legs still weak, my butt slick with Vaseline and throbbing, when my mother came home. "I worry about leaving you along so much, sweetheart. Why don't you have one of your friends over?"

In January, Mike's chronically unemployed father got a job offer in Abilene, and two weeks later, the Carson's house sat empty, a *For Sale* sign stuck in the weed-covered lawn. Just as suddenly as he'd dropped into my life, Mike was gone. I was stunned by my unforeseen reprieve; the steaming cracks in the earth closed up, and the ground trembled quietly. The following week I held hands with Fleur Patton at a party and asked her to go steady, but she declined in an enigmatic note.

One clear, cold March day I trudged up the short flight of steps from the subterranean locker room to the gravel school-yard, relieved as always to have made it through one more PE period relatively unscathed. We'd been playing basketball, and while appearing to run after the ball wholeheartedly, I'd managed to avoid contact with it completely, except for once when someone slammed it into the back of my head. Down in the changing area I'd pulled my clothes on without drying off much and then stood at the sink a little longer than usual getting my hair parted just right, a mistake. Anyone paying too much attention to his hair or just standing in front of the spotty mirror too long risked trouble. I knew I'd stepped over the line when I caught Ricky Bradshaw's glance in the mirror as I combed my bangs across my forehead a second time, and he looked hurriedly away and spit noisily on the floor in disgust. Ricky was one of those jocks who practically wept if his team lost, and he despised me for sidestepping the ball at crucial junctures, as if I were fumbling it on purpose. "You could've had that one, asshole!" he'd shout at me. I knew he'd jump at the chance to knock me down and kick me.

I was still standing there in the gravel when a hand snaked around the back of my head, fingers running roughly through my damp hair. "You sure got your hair fixed real nice, Barkley. Makes me want to mess it up." It was Bradshaw.

"Hey, cut it out! You're not funny!" My own words rang mock-ingly back at me in a lispy, screechy fag voice. Or was that me too? I was surrounded by jeering boys, somebody's arm around my neck in a chokehold, lifting me off my feet. Hand after hand shot out and ran through my hair; lips smacked inches from my face with exaggerated kissing sounds. "Hey, he needs a hair treatment!" someone yelled, and then they were spitting on my hair and rub-bing it in. I lost my balance, tossed from one set of gripping arms to another like some awkward Martha Graham performance. All the fit, sinewy boys I'd feared and craved surrounded me, pawing, pinching, jabbing, and roughly caressing my head, their faces, lips, open mouths livid and up close. I was turning dizzily, clinging to my smart-boy dignity, *Cut it out!*—but the ground had split open and the other me spilled through. I wondered if I would cry. My dick was hard. Terry Swain's evil, beautiful face shoved impossibly close, his lips almost touching mine. He hawked and spit. "Fucking fag!"

The bell for fourth period rang. I picked myself up and wiped the blood from my skinned palms on my pants, tucked my ripped shirt back in, and walked into the biology lab, climbing onto a stool next to my table mate, who pretended not to notice my spittle-covered hair poking out all askew. I didn't go home till lunchtime, and I didn't cry till I got there. I didn't have sex with a man again till college.

Evesham
Encounter

DAVID WATMOUGH

I am so pissed off with revisionism that I have decided to go ahead and tell this story about Ken and me which occurred way back in 1952. Yes, well over forty years ago (depends when you read this, of course) and when we were both in our early twenties. I might also add for the benefit of the children of our kind that Stonewall was as futuristically remote as a moon landing, AIDS was still an unrealized nightmare belonging only to the imaginations of a few revenge-crazed Christians, while Gay Rights was as remote as public Gay Loathing was acceptable and commonplace. And yet . . . And yet . . . Well, hear my tale. . . .

One thing in common then with my current life in the Northwest of the American continent was the ubiquity of green fields and gray rain—even in the lush of summer when one was least expecting it. It was just like that on the June afternoon after we left Worcester and discovered a narrow road (perhaps broad lane would be more accurate in that English context) leading vaguely in the direction of the major highway we hoped would eventually, if circuitously, bring us to Oxford. Suddenly we were drenched to the skin to the tune of thunder and the savagery of lightning.

As the water soaked down to cool young flesh, flattened hair, and short pants, so that we both bulged prominently at our flies above cold wet knees, we laughed out loud and blew the spray from each other's noses. The leafy lane with its verge of tall cow parsley was deserted, for it was lunchtime. Not that we two would

have cared if it had been Times Square or Piccadilly Circus, for we
were young men with futures. More than that. We were in love.

This is not exactly a romantic tale but that fact was important.
For our being in love, the state of our hormones and the romantic
excitement, now over a year old, was the all-encompassing con-
stituent of our youthfully insouciant lives. There was only balm in
Gilead for Davey and Ken. No mean serpent in the Eden that
their ardor had created. I don't know what prompted it. Perhaps
the sudden cessation of the pelting rain coinciding with a bright
gleam between the charcoal frown of cloud. Anyway, without even
a glance in front or behind down the already steaming, sun-
brushed yellow road surface, we both dropped our knapsacks and
embraced. The cool of raindrops still dripping from hair and eyebrows soon melted in the heat of our joined flesh as with closed
eyes, first our lips and then our tongues conjoined in that sense of
unity we so craved.

I mention the shut eyes because if they'd been open we could
hardly have failed to see the vehicle approaching. What is more
surprising perhaps, is that we didn't hear anything for when the
car did draw up to us and jerk to a halt it proved to be an angular-
shaped auto of ancient vintage with an engine that chugged like a
tractor. But I guess the roar of lust unfurling in the recesses of our
eardrums drowned out the motor, the creaking bodywork, and
the eventual squeal of primitive brakes. If that vision was undoubt-
edly surprising as it ruptured our preoccupation, it was nothing
compared to what happened next.

At the wheel of the car sat a strange apparition. Sitting bolt upright in the manner of Dowager Queen Mary was a woman dressed
in a black silk dress that disappeared from sight below the car
door. The only relief from this atramentous sea was a pair of white
kid gloves and it was a hand enclosed by one of these that waved
imperiously in our direction, indicating that we draw near.

It was only then I realized that both of us, now over a week on
the roads of Britain, had instinctively drawn up our arms and indi-
cated by extended thumbs that we were seeking to hitch a lift. Self-
consciously lowering our arms as we disengaged from our sponta-
neous embrace we advanced toward the imperious figure driving
what I now saw to be a Daimler limousine dating, I estimated,
from the late 1920s. There was not a curve to any aspect of its
shape above the wheels; the running board was massive and the

whitened spare wheel carried on the vehicle's side. But of infinitely greater interest than the antique car was the young man who sat in the far side of the vehicle. He appeared to be in his midteens and wore a canary colored shirt with short sleeves below a rather pretty face, which itself was crowned with a mass of curls of a light auburn hue which distinctly looked as if it had been given some external help to produce its distinctive effect. His lips, too, were almost preternaturally pink.

The stately chauffeur now lowered her window slowly to address us. "My son has suggested that you wish to be driven somewhere—and in our car." The voice was crisp, well modulated, and obviously used to command. However, in light of what its owner must have recently observed as we stood in our tight clinch, it was remarkably friendly.

We both started to explain our direction at the same time. Then I faltered and let Ken take over. It had been our experience since leaving my parents' house in Cornwall that Ken's classless American accent was much more effective for hitchhiking than mine. That's to say it had been for the lorry drivers, van owners, and general road users (all of them men) that we had hitherto successfully flagged down.

"I presume you are heading toward Evesham for that is the direction in which we are going."

"That would be perfect, ma'am," said Ken. "For we are aiming eventually for Oxford but there's no hurry."

"Ambrose had suggested you were probably students at that university," she informed us. "Your attitudes did not convey a local flavor."

For the first time her passenger spoke up. "They are probably wet and uncomfortable, Mother. Would it not be sensible to invite them into the car and out of the rain?"

It had quite obviously stopped raining for the clouds had now fully parted, the sun beat down, and wisps of steam were rising not just from the road surface but from parts of our clothing as well as from the foxgloves and cow parsley and the intermittent clumps of sedge grass forming the jungle of vegetation in the verge.

"That is precisely why I brought the Daimler to a halt, Ambrose, if you remember. Now put those bundles beside you in the boot, take off your outer things and put them in there also. And then climb in behind us. Ambrose will help you."

I was about to protest that we could heed her bidding unaided but her son was already out on his side and waving a key. He leapt to the car's trunk and stood awaiting us as we gathered up our discarded knapsacks. That was the first time I had to really give him the once over. Now I have already stressed that Ken and I were madly in love and could have added that we had sex at least twice a day if opportunity presented itself and fucked like bunnies (as the expression has it) when we did so. But that didn't make either of us candidates for white canes or seeing-eye dogs. One of the joys of our togetherness was the discovery that we had similar tastes in so many respects—and that included the male portion of the human race.

As we both bent to push our knapsacks into the less than spacious compartment of the trunk we took time out to wink at each other—and to convey unspokenly, the thought that Master Ambrose could very easily share our sexual persuasion.

Once installed in the back seat of the Daimler we took advantage of its relative smallness to press our bare knees together in gay solidarity. Nor did we move them when Ambrose put his arm along the back of his mother's seat and half turned to address us more easily as our driver accelerated to a full twenty miles an hour—a speed she didn't exceed for the time we spent in her vehicle.

I have no doubt that Ambrose observed our propinquity—then from his mother's earlier remark I thought he must have a pretty fair idea of the score and that from him at least, there was no crying reason for an excess of prudence. Mind you, if his Mama had taken her eyes from being glued to the road ahead and attempted to observe us, either might have made some small gesture of propriety. But Madame was not the kind of lady who would have ever entertained the notion of neglect toward her duties as a driver along the King's Highway, which had just become the Queen's Highway by virtue of the death of King George VI. Instead she addressed us—albeit with disconcerting directness—as to our relationship. "You are chums, I take it? Or is the relationship closer?"

A small silence fell over the Daimler's interior. I broke it. "I beg your pardon?" I croaked.

A hand waved fractionally before returning to the ebony steering wheel. "Hardly brothers—cousins perhaps?"

"Mother," her son expostulated. "They don't sound at all alike.

The tall one sounds—well, from overseas. The other . . . more—more like ourselves."

"It will not have been the first time that members of a family have emigrated and left siblings behind. The whole Empire is criss-crossed by such family ties. You have only to think of your own family and Uncle Marmaduke."

Young Ambrose looked sulky. "Only the other day you were instructing me NOT to think of Uncle Marmaduke."

"The context was wholly other. I am not now thinking of those who departed our shores for devious reasons."

"Perhaps I can help you," put in Ken amiably. "I do not come from the Empire but California. My family originated in Scotland but, frankly, I haven't a clue why they decided to cross the Atlantic."

"There!" expostulated Ambrose. "I knew he was a Yank! Didn't I tell you so, Mummy? When—when they were standing there, huddled from the rain?"

In spite of myself a hiss of relief escaped my throat. Somehow I didn't feel the confines of the ambling Daimler suitable for gay confessions with perfect strangers. Rather rarefied ones at that. Ken, I think was of similar mind. At any rate, he suddenly reached out and brushed Ambrose's flipper.

"By the way, we haven't even introduced ourselves to you good people. I am Ken Bradley of San Marino and this is my Cornish friend, Davey Bryant. We met at the Sorbonne and are now vacationing together before I have to return to Stanford and start work on my Ph.D."

I suddenly felt desperately sad. A tear trickled down my cheek and in my misery I saw Ambrose curiously charting its progress. The only cloud in my life at that time was the thought of Ken's incipient departure—though I had already started to plan how I would join him in the Golden State, as I now proudly called my future home. But it was a horrible subject, one I refused to contemplate on this, our protracted honeymoon. And now Ken had inadvertently opened the wound. I listened to the rest of them as if I was sitting as far away as the moon. "And our name is Hetherington-Gore. I'm Ambrose, of course. And you are being driven by my mother, Lady Gertrude Hetherington-Gore, who is so grand that she will not let me take the wheel when she is present . . . I say, are you feeling all right?"

It was several seconds before I realized it was me being addressed.

"Oh, I'm all right. It's just that you reminded me of things I don't want to think about."

I think Ken thought he was pouring oil or just taking the heat off me and my discomfort. But he just sounded brash and oh, so American!

"Lady Gertrude—my goodness, I can't wait till I get home to tell my mother! She'll be so thrilled!"

The second reference to his departure didn't help me a bit. I knew I was in danger of flooding with tears. I sniffed hard. "Does—does that make you something, too, Ambrose? Are you an Earl or an Hon. or one of those things?"

In my heart I was thinking—in spite of my distress, or maybe because of it—you should be at least 'Your Ladyship' with those pouty pink lips and that waggly wrist! Even so, I was quite surprised by his reply.

"My mother thinks I'm a Bolshie. I refuse to use all that title stuff. Ambrose Hetherington-Gore is already too much of a mouthful. Now I'm eighteen and finished with Harrow I can bloody well please myself!"

A long-lashed lid came down in a wink over his left eye. "My friends call me Amber!"

I thought for a moment that Lady Gertrude had increased speed, but when I craned forward to look I saw it was only my imagination. Her mind was not on speed but on her son. We were to learn that it was rarely anywhere else—although it did not always appear that way when she addressed this or that.

"I am fascinated by your Californian provenance, young man. That would be down the road from British Columbia, would it not?"

Ken was far too polite to smile. "That's one way of putting it, ma'am."

I felt I'd scream if he trotted out that phony "ma'am" once more. He'd never used it from the first day I'd met him. I hated to think he was being influenced by the English caste system.

"I ask because Ambrose has a sister in that colony."

"Mother, it ceased to be a colony God knows how long ago!"

"I'm sure He does. But then I have never claimed to be God."

"You could have fooled me." Only he said that, *sotto voce* in a pseudo-American accent, looking at us, a wicked smile about those cupid lips. I don't think she heard him. At least she wasn't going to admit it. Instead she continued with her interrogation of my lover.

"I have examined maps. Both border the Pacific, I gather. I presume they are joined by roads?"

"And by two states, my lady. Oregon and Washington. It is some thousand miles, I believe, between them."

I thought he sounded like a fucking butler. Seen too many British movies, I concluded sourly.

"Am I not correct in thinking that is virtually next door by your North American standards of giganticism?"

Ken paused, obviously thinking of past conversations with me, I concluded ruefully.

"It is hard to make the transfer from one continent to the other. The differences that prevail are so radical."

Christ! He was beginning to even sound like her!

"Quite,"said Lady Gertrude. "Quite."

At which very moment we entered another downpour, even heavier, if possible, than the one that had caught us standing in it. The hiss of the rain on the ground and the rat-a-tat-tat on the roof of the car put an end to any semblance of conversation. In fact our chauffeur almost barked her next words. I was relieved to hear that they were addressed to her son.

"Ambrose, the windscreen wipers!"

With that her offspring whipped his arm off the back of the seat and started to physically turn both wipers manually in each direction.

"The mechanism is broken down and my mother refuses to have them mend it," he explained loudly.

"The vital parts are being transported," Lady Gertrude shouted enigmatically. "But you see the reason why I will not let him drive the machine. I do not have the dexterity to do what he is doing now, and it would be quite impossible—given the vicissitudes of our British weather—for either to drive solo."

So there was silence in the chugging Daimler for the next portion of miles. I was glad. I didn't like feeling irritated with my darling Ken. It made me feel disloyal—the supreme vice for me. Instead I took the initiative with a little more knee play and we "embraced" with our entwined fingers. I even daringly disengaged digits at one point to brush his rain-moistened crotch. We were below the potential theater of vision should either front-seat occupant have glanced back, but prudence was certainly not high in my considerations. Anyway, they were both too preoccupied with their several tasks to have risked even momentarily turning around.

Then once more we were back in sunshine. Ambrose ceased his to-and-fro activities, and we still steadily trundled forward at twenty miles per hour. I had just time to glance down fondly at my satisfying efforts to stir my lover into an encouraging hard-on when our driver reinitiated conversation.

She ignored the interruption by the weather entirely. "Do your people have much land? You don't call them estates, do you? Ranch is the term out there, is it not?"

"My father is a doctor—orthopedics. Lots of his patients are movie stars." (I think he added the rider for "Amber" rather than Mumsey.)

"A pity," commented Lady Gertrude.

"I'm sorry. I'm in no way responsible for his profession."

Bully for him, I thought. That was more like my real Ken!

"I was merely referring to his lack of acreage to support livestock. Ambrose has neither knowledge nor ability for other than basic animal husbandry. There he is truly the son of his late father. Sir Perceval knew the Hereford stud book like the back of his hand but could never make out the schedules in his Bradshaw on those rare occasions we had to take a train to London. The man died smelling of cow."

"My mother would like me to join up with my sister, Hermione, in some God-forsaken spot named Williams Lake. My brother-in-law has settled there and rides herd over three thousand steers— or steers herds over three thousand rides—I have difficulty in making out what sister Hereby is saying in her ill-written letters."

"My son-in-law is some kind of Cecil and has joined members of his family who have found God in conjunction with some excellent cattle country in those parts. It would be perfect for my Ambrose. Especially as he repudiates all talk of the Varsity. A terrain of vast spaces—capable of absorbing even his most arcane appetites. It is the only alternative."

She stressed the word "arcane" so heavily I decided I must look it up as soon as I got chance. Perhaps it meant something deliciously filthy.

"I have no desire to travel farther than the snug at the Feathers in Ludlow," her offspring said sullenly. "I am a home boy."

"Not the famous Feathers? The hotel with all the marvelous half-timbered work?" I inquired—knowing bloody well that it must be.

"What is a snug?" asked Ken, in honest ignorance.

Lady Gertrude answered us in one combined stroke. "An ancient hostelry with one smoky room serving nowadays as a center for dissolute American servicemen who are rendered lascivious from idleness. My son is rarely out of the establishment and that one room, and his patronage of the place and its clientele is distinctly unhealthy. Not least for a minor as far as the law is concerned."

Ken responded with more vigor than I would have liked. Plans were dimly formulating in my head and a precipitate discharge from the Daimler was not among them.

"Lascivious behavior, Lady Gertrude, might have the desire to leave foreign lands as its basis. Homesickness, that is."

"Doubtless they are bored and anxious to depart our beloved Vale of Evesham and return to their own wilderness."

"They are not all from the open range, Mother. Some are city sophisticates from New York and Boston." Ambrose paused for a moment, before quickly flashing me a smile. "And from Los Angeles," he added.

"I do not doubt you should know," his mother said. Her voice still plangent with disapproval. "I understand you have addressed most of them at one time or other. The city slickers and the country boys both. Your appetites seem omnivorous according to that landlord Finch."

"Is village gossip the bane of life in California as it is in the bloody Vale of Evesham?" Ambrose inquired sniffily of Ken, his mood quite changed.

I saw I must rescue the conversation, which was threatening to have dire implications beyond the snide shots between mother and son if left to its own dangerous devices.

"It most certainly is in the parish of St. Keverne," I contributed sharply. "It's why I'm so anxious to leave the place which has, after all, known my family for a thousand years. It has brought about everything from divorce to suicide in our village, and mother says it is now threatening to wreck the Women's Institute."

I didn't dare look around for I knew that Ken must be staring incredulously at me. Only the night before I'd told him that we could trace the Bryant family back at least a couple of centuries since they'd made the epic trip forty miles north up the Atlantic coast from St. Agnes. In any case my mother was a Londoner who had gone as a young bride to the Duchy. But what is a drop of exaggeration when the stakes are so high? I Cornishly ask. And I truly believed that young Ambrose might easily explode if his mother continued to pressure him over his "arcane" activities at the Feathers when his working hours of animal husbandry were over.

But inadvertently I touched a tender spot with Her Ladyship. "Women's Institute? Did you say the Women's Institute?"

It was hardly possible within the confines of that snail-crawling Daimler that she could have confused my words with any other— but I seized upon hers with the speed of a weasel about to dispatch a rabbit.

"I did indeed, Lady Gertrude. I did indeed." (Repetition was seemingly catching!) "Mother has run the organization for many years."

"Then she is a jam maker? And puts up her own fruit, too, I'll be bound!" Enthusiasm—in the guise of an almost girlish tremulousness—now occupied her voice.

This was safer terrain. I longed to encourage her. "Mother much prefers the Institute to the Mothers' Union—of which she is also the local president." (And for good measure.) "She is also Commissioner for the North Cornwall Girl Guides and Honorary President of the Business and Professional Cornishwomen's Association—but nothing equals the jolly old Women's Institute for her."

I paused. Not so much for breath but because I had momentarily run out of invention. It was Ambrose who took up the slack.

"I love the W.I., too. Ask Mother about my darling pear chutney and my delish apple and quince marmalade. Lady Hewitt swears it the best she's ever tasted and says that if only I'd agree to market it would put me on the map. It would also put the Vale of Evesham on the map."

"I was not aware that it had ever left it, darling," his mother remonstrated. "Then we must never forget that Dotty Hewitt started life as the rather ugly daughter of Gigantic Groceries and has always sought to excel in her daddy's eyes. The misfortune of those foxy Welsh provisioners, the Hewitts, was to have just the one child. Sometimes I think mine was to have two."

I held my breath. Any second, I thought, the atmosphere would explode with filial rebellion for such hard taunts. But mercifully our driver had decided upon something of a conciliatory mood.

"On the other hand, Ambrose, darling, our current W.I. President is right. You do throw the most masterful confections. It is one thing you inherit directly from me and mine. Your father did not know Cumberland sauce from plum jam. Or my lemon curd from sheep-maggot ointment which I once saw him apply to his toast."

Ambrose seemed mollified. At least, the sides of his temples were not working as angrily as they were a few minutes earlier. "And my greengage jam, Mother ? Or my crabapple jelly? Is there better in the whole wide world?"

"I do not believe so. Not since that of your grandmother, the Dowager Marchioness. It was said at the court of King Edward that she parted her legs more freely than she parted with her recipe for greengage jam. I have always felt that has characterized the spirit of the Vale of Evesham's Women's Institute from day one."

"One must never forget our good fortune in belonging to the Vale, Mother. For generations we have been privileged to enjoy the finest fruit in the kingdom. Kent pales in comparison—in spite of its pretentious claims to be the 'Garden of England.'" The insincerity dripped from his words.

"Have you always had a penchant for fruit?" I asked wickedly.

But Ambrose, prematurely sophisticated though he might seem, was apparently unaware of the gay allusion. "We have the most marvelous orchards. Full of ancient fruit trees and exotic things like mulberry trees and medlars."

Master Ambrose with the long lashes himself seemed pretty exotic to me as we drove through the heart of the English shires—but of course we were on different wavelengths at that moment.

So was Lady Gertrude. "A brilliant idea occurs to me! We can make a fine old slaughter of birds with just one stone. Ambrose can show off our famous orchard while I can talk to Mr. California about certain matters over which I would like his advice and perhaps his assistance. I have decided, dear boys, to break with conven-

tion and invite the two of you to be our guests at Badely Grange.
Now does that not satisfy you, child? Was it not what you wanted all
along?"

Her son paused before replying. Their conversations seemed
very well honed—each knowing the pitfalls the other could lay. "I
did say, Mother, as we saw them huddled in the rain that they
might care to come home and get dry. I also might have added
that it would be a pleasure for me to talk to people closer to my
own age for a change. But you obviously have a plan now of your
own. Perhaps at this juncture we had better ask them whether
they have some, too."

I was about to prevaricate. Not because I had some real excuse
as to why we should continue our hitchhiking progress but because I am inveterately cautious. Not that it mattered. Ken was in
there instantly, expressing his enthusiasm to visit what he obviously took to be one of the "Stately Homes of England." "We'd
love to, Lady Gertrude. And I would certainly love to take Ambrose's recipes back to Mother. And give you any advice about the
United States that I can. By the way, please call me Ken, like everyone else. As a matter of fact the only 'Mr. California' I know is an
Afghan hound who wins awards at our local dog shows."

"Well, I certainly would not wish to imply I saw anything canine
in your character, young man. To the contrary—I find you open,
articulate, and well mannered. I wish that our British youth were
of similar disposition. Ambrose is a polite child but he is inclined
to be far too devious. Harrow has not helped."

"That is because you are always cross-examining me, Mother. I
would yield more if I were pressured less."

Again I thought it time I enter the arena with oil for potentially
troubled waters. "We would most certainly love to see Badely
Grange, Your Ladyship. I believe I've read of it in Naythorpe's *History of Country Homes*,"—a title I invented that very moment.

"Then that is settled," our driver announced. "Ambrose will
lend you outer garments while yours are drying and after a turn in
the gardens and orchard we will take tea. We do not dress for dinner in these austere times so there will be no problem for either
of you there. I presume you will be our guests overnight and my
son will put you on the Oxford road bright and early tomorrow
morning."

I was still digesting the implications of all that assumption when we suddenly swung from the lane onto what was hardly more than a refined cart track leading after fifty yards or so to wrought-iron gates and a mellow red tall brick wall.

What lay the other side I can only describe as an architectural gem in the most blithely congruous of settings. The softly weathered brick of a seventeenth-century manor house glowed rutilant in the afternoon sun (the rains clouds now utterly fled), and the caressed and cultivated park that lipped the long, leaded windows provided a verdant mantle along its western facade. I'm not good at verbally coping with things like beautiful views: want to say something cynical or at least smart-ass. I kept thinking of National Trust calendars of noble English mansions or ads for such in the glossy magazine, *Country Life.* I often regret the loss of innocence and the advent of stupid self-consciousness.

In the event it was as well I fought against some dumb wise-crack and kept my mouth firmly shut. For Ken came up with the perfect response—perfect, that is, for someone sitting in a car next to the Lady Gertrude and her fey son, the Honorable Ambrose Hetherington-Gore ("'Amber' to my friends").

"Living in such a paradise as this must be a great challenge to one's character. Not to be superior thinking—on the other hand, not to take it for granted. To treat beauty with respect, even though seen on a day-to-day basis."

"They are exactly my sentiments, Kenneth," our soon-to-be-hostess replied. "I am afraid that although Ambrose handles the first hurdle well enough, he is all too inclined to fail the second challenge. He might be living in a crofter's cottage as far as that goes."

"Mother, I have always had reverence for the Grange as our family inheritance. In fact it isn't me who wants me to leave now. I love this place even if I don't hoo and ha over it like an estate agent."

"I am dying to see the medlar trees," I interjected wildly. "I don't think I have ever seen one in its natural habitat."

"Nor I a mulberry," added Ken valiantly.

I flashed him a grateful glance.

"It would be just smashing if we could see the more ancient trees," I added. "I imagine they were already saplings during the Civil War."

"The Grange was Royalist, of course," Lady Gertrude informed us. "It is reputed that King Charles the First was succored by our greengage plums. The Roundheads pilfered our apples and it is said they suffered colic in result and that was a small contribution to our victory at the Battle of Marlborough in sixteen forty-two. If we only had had enough unripe plums and green apples I am sure we would have won the war."

"Mother is an amateur historian," her son explained—I swear about to add a rider as to her inadequacies in that field. But my Ken was now fully in form.

"How lucky we are then! Lady Gertrude, can we beg you to escort us and bring the past alive for us. It is something I will never forget as long as I live—just as I will never forget the absolute grace of this ancestral home!"

It was fortuitous that even as he spoke, Her Ladyship applied the brakes, relaxed back from the steering wheel, and put the tall gear stick into neutral as the car halted on the sandstone curve of the drive, just a few feet from what I presumed was the front door. Ken was out before she had time to reply, and opening her door, held it so for her exit as he bowed deeply. I have never seen him act so campily and I have never loved him more than at that deliciously exaggerated moment.

In the open air the owner of Badely Grange took on a different aspect than when cooped in the confines of the ancient Daimler. She was considerably taller than I had estimated and her spine evidenced no suspicion of a curve once she stood there in thin angularity, her unfashionably long black dress wafting gently about her gaunt figure.

Now also was the first time we had to study her facial features properly. They, too, could be called severe, though a smile about her faintly mustached mouth (inspired, I decided, by the proud ownership of that splendid pile of historic masonry) softened the lower half of her sun-lined visage. It was the face of a country woman, used to hours in the fresh air, in spite of the degree of gentility her blood carried. But that mouth, however currently curved in satisfaction, like the cool blue eyes that congruently sparkled at that moment, were equal evidence of an accustomed authority. No one would have mistaken her—in spite of the undistinguished dress and rustic complexion—as other than the mistress of Badely Grange.

These reflections on my part, however, were abruptly sidetracked by the action and utterance of her son who mysteriously materialized at my side, grabbed my hand, and tugged suppliantly at it. "Now, Davey, why don't you come with me to see Tinker, my pony, while my mother shows Ken the kitchens and those recipes? Besides, he's probably sick of horses, living in California. Then we can meet up by the paddock gate and enter the orchards together. Please!"

I was given no time to debate the matter—even to obey my primary instinct to stick with Ken at all costs. It was he who answered on my behalf. "Why don't you do that, Davey? Then Lady Gertrude and I can get the domestic details out of the way. You hate that kind of stuff anyway—or so you're always telling me. Then we can do the orchards and these kind folks can show us the actual house and explain some more of its history."

I was tempted to sharply instruct him to stop sounding like some old midwestern blue rinse of the kind he'd pointed out to me in Paris in their first postwar invasion of Europe, but again I was frustrated from utterance. This time by Her Ladyship herself. "It is not often that I agree so readily with my son, boys. Then it is not often he comes up with such a sage suggestion! With these utilities out of the way we can participate in more general conversation—before and after dinner. I am an inquisitive woman. There is much I wish to know about both of you."

You haven't even mentioned Cornwall since we climbed into your bloody car, I thought. It's been all California and America! However, I didn't feel like being odd man out at that juncture and turned with a gesture of acceptance to the willowy Ambrose, whose brightly auburn curls rustled in the summer breeze, rather like his mother's dress. He was still holding my hand, I noticed.

"I am literally in your hand," I observed, "but it will be easier for you to lead and guide me, Ambrose, if it's otherwise." And as I spoke I gently disengaged, placing my hand firmly in the pocket of my khaki shorts.

He did not seem to take offense. Just tossed those curls for the umpteenth time and waved his own freed digits at Ken and his Mummy. "See you in a jiffy," he warbled, "and make Mother give you enough time to write things down properly. I don't want all of California suffering from diarrhea on my account—just because of a wrong recipe for apricot chutney!"

As we walked away from them I saw Lady Gertrude take my

lover's arm (it must have been a family habit) and leading him before the portal of the house, point up to the sundial above the fan vaulting that crowned the white doors. By his expression I knew Ken was in his element. With jutting chin and fierce jabs to indicate things, she looked in her element too.

Ambrose led me in the opposite direction around the side of the stolidly oblong house, toward various creeper-clad outbuildings which reflected different architectural styles, two or three looking much older than the Grange with even Tudor facings to their windows and squat doors. My guide must have seen my sight travel to such details for he suddenly called out, "These are the original barns and stables. Now we store our Worcester Permains and other apples in some of them, though the horses are where they've always been. Tinker's over there, by the way."

But I was already looking at the hoof-scarred paddock which formed one side of a cobbled courtyard, which had a charming dovecote at its center and what I presumed to be Tinker's stable open toward the small field, where a piebald pony munched unconcernedly at clumps of grass and sorrel. There was a good deal of shade among the outbuildings and I grew aware of just how quiet it was there in the heart of the country in the deep of a summer's afternoon.

I grew aware of other things, too. Especially as we entered the cool shade at the mouth of Tinker's stall. Ambrose changed, for instance. At least, his voice did. "Where'd you meet the Yank? I bet he's something in bed!"

At that point I felt infinitely more than twenty-four and infinitely proud of my Ken—though I wasn't about to drag our relationship down to the level of stable talk—even if the stables were sixteenth century and I was talking to an "Hon."

"I thought it was already mentioned that we met in Paris last fall." I deliberately eschewed "autumn" as too English for my recently acquired status of someone-with-an-American-lover and who was shortly to emigrate to the United States and never say "petrol," "lorry," or for that matter, "autumn" again.

In similar vein I proceeded to correct my young companion. "By the way, 'Yank' or 'Yankee' is strictly a term for those from New England." I certainly wasn't going to answer his question about bed. For one thing I was rather prudish about such things. For another, I was also determined to be prudent. Being that young he was quite likely to go tell his mother whatever I said and being that young I wasn't about to treat him as an equal in a discussion of things sexual.

I needn't have worried. He did not pursue the point, save to inform me that he knew at once we were queer when he saw us in embrace in the rain. It was soon obvious that he had not dragged me off from the others either to ply me with questions about my love life with Ken or even to see his bloody pony. What he was determined to do was unload several salient features about his teenage self.

Without hesitation he described some recent experiences of his at Harrow School. "I'm not a virgin, you know. I understand all about 'the game.' In fact I've been on it for some time."

Now he had me at a loss. I wasn't quite sure what he meant by "the game" and was about to seek some devious means of finding out when he inadvertently let me off the hook.

"Little Leicester and I have been going up to Town and landing a bit of rent to bring back to the school for ages. Then last year we branched out. Leicester has gone in for either the Coldstream or the Irish Guards. He claims they're the biggest—besides, he likes to be fucked all night and they know their way back to the barracks from Harrow without any fuss. I, on the other hand, like cock sucking a whole lot more. And instead of cruising Green Park or Buckingham Palace Road as Harry Leicester has to do, I go straight to Piccadilly Circus from school. There's only one change of tube line, you see. I know I can find all the American airmen I can handle—as it were—down there in the lavs at the Underground. Then we just nip back to school if we like each other. What's more—unlike Leicester—I don't have to pay for it. Then, when we've sucked each other off, my airmen just bugger off. And do you know those Yanks—sorry, Americans—" (he looked at me apologetically) "are so generous they often leave me whole cartons of fags called Lucky Strikes, which I give to Guy Wilberforce as I don't smoke, and some revolting chocolate called Hershey. Not a patch on Nestlé or Cadbury. But of course I don't tell them. Can't hurt a chap's feelings when you've just swallowed his seed, can you!"

I stared at him, probably looking like a village idiot as total amazement flabbed my facial muscles.

"Well can you? I mean there is such a thing as being polite which you don't just abandon because you've had sex, do you?"

I realized as I stared into those wide gray eyes amid the scrubbed, puppy features, that he was being genuinely sincere. As I struggled for words it was to discover that most of the silt of the local Avon river had mysteriously managed to insert itself in my throat. All I could manage was to croak through it. "I—I suppose so. I wouldn't know. I've never—"

That seemed to satisfy him. Ambrose continued airily, as he sat himself down on the manger of the loose box and invited me with a pat of the ancient wood to join him. "Of course I knew the two of you were queer the moment I clapped eyes on you. Even without the embrace—well, you know what it is, how we chaps recognize one another? But then, when you piled into the old Daimler and I realized that your Ken was a Yank—sorry again, old boy—bit of a habit I'm afraid—well, I got really excited. 'Cos that's what I'm looking for too; I want an American boyfriend who will take me home with him. I suppose that's what's going to happen to you two?"

That was the first time a third party had entered my hopes and fears of my future with Ken. It didn't make anything easier. In fact the notion that this feckless, sex-starved, promiscuous boy was party to my covert schemes scared me. The truth was the best that I could extract from Ken was a sort of noncommittal grunt of acceptance of the fact that I would follow in his wake as soon as humanly possible. But my secret fear remained that the minute he stepped back on his native soil he would regard me as part of the interesting package he had known in his year or so in Europe. That new horizons such as embarking on a Ph.D. might well exclude me.

It was certainly not that he'd said as much but at twenty-four my life was wracked with uncertainty. It was this that made our hitchhiking trip around England so crucial to my existence. Someone had told me—or I had read—that shared experience was the most resilient form of social cement. And I was taking the observation totally to heart. For that reason we had traveled the length and breadth of France as well as dug into every historical nook and cranny that Paris had afforded. In the twelve months we had been together, at my insistence, we had already accrued over three hundred photographic slides, given each other books with prolix dedications and carefully retained not only the programs for the plays and concerts attended but the ticket stubs, too. The shorts I was wearing Ken had given me as an Easter gift and he was wearing the expensive leather belt I had bought him at Medelio's.

The only thing he had balked at was our wearing clothes of the same cut or color. He had looked uncomfortable every time I suggested it (which was initially quite often) and he would mutter something about not looking like the "Bobbsey twins" (whoever they were).

Master Ambrose wasn't finished romping through my privacy.

"Do you think you will both end up teachers or something? Or will he just want you home to look after him. Do the cooking and all that stuff. My trouble, you see, is I'm not a brainy chap. But as you will soon see I am a pretty dab hand in the kitchen. I had a nice airman I picked up in the Feathers over to the Grange when Mumsey was away and gave him dinner. He thought I was a marvelous cook."

Ambrose swung a sandaled foot from where he perched on the manger. "The only trouble was he was normal and wouldn't let me do him. He thought I was normal too—up to the point I tried to take his thing out. That's the trouble, you see. Most people don't realize I am a queer. I'm not like you—and your Ken being American doesn't count. You know what the English are. They think cologne is enough to make a man homo!"

I was still smarting at the implication that I was so obvious. "Well, I knew what you were right away. You didn't have to wave your twinky in my direction over the car seat to let me know! In France they'd call your type a tapette."

But Ambrose sailed different waters—those unknown to a Cornish farmer's son—or even a London University graduate with a stint of gay life in Paris. He continued as if my bitchy little protest hadn't occurred and sought no explanation for "tapette."

"That's why her bloody Ladyship wants to farm me out to British Columbia and put me in the hands of that religious freak my half-witted sister has married. And why I've gone along with her up to a point. I mean I want to find an American husband in a gorgeous place like California—just like you have. But I don't want to see another cow as long as I live and Tinker out there can go to the knacker's yard for all I care! I love Badely Grange, of course, and I am crazy about bottling fruit and jam making when the time comes 'round. But I can't live on old bricks and damsons—even if Mother can.

"I tell you, Davey, this love-starved lad isn't cut out to play the Duchess of Evesham when the old girl's gone. I want my Lucky Strikes and that delish Mennen after-shave and all those deliciously circumcised wee-wees in the United States. That's not asking too much, is it? Can you help me?"

"I—I don't think I can be much help, Ambrose. I mean my own problems—"

"I'm not asking you to tell me right now. But later perhaps? I can slip into the guest room when we have all retired for the night and listen to what you and Ken have to say. I'm sure that between the two of you there'll be something to help a poor young damsel who's pining away in this godforsaken Vale of Evesham where everyone smells in greater or lesser degree of cow dung or pig shit." He put a clenched hand melodramatically to his forehead, batted those long-lashed eyes, and sighed extravagantly. "I mean Davey, what in heaven is a girl to do?"

My first thought was that I was getting the benefit of the latest movie he had seen—then that Ambrose was sufficiently the real thing not to need much by way of external props or inspiration. The third and most important notion that came to me was the implication behind his proposal for a bedtime visit. And the notion was a disturbingly erotic one. "You must give us some time to talk first between ourselves," I told him. "Then when you come we can see what we've come up with."

Ambrose was obviously delighted. He jumped down from the manger and almost dragged me from the horse barn in the direction of the kitchen garden which I could see led to the orchard which was crammed with ancient and much-gnarled trees whose trunks were furred with silvery lichen. Lady Gertrude and Ken awaited us. Her Ladyship looked pleased with herself. My lover's eyebrow was cocked enquiringly in our direction as we approached.

Both factors were soon explained.

"I am so glad you two young men have agreed to stay the night and dine with us. Ambrose will demonstrate one of his less-manly skills and go mad in the kitchen. I promise you his high-pitched screams of anger and frustration will ultimately prove worthwhile. Our man Benson is off tonight so there will be just the four of us at the Grange. We shall have a cozy time here at Badely!"

I looked up at the impressive pile of masonry which stretched as far as the eye could see along the north front. "Cozy" was the very last word that any of it evoked for me. Then I thought of her opening remark. She knew bloody well that Ken and I had had no opportunity to discuss actually staying overnight. Fortunately my little chat with her son had persuaded me to suggest doing so to my lover. And apparently he had already concurred with her proposal.

In the event things went very much as she had prophesied. We sat in her sitting room, painted in dark green, paneled in dark oak, and stuffed with heirlooms and several Stubbs paintings of horses and a family portrait she informed us was by Wright of Derby. Ambrose came and went in dizzying rapidity as he prepared dinner. And every now and then from the dim recesses of the great house we heard the shrill vents of protest she had promised.

We sat down to homemade venison pâtè, followed by jugged hare (also local) in conjunction with scarlet runner beans and new potatoes, followed in turn by peach pie and fresh cream and a wheel of Stilton cheese that a cousin of the family regularly sent from her Leicester estate.

Afterward we repaired again to Lady Gertrude's room, where she announced she had a special treat for us.

"This is an auspicious occasion," she announced, "and I am therefore going to celebrate it with something very special."

Ken and I eyed each other. We had not had long to talk after being shown our enormous bedroom with its damask-covered four-poster before being summoned downstairs again for drinks before dinner. But I had found time to describe Ambrose's outrageous conversation and his request to visit us after what I described to Ken was "lights out" in the great mansion. He had mildly disappointed me, in being highly enthusiastic over the scion of Badely's proposed visitation—but my earlier, somewhat lubricious speculation, cheered me up and persuaded me to think of Ambrose's arrival and our reception as something hopefully to chalk up as yet a further sample of shared experience which would eventually prove yet another bond uniting us.

It was in the expectancy of that that I now grinned at my lover, and in the gentle buoyancy of homemade cider before dinner and wine during it, relaxed once more in her comfortable den and awaited her surprise.

Our hostess was expatiating on the virtues of English country cooking when her son finally rejoined us permanently, flopped down in the remaining leather armchair in her sitting room, and opened his rather long legs to sprawl the more comfortably. "We mustn't be so insular, Mumsie. It really is the English besetting sin." He sighed reprovingly. "I cook these things because they are conveniently to hand. But I would love a shot at bouillabaisse or a really spiffy paella."

"I see no reason to pursue all that Latin fare. Then I do not have your interest, Ambrose, in the exotic—whether it be foreign food or flesh." With that she dismissed both the subject and her son's criticism. Without the slightest intimation of inconsistency she addressed the two of us sitting directly across from her. "Now you shall have my special treat. I have had Ambrose bring up the brandy that Great Grandpapa brought back to celebrate the victory over Bonaparte in eighteen-fourteen—Waterloo, you know.

"The marquis was a great friend of Castlereagh and got him to secure a cache of cognac from that old rogue, Talleyrand, who needed British help at all costs."

It was evident that Ken was following her words closely. "Then this doesn't date from eighteen-fourteen? Presumably a little later—after the Congress of Vienna in the June of eighteen-fifteen, if I recall correctly."

For me it was even more evident that my lover had made a hit of major proportions with Lady Gertrude. No question now of her bickering with him and his mild criticism as she had in response to her son's strictures over English culinary chauvinism.

"Yes indeed, young man! It is so refreshing to converse with someone familiar with our history and has an accurate eye for dates. The transaction was effected in July—right after the Conference. It was still in Vienna and Prince Metternich was present as well as Great-Grandpapa Ambrose."

She nodded at the brandy we now held. "Let it relax, boys, in the snifter before your lips embrace it. Just a slight warming with cupped hands—thus—and a good sniff of elixir before consuming it."

We dutifully held our glasses of the almost colorless liquid in the embrace of our fingers before emulating the remainder of her protracted actions with the Napoleonic brandy. To me it tasted like undiluted fire. Indeed, taste was an inappropriate word: it burned. Ken, on the other hand, referred not to the effect the venerable liquid had on his mouth and throat but to the vision it evoked for him. He spoke of candelabra and white britches, of the glint of silver and gold at state banquets, of velvet and lace, of the gleam of tiaras, and insignia on the high slashes of color of the sashes adorning dignitaries and their escorts.

Obviously seen on a movie set back home in Hollywood, I thought, but Lady Gertrude was thoroughly impressed. "What a splendid eye for detail!" she again enthused. "What an asset that is for the budding historian. I presume it is a university chair of history you will be seeking on your return to your country?"

I craned forward, keen to learn of any plans my lover might have—a subject on which, with me, he had been frustratingly silent. I was rewarded by my attention. "That could very well be, Lady Gertrude. My time then at the Sorbonne wouldn't be wasted. I learned a lot about eighteenth-century French life there though of course it was excessively patriotic in its presentation. You just have to make adjustments as you listen to how France won everything, created everything, and thought everything."

"How true again, young man! That the French cannot be trusted is an axiom I have always embraced."

My Francophilia smarted. I tried to emulate her tone in moving to attack. "How strange, then, that it is this island which has been designated Perfide Albion! Not only by the French but the rest of the civilized world."

Ambrose was quick to back me up. "They say an Englishman's word is his bond—but only to another Englishman!"

"Drink up your brandy and do not be disputatious," his mother said, ignoring me. "You do well to listen to Kenneth here. An old head on young shoulders if ever there was! Perhaps we can persuade him to visit you in British Columbia after he has returned home and rested from the journey. He could bring learning and culture to an otherwise barren place consisting of cattle called steers and something called sagebrush which would be a stranger to your Elizabethan herb garden."

He was ready for that. "If the place Hermey calls the Caribou is so utterly ghastly, why banish me there?"

It was his mother's turn to sigh extravagantly. "You know very well that nowhere else will take you. That you need your sister and her demented husband to sponsor you with your unsavory school record. Your current antics in the Vale of Evesham suggest that only a human desert like the Caribou will preserve you from crimes of the aroused flesh and hopefully stiffen your character instead!"

"Mama, I am now of a thoroughly urban persuasion. That is what your insisting I follow Papa to Harrow has done to me." His voice rose a half octave—which meant it was now very high. "I pine for banks, buses, and busy streets. Fields depress me and the vista of some vast open range makes me positively suicidal."

"You see few enough open anything, darling! I find little difference between that smoky snug at the Feathers and urban life elsewhere."

This recurrent repartee was getting on my nerves. And to me at least, if not Ken, it sounded decidedly artificial—as if mother and son were using us as some kind of sounding board for their much practiced feuding.

"Is A. E. Housman still remembered hereabouts?" I inquired. "I gather we are not too far from the realm of 'A Shropshire Lad?' And wasn't it Housman's closest friend, Moses Jackson, who left him, got married, and ended up in Vancouver, British Columbia?"

Ambrose quickened at that—though I was pleased to observe a frown crease the maternal countenance, even if its owner this time remained determinedly silent. "Oh really, Davey, is that so? 'A Shropshire Lad' is absolutely my favorite poem. To think of that dried-up old classics professor revealing the state of his heart over his lover, so close to us as that! Gives me goose pimples just to think about it. I've personally never seen a handsome young man in all of Shropshire—and believe me, I've searched! I suppose they all emigrated somewhere far away like that poor sod Ambrose Jackson."

Lady Gertrude Hetherington-Gore twirled her snifter before emptying its contents down her gullet and rising, just a trifle unsteadily, to her feet. It was at that juncture I was reminded that the Napoleon brandy had been preceded by several glasses of claret at dinner, and a couple of generous gins and tonic (while we drank cider) before we ever reached that sea of polished mahogany where we had sat to consume Ambrose's culinary handiwork.

"I think all this talk of coming and going overseas has unduly fatigued me," she announced, "And I shall now retire. Ambrose will show you to your room, in case you have forgotten its whereabouts off the Holbein Gallery. I will doubtless see you in the morning before my son deposits you on the highway. I do not breakfast in public so we will meet at the very point of your departure." Even as she spoke, our gently swaying hostess extended much-beringed fingers for a faint brush with our own. "Adieu then, boys. Ambrose, you may now kiss me good night."

We chorused our good nights and her son dutifully delivered his peck on her lightly powdered cheek before we three males were left alone in the clock-ticking silence of the comfy antechamber of a room.

"No need to show us the way," Ken informed our remaining host. "Besides, before we hit the sack we can give you a hand with the washing up."

But Ambrose fiercely demurred at that suggestion. "I will be drifting up very soon, too," he told us. "She thinks I'm going to wash up all that stuff but she's wrong. Benton will do it when he gets home to prepare breakfast. He always does but she doesn't know because she never crosses into the east wing except to give him instructions in the butler's pantry. She only enters the kitchen for jam making with her W.I. cronies or to criticize my chutney making. Today with you chaps must be the first time in months!" he added with a scowl.

In a rather self-conscious way we shook hands with him there in his mother's sitting room before he escorted us to the bottom of the circular sweep of staircase (I thought of *Gone With the Wind*). Then blowing us kisses he skipped off in the direction of the green beige door leading to the kitchen wing.

We quickly undressed but I took much longer than usual with my nighttime toilet in the lofty bathroom with its enormous, old-fashioned brass fittings before joining Ken, who had preceded me in brushing his teeth and hair, in the feather-soft and canopied bed. We exchanged a few giggles as we retraced the contours of what had proved a quite extraordinary day and an even more singular evening in the palatial house, before, without mention of it by either of us, awaited the arrival of the scion of Badely and his seeking advice on emigration while we (although perhaps I should speak only for myself) anticipated the uncharted seas that would comprise his presence upon the bed between us. . . .

It couldn't have been more than a further five minutes—though it seemed to me like twenty—before the heavy bedroom door clicked loudly open. I quickly moved away from Ken, to afford a larger and hopefully more inviting space between us. I had deliberately left only a single candle burning—a sort of nightlight, which bathed the room in a romantic glow and thus a congruous atmosphere for the anticipated events now rapidly congealing in my head. But the light was quite sufficient to reveal the figure, not of willowy Ambrose but a ramrod Lady Gertrude standing there at the foot of the bed. All the earlier waving seemed to have departed her and in a foot-length white nightgown she seemed more stately than ever before; indeed, so imposing I instinctively moved back closer to my lover again for succor.

She addressed us in a stage whisper. "I am so glad you are still awake. I myself had to feign fatigue downstairs but it was imperative I speak with you without Ambrose being present, as it is my son I so desperately wish to discuss."

Ken and I looked at each other, embarrassed and anxious; both of us, I think, wondering what on earth would happen when the door opened again to admit Ambrose and his agenda. One thing was certain: There was no room for both of them on the bed.

Lady Gertrude, however, accorded no time for random speculation. "I am here to invoke your aid. My son must be persuaded to depart for Canada and the shelter offered by his sister. If Ambrose stays here I have not the slightest doubt he will shortly be apprehended and imprisoned by the authorities for his sexual appetites, which grow lustier and more louche as day follows day. Now I do not know what bond exists between you two young men lying there but I am now convinced (as was Ambrose from the outset) that you share this thing men get and which, in fact, inflicted my brother and indubitably—as you must both be aware—his nephew too.

"Now I do not know the laws that obtain over the matter throughout North America but I have been long aware that the colonies and dominions have long been asylum for Britons of that persuasion who have thus become remittance men. Because of this imperial tradition my mind turns to British Columbia rather than your state of California, Kenneth, where I understand the solution for those afflicted with these male appetites is usually the electric chair."

I was so relieved when Ken stirred restlessly and found the presence to answer. I had thought since meeting him, falling in love with him, and introducing him to straight relatives and friends that somehow the fervor of my love had wholly liberated me: made me bold in the ardor of our romantic partnership which I happily held up for the world to see. But it was at that moment in bed that true revelation came. Facing that tall and imperious relic of aristocratic England, who was at the same time a fiercely determined mother who'd catalogued and confined our kind of love as a quasi-disease, a male affliction for which a cure (unlike penicillin for syphilis) had not yet been discovered, my bowels melted and my pride in what linked us and sustained us suddenly fled away.

Not so Ken. "I do not think you have a very accurate picture of California, Lady Gertrude. Nor the United States, come to that. And although I can't speak for Canada, of course, I think you'll find the idea of the remittance man most probably seen as a little old-fashioned up there, too."

"I read the *Times*. And *Punch*, too," she replied primly. Obviously unconvinced.

He chose to ignore her. As my cold foot between the sheets found his equally cool one and played with it, he warmed to his topic. "But far more important, I think, is the fact we are strangers to the two of you. In spite of your wonderfully generous hospitality you really know nothing about us—nor we of Ambrose."

"I have the evidence of my eyes, as does my son!"

"We are all so very, very different," he persisted. "Quite honestly, I don't know much about the subject you are talking about. Factors that certain of us seem to own that make us different from the majority of men. Things, if you like, that you see as problems of one kind and another for Ambrose that maybe Davey and I don't share. I therefore wouldn't dream of—"

"You prevaricate! You refuse to help! Such selfishness—especially when it concerns your own kind of depravity—is lamentable to say the least. It is obvious to the whole world, young man, that you two share the same vice as my unfortunate son."

Ken rose a good six inches on his elbows, his beloved crewcut head now far from the pillow. His good old American voice flooded with fresh color. "No, ma'am. That is only your perception—coming from where you stand as a mother—and a mighty judgmental one at that!"

I felt so proud of my man I pressed my toes hard against his ankle.

"I am indeed a proud woman! The Hetherington-Gores, may I remind you, have had every reason to be. I do not intend to sit quietly by and see the family's reputation besmirched either by colonial rebels or by a freak of nature!"

"Please let me finish, Lady Gertrude. You came in here and asked for our aid. Well, what I'm about to say is about the only aid or advice I'm capable of giving. You are obviously a mature woman with equally obviously a lot of experience. We are both still young with very little. But this I do know. Davey and I love one another. We have every intention of living together—for always. We are taking our last shared holiday before we face our first separation since we met a year ago."

I felt his body next to mine grow even tauter. This was not an easy speech for him. "You can count on one hand the nights we haven't been able to sleep in the same bed. We have to thank you, Your Ladyship, for keeping that number down even further."

"All this is very interesting, but . . ."

Ken went on undaunted. "Yet I have no way of knowing whether your son is in love with another man as we are. Or what he would intend to do if that happened. I don't like to generalize. We are all so different as I said before—and that's why it's so dangerous to give advice. Perhaps Davey and I are just two of the luckiest people in the world. I often feel so, anyway."

I felt like swooning with joy. Ken *never* talked this way to me. It would have saved me countless hours of lying awake through the night agonizing over the degree of his love. Neurotic me, forever insecure, in love with self-torture: a mass and a mess of debilitating doubt. But now, hearing the words of my earthbound angel, my fears were quieted, my hope replenished as we lay side by side in a strange bed in an enormous mansion, confronted between the dull crimson curtains at the foot of the bed by the most frightening human apparition I had ever met.

Lady Gertrude shook her head—as if repudiating my lover's brave declaration. But before she could back that up with so many words, my ears caught a further activity at the door. So did Lady Gertrude's and so did Ken's. All three of our heads turned to watch Ambrose, in pale green silken pajamas, glide into the room—whereupon he gave a startled shriek on seeing his mother. It was she, though, who got in the first word.

"Get out, Ambrose! You have no right here."

"Stop interfering with my life, Mama! I will make my own plans. I will go where I please. Now go to bed and leave me to talk with my own."

Her Ladyship snorted. "You are still a child—if a depraved one. These two buggers are by no means sure you share what they have. It would seem they at least lack the slattern that courses through you."

"I'm very tired," I pleaded. "It has been an awfully long day."

They both ignored me.

"I am not in love as they are, Mama. But after what you did to Uncle Marmaduke, your own brother, I would never dream of telling you if I were. You broke my heart once. I won't let you do it again."

Her Ladyship's next words were heavy with contempt. "You were a child! You were fifteen and Marmaduke was a pedophile. If I hadn't sent him to Cousin Ethel in Tasmania he would be in prison this very moment."

I tried again. "Could you have this family talk somewhere else? We need our sleep."

This time I had an ally. "Please listen to us, ma'am. You are taking advantage of our position as your guests."

That had an immediate effect. "I was hardly expecting my son to sneak in on my guests and exploit their vulnerability by starting an argument with me. But that apart, I see it is impossible to dent your obsession with one another. You are patently too far gone in infatuation. Come, Ambrose! There is nothing here for either of us."

She turned without even looking up the length of the bed again and marched to the door. There she stood, holding its oaken weight open. For a moment nothing happened—creating a candlelit tableau I shall never forget. Ambrose stood there, tall for his age, youthfully slim, slumped in dejection. He looked from us, to her, and back again.

"Ambrose!" That was the last word I ever heard from Lady Hetherington-Gore, as she failed to materialize in the morning. Her son flapped dangling hands against his thighs in some kind of helpless frustration. Then did as he was told and mutely passed her before she yanked the door savagely behind the two of them.

Neither did we two have much to say to one another that night, and nothing relating to them. As we turned spontaneously toward each other, our mouths opened. But it was not to speak. . . .

When we descended the staircase the next morning (our knapsacks already firmly on our backs), it was to find a listless Ambrose awaiting us in the kitchen. He offered us breakfast—but without energy. Without consultation we chorused a polite decline. A similar pattern persisted as we sat in the back of the Daimler with the sole Hetherington-Gore behind the wheel—in spite of his mother's strictures. Ken briefly explained that we would now skip an exploration of Evesham and travel straight to Oxford, having spent the night at Badely Grange.

Ambrose responded by asking us for the third time that morning whether we had spent a comfortable night. For the third time I told him yes—though without specifying wherein the "comfort" was contained. I have never felt more honest in response to that oft asked question!

The journey was shorter than it seemed and the remainder of it passed in silence save for a couple of neutral comments from the back seat about the beauty and freshness of that summer's day. Ambrose drove us right through Evesham and stopped the car on the verge of what he flatly and dully announced was the main Oxford road. As we got our stuff out and prepared to say good-bye, a flicker of life reappeared in the disconsolate young man that stood behind us.

"Can we at least exchange addresses?" he asked.

Ken was already writing his on a scrap of paper he'd found.

"I won't give you mine," I explained, "because it will be the same as Ken's in such a very short time."

When he handed Ken a folded sheet of blue notepaper, I noted that it was embossed with the family crest and that he had added his name above it. I thought he was about to jump forward and embrace us as the traffic whizzed by, but he didn't. He just said: "It will be nice to have people to write to. It will make things a bit easier. Until I get over there." After a pause he added: "Because I'm coming to California one day." He met the eyes of both of us. "I shall definitely see you again."

I am wishing so hard as I write down these recollections that I could have said that he did so. That the final, formal 1950s shaking hands on the foxglove edge of an English highway wasn't the end of Ambrose in our lives. He never wrote to us either.

Parting Gifts

DAVID VERNON

Joan and I were at a dinner party when one of the guests asked if we had ever thought of going on a game show.

"Us?" I asked in disbelief.

Joan, wearing her dazzling new black dress, sat up and in not such subtle body language crossed her legs. "Game show?" she asked. "And this had been such a *nice* evening."

The man, a friend of the host, explained that he worked for a company that found promotional considerations for various game shows.

"Promotional considerations?"

"Prizes," Joan said flatly.

The man apologized up and down, trying to convince us that he was not stating a personality flaw, rather he was offering a business proposition.

He said he knew of a show that was looking for contestants.

"But game shows are for people without any self-respect," Joan insisted. "They're for merchandise gluts who tremble at the words 'washer-dryer,' 'microwave oven,' 'home entertainment center.'" Joan noticed my hand flinch with the dramatic rendering of her itemized list and put her hand on top of mine. "They're not for people like us."

The man gave us his card anyway.

Joan stopped by my apartment unexpectedly at 3:15, just fifteen minutes before the game show in question was to come on.

"Ben, do you want to take a look at it, just as a goof?" she asked.

"Why not?" I tried not to betray the fact that I'd planned my entire afternoon around it.

The show was called "Breaking and Entering." The host, Bill Modell, was a gorgeous blond with a winning smile. His sidekick was the lovely and very Nordic Anke Mitmar. The contestants, two couples, were dressed as burglars in black slacks, black T-shirts, and black knit caps. The first round involved pantomimes that were worth twenty points. The second round involved a stunt worth twenty-five points. The last round was the lightning round, each answer to the fast-paced questions worth ten points. (My favorite moment occurred in *this* round where one couple, posed with the question "What year was the bicentennial?" answered 1985.) The team that won the most points got to go on to the bonus round to "break and enter."

The breaking and entering part was a game-show twist that only could have been written by some demented, victimized L.A. writer who was about to head back to the midwest on a Greyhound bus after years of overwhelming rejection. In the show the winners had ninety seconds to climb through an open window into the set of a house. Every item open for theft had a sealed envelope on top of it and the team got to steal six things. They got a ten-second warning and if they both didn't climb back out the window before the ninety seconds are over, a security alarm went off. If their theft totaled more than $2,500 then they won the prizes as well as a bonus vacation.

"This is the worst show I've ever seen," I commented.

"I feel dirty just watching it," Joan whispered, transfixed.

"If pressed, I'd have to admit that the host is pretty cute. If pressed."

"Yeah, and I'm warming up a bit to Anke Mitmar. I'd say she's ready for the big time."

Bill and Anke totaled up the winning couple's loot, which ended up barely passing the $2,500 mark. Anke handed Bill the sealed bonus envelope.

"I'll bet it's a one-way ticket to Stockton."

"A weekend in Torrance," I wagered.

Of course we both nearly fell off the couch when Bill opened the envelope and announced that Robber Couple Number Two were going to Ja-Mai-Ca!

Anke Mitmar applauded, a skill Joan noted that she executed quite well. The credits rolled and Joan and I struggled for breath.

It was the middle of the night and I was dreaming that I was on the game show "Jeopardy." The other two contestants were Dr. Kate Hutton, member of the seismology lab at Cal Tech, and Lettie Fields, a ten-year-old girl scout from Woodland Hills. The categories for Double Jeopardy were: the Persian Empire, Canadian Folk Heroes, Edna St. Vincent Millay, Starts with a "Q", and Films of Ernest Borgnine. The sixth and final category was Ben Chambers, a whole category devoted to my life.

At first it was a three-way battle, Kate Hutton just a little bit in the lead. Finally we got the category about me. I had control of the board. Much to my dismay, I didn't know the answer to a single question. The girl scout chimed in and answered each of the questions in my category in rapid-fire succession: *Where Is Silverlake? What is "What a Difference a Day Makes?" What is the back seat of Vince Mozzarella's Honda Civic? What are bee stings and shellfish? What are six inches?* The buzzer went off, signaling the end of Double Jeopardy and waking me from my nightmare.

The phone was ringing. It was Joan.

"I've been thinking, Ben, what do we have to lose?"

I didn't disagree with her. I had been asking myself that question all night.

Joan and I have been friends for seven years and during that time we have seen success and fame elude us time and time again. I was still working as a freelance journalist with a bank balance seldom bulging past three figures. Joan was a freelance layout designer and a part-time writer. Her most recent gig had been doing Cher's mail-order catalogue. She was fired for designing a page detailing Cher's living room (leopard rug, leather couch) that included a cubbyhole prison cell. Inside the cell were several twelve-year-old boys in loincloths, lunching on turkey bones, being fatted up for their high mistress. ("You would think that Cher would have to have a sense of humor about herself," Joan said at the time.)

My lack of success in my career has only been rivaled by my track record in romance. It was sad when I realized that my longest relationship was with the guy I've been flirting with, but have never talked to, at the Speedy Queen Laundromat. The last real date I had was eight months ago. I don't believe in astrological signs, but this guy was a Leo, and I'd never do that again. They need too much attention. We were at his apartment. He put on a CD of the *Three Tenors Live*. We started having sex on his bed. "La Donna é Mobile" was playing in the background. The sex was good but it was taking him forever to come. Finally, it happened, just as the song was coming to an end and the three tenors were receiving a thunderous ovation. We had two more sexual encounters identical to this one. Finally it dawned on me. I wasn't the one that was making him come, it was the sound of all the applause. Leos. They never can get too much praise.

Joan, on the other hand, just entered into a relationship with a political activist named Martica. Now I've met many lesbians with sharp wits and spectacular senses of humor, but Martica is not one of them. Joan defends her by telling me that if she wanted fun she'd go to Disneyland. "I'm looking for someone serious and stable. . . ." Joan says. "And rigid and judgmental. . . ." I add. While the actual dating was going well, Joan is worried that she doesn't have the resources to keep up with Martica's active social life.

In all the years I've lived in Los Angeles, I've felt as if I've been waiting for something marvelous to happen. It's like I'm one of those tourists in Las Vegas, vigilantly playing the same nickel slot machine through the night, afraid to walk away because I might be just one nickel away from the jackpot.

"Let's do it," I told her.

The guy at the laundromat was there again today. I got a chill as I watched him fold his stack of plaid boxers. Joan keeps wondering when I'm actually going to talk to him. As I've told her, I am just waiting for the right opportunity to present itself. Today he's washing a pair of black jeans that I haven't seen before. He sees me staring and he smiles then looks back down at his laundry. Little does he know that he's flirting with someone who's on the brink of fame.

"There's a few hitches," I told Joan as I hung up the phone. "The team has to be within ten years of each other."

"No problem." Joan and I have been twenty-nine for two years now.

"And they want the couples to be peppy and preppy."

"Peppy *and* preppy? I guess we can work on that."

"And they want their couples to be couples."

"Couples?"

"They've filled their quota for couples that are friends. They only want couples that are couples."

"And you told them . . ."

"I didn't tell them we weren't," I said, squirming. "I'm sorry. I was on the spot. I saw that cruise ship to the Bahamas. I saw our friends waving. The boat was leaving without us. I panicked."

So now we are a couple.

Driving home from Joan's, I found myself thinking about our friendship. If Joan had any real flaw it was her tendency to let me draw her into my various schemes. Like the time a few summers ago we were both broke and I got a gig working the Garlic Festival. We were dressed in unbearably stifling costumes as friendly garlic cloves handing out Breath Savers. It was a hundred and two degrees and after a few hours Joan became dizzy. I tried to help her out of her costume, but the zipper jammed. Joan passed out and I rushed her, still in her garlic costume, to Cedars Sinai, where she was attended to by a not very amused Dr. Gallagher, the woman Joan had recently started dating. There was also the time that I found a harmless-looking plant on one of our day trips to Mexico and I asked Joan to help me bring it across the border. Needless to say, I was amazed that after everything I'd put her through that we were still friends.

By coincidence the *Los Angeles Times* metro section ran an article about people who make their livings as game-show contestants. Apparently there are laws restricting how many game shows one is allowed to do a year. There is a whole subculture of these people. They have a support group that meets to discuss how to get around these laws. Who knew this was so involved? One guy the article featured, Jersey Wasserman, has supported himself for years doing "Jokers Wild," "Supermarket Sweep," "Press Your Luck," and so on. He was such a good contestant that game-show producers begged for him to be on their shows. He mulled over offers. One loophole he found was that many companies shot pilots for game shows. Pilots didn't count as an official game show since contestants didn't get to keep the prizes they won, but producers sweetened the pot by shooting these pilots in Scotland or Hawaii. Jersey Wasserman had made it to the big time.

When I arrived at Joan's house to practice for our audition, she was working on a proposal to teach a writing workshop.

"Ben, what are the three classic conflicts, again? Man versus man, man versus nature, and what else?"

"Man versus wardrobe."

"That's it," she said.

I pulled her from her work desk. "We only have a few days to get this down."

Joan joined me at her coffee table.

"First, we have to rethink what we might put on our application."

"Why?"

"Because if they ask us what our hobbies are I might be inclined to write cooking, Stephen Sondheim musicals, and boy watching. Yours would be golf tournaments, 'Two Hot Tamales,' and an unhealthy fixation with Princess Diana."

"Oh, let's not bring *her* into this."

For the next two hours we reinvented our likes and dislikes. We practiced jumping up and down in the throes of excitement. We discussed how we'd split the prizes. (We'll list what we each want. Any prizes we both want will be written on slips of paper and drawn from a hat. What neither of us want will be sold or given away.)

At 3:30 we turned on the television. The first image to appear on the screen was Father Felice, also known as Father Hollywood. He's the Catholic priest who relentlessly speaks out against the gay community. Somehow, whenever Father Felice shows up anyplace, the media have been alerted and the good Father feels compelled to issue a statement. Joan and I booed and hissed at the TV screen and I switched channels until I found "Breaking and Entering." In this episode a couple made it to the bonus round then failed to escape back out the window before the security alarm sounded. Their parting gift was a six-month supply of Ricola cough drops. That could be us if we're not careful.

Auditions were in studio four in the Warner Hollywood lot. Joan and I both wore khaki pants and bright T-shirts in our attempt to dress "preppy." At the studio gate we were directed onto the lot, where we found a line full of other couples wearing khaki pants and bright, colorful T-shirts. We didn't talk to anyone. To talk to them would be admitting we were one of them. At this point we were both in serious denial about the fact that we were trying out for a game show.

Soon we were brought into a large, drafty sound stage and told to sit in the folding chairs, leaving a space between us and the next person. Tests were passed out. We had twenty minutes to complete the test. When I opened the test booklet I was instantly relieved. This test was obviously designed to weed out the pop-culturally impaired.

Winnie the Pooh is . . .
  (a) A rock star.
  (b) A cartoon character
  (c) The ex-wife of Nelson Mandela
George Orwell wrote . . .
  (a) My Sharona
  (b) The Gettysburg Address
  (c) 1984
Johnson & Johnson is . . .
  (a) A company that makes baby powder
  (b) A slang term meaning, 'where's my money?'
  (c) The employment of the literary device called repetition

After the test we were introduced to the producer of the show, a lavish woman named Lorraine Aqua Viva Heidegger. Lorraine was tall and in her early fifties with shoulder-length blonde hair. She was a fireball of nervous energy. Studio four hardly seemed big enough for her.

"Welcome," she said, in a raspy voice. "Not everyone here will be chosen. I want to tell you that if you're not, it's no reflection on you. But then again, if you can't get on a friggin' game show, then I don't know what to say."

She called up the couples and asked them to say a few words about themselves. Then she asked one of them to pick a card from a deck and pantomime the word written on the card.

It was easy for Joan and I to spot out our real competition. Most couples seemed too bizarre for daytime. An Indian wearing a turban was paired with a punk rocker with green hair. Not that I feel superior to Indians in turbans or punk rockers with green hair; I don't, you just don't see too many of them on contestants row at "The Price Is Right."

The audition dragged on. Toward the end, Lorraine starting calling up two couples at a time. Joan and I were called up with another couple, whom I had tagged early on as our most serious competition. They were cute and bouncy, holding hands as they energetically ran up to the front of the studio. By this time, Joan was so exhausted I practically had to pull her from her seat.

Lorraine asked the cute couple how long they'd been together.

"Three years," the cute guy piped in, eliciting a big "wow" from Lorraine.

She turned and asked us the same question. In a severely competitive mood I looked at Lorraine and said, "Actually, we're engaged." I grasped onto Joan's hand.

"Engaged? Fantastic!" Lorraine made a notation in her file.

I smiled the best I could given the fact that Joan's nails were digging into my palm.

The cute couple had the first pantomime. So far, all the words for the pantomimes had been slightly risqué, probably to keep the jaded staff from dozing off. The cute couple drew the word "virgin." Lorraine clicked her stopwatch. The cute guy jumped into action, pointed directly at the cute girl, and of course, the first word to come out of her mouth was "virgin."

Our turn for the pantomime. Of course, the word I got stuck with, the only word it could possibly have been, was "lesbian." I knew I could have also just pointed to my female partner and our round would have been over in three seconds, but then we also would have been bounced from the game. Five minutes into me playing every demeaning, woeful stereotype I could muster, Joan finally let the word "lesbian" leave her horrified lips. We stood on the stage, physically and emotionally spent.

"C'mon," Lorraine shouted, "Imagine you just won the game. Hug, jump up and down. Be a little ecstatic, for christsakes."

Joan and I leapt in place in a manner that suggested calisthenics more than outright joy. Then it was all over.

We had dinner with Martica that night at the Sawtelle Kitchen, her treat. She was celebrating getting a grant for one of the organizations she chaired. She pointed out to us that none of the money for our meal was coming out of any grant funds, and that she was planning on paying for the dinner with her new Rainbow credit card, which donated 5 percent of their profits to lesbian and gay organizations. The guy Martica tried to set me up with didn't show.

"It's too bad, I think you'd like this guy. He used to work for G.L.A.D.D., and before that G.L.C.S.C., now he works for A.P.L.A. And he has an M.B.A. from U.S.C."

"Sounds D.U.L.L.," I pointed out.

Martica smiled weakly, as an afterthought.

The mood of the evening was high-spirited. Joan and I were celebrating something too. We'd found out that we made the cut on "Breaking and Entering." We both felt thrilled and terrified. What were we getting ourselves into?

Joan opted not to tell Martica about the game show, especially now that we're engaged. She was certain Martica would have issues. Since Martica didn't watch any daytime television it seemed safe to say that she'd never find out.

Joan and I started training for the show. First and foremost we dieted. Even though black, the color of the "Breaking and Entering" costume, is thinning, the camera does add five to ten pounds, something neither of us could afford.

We crammed by watching the show, gaining invaluable insight into the types of questions posed, as well as developing attachments to Bill Modell and Anke Mitmar. We rehearsed climbing in and out of the window to my ground-floor apartment, keeping track of our times. We practiced our joy level by acting excited over the slightest things. We went for lunch at the Astro Diner and when our waiter informed us that our steamed vegetable plates were on their way, Joan and I leapt to our feet and high-fived each other.

We were ready.

The way the show works was that if you won the game then you were asked to return for a second game the following week. If you won the second game you'd come back the next week for a third and final game. By winning the third game, you won a special grand prize picked out just for you. Some of the grand prizes were built around fairly elaborate stunts. On a recent show one of the champions was a pregnant woman from Huntington Beach. In

the last ten minutes of the show, as the grand prize, Bill Modell
and Anke Mitmar threw her a baby shower, bringing in friends of
hers while supplying some high-end presents.

Our first day on the show. Most of the staff were gracious. Then
I was fitted for my burglar costume. In the changing room Joan
and I were given black wool caps. It was explained to us that these
were the latest addition to the "Breaking and Entering" costume.
The outfit was embarrassing, but the wool cap somehow moved it
over into the category of humiliating. I walked to the green room
in the black slacks, black T-shirt, and black wool cap, and one of
the crew stopped and stared at me. He was 250 pounds, eating
a bag of Sun Chips. "Some people will do fucking anything for
money," he said. I wanted to remind him that he wasn't exactly
working Wall Street himself, but I stopped myself in case this was
part of the testing procedure.

Joan and I were asked to meet with the associate producer of
the show to sign some kind of contract.

"Good," I told Joan," I want to complain about this cap. I'm not
going on national TV wearing this."

A production assistant walked us over to his office and knocked
on his door. A voice told us to come in, and the production assistant led the way and introduced us to Matt Barnett, associate producer of "Breaking and Entering." The first thing I noticed about
him is that he was younger than I expected, probably no older
than twenty-eight. The next thing I noticed is that he was one of
the most attractive men I'd ever laid eyes on. Wavy black hair. Athletic build. A warm and generous smile. I couldn't stop looking at
him. He extended his hand and introduced himself to me. I felt
feverish touching him. This was a moment that kept extending
and extending. Not a word was spoken but I felt that everything I
needed to know about him was being passed to me through this
exchange. Joan broke the silence by stepping between us and introducing herself to Matt.

Matt dropped his hand from mine and gave Joan a quick handshake. "I see you've got the wool caps."

"I was going to talk to you about these . . ."

"I had to fight Lorraine about them, but I thought they added
something to the look of the show. It's my first real contribution.
Do you like them?"

Joan stepped back and stared expectedly, knowing full well

that I have never been one to alter my point of view for anyone, even someone as handsome as Matt.

"You should be proud," I gushed. "They're an inspiration!"

"You don't think they're too much?"

"Too much?" I said, straight faced. "They make the whole costume!"

"I'm glad you think so."

At this point I couldn't even bear to look over at Joan. Matt picked up our file, looked at our application, then his face dropped. "You're engaged?"

We nodded.

"Engaged?" He stared at us like he was expecting a punch line. Neither Joan nor I denied the accusation. "That's great," he said unconvincingly. "Just great. Congratulations." Matt went to his desk and found the contracts for us to sign. He wouldn't look me in the eye.

"What are these?" Joan asked

"Usual stuff. Permission to use your likeness in the show and in any promotions for the show. The understanding that you are liable for your own taxes for any prizes won. Our right to revoke your winnings if we find that you've misrepresented yourself in your application."

Matt looked down at the floor as Joan and I reluctantly signed the release forms. I handed him back the forms and his pen and he smiled weakly. On our way out the door he wished us good luck and told us that he thought we'd be very happy together. Somehow, that last remark hurt most of all.

Before the show we met Bill Modell, who was huddled into the corner with his assistant, and Anke Mitmar, who was on a cellular phone and waved to us. Back in the green room we met our opponents, Donna and Kevin.

"We're from Rancho Cucomonga. Everyone we know is in the audience," Donna said nervously to me just moments before the taping was to start.

"That's a real morale boost," I whispered to Joan. "We're going to have half of Rancho Cucomonga booing us out there."

Joan looked too terrified to respond.

The show started and when our names were called we rushed out from the wings.

Bill Modell introduced us to the audience and asked me how long we've been engaged.

"A year," I replied.

Bill smiled in approval. He turned to Joan. "What do you think, Joan? When are you two going to do it?" The audience tittered. "Get married, I mean."

Joan cleared her throat to make way for the answer we had rehearsed. "As soon as we can afford a honeymoon, I guess."

"Well, maybe you'll get lucky today," Bill said before moving on to Donna and Kevin.

The game started. I sensed the other couple was no threat to us but by the end of the first round they were in the lead. Even though Joan was trying her damnedest, there was an element of her personality that prevented her from throwing herself on the floor and imitating a goat in front of a studio audience with the required level of enthusiasm.

We caught up in the second round where, blindfolded, I had to guess the flavors of ice cream Joan was scooping into my mouth. I'm embarrassed to admit that I got seven out of seven right, earning us a whopping twenty-five points.

During the commercial break Joan turned to me. Her face was completely white.

"I have an idea. Why don't we walk outside, like we need some fresh air or something. Then we could casually walk over to the car and drive home. What could they do? There's no law about walking out on a game show, is there? We'd never have to tell anyone. We'd make a pact to never speak about it. In a few years it would be like it never happened."

Before I could answer her we were visited by Lorraine Aqua Viva Heidegger. She looked at Joan and put a hand on her shoulder. "Are you going to be OK?" Joan nodded, gazing at the floor. "You gotta have more fun with it, dear. Think of it as sex. Think of the whole thing as one big fucking orgasm."

"Great," Joan whispered to me as Lorraine walked away. "There goes my sex life."

We were five points ahead as we went into the lightning round. In just a few seconds the game would be decided. Truthfully, I didn't expect much help from Joan. Winning or losing would be equally terrifying for her at this point. Then the lightning round began and Joan all of a sudden came to life. She buzzed in with an answer to each question. Kevin and Donna didn't have a chance.

"Who won the Academy Award for the *King and I*? Who wrote the novel *Native Son*? What's the airport code for Jakarta?"

Joan was unstoppable. She had all the right answers. "Yul Brynner. Richard Wright. HLP."

Joan kicked Rancho Cucomonga ass and sent Kevin, Donna, and all their friends on the next bus home.

Joan screamed and jumped around the stage in a way I had never seen before; not in rehearsal, not in real life.

We took a few deep breaths before the bonus round.

When we returned from commercial, Anke set the alarm for ninety seconds. Bill waited a beat, then told us to start. Joan and I leapt through the window into that day's set, which was dressed as a kitchen. Joan's expertise in catalogues seemed to give her a sixth sense as to what the most expensive items in the room were. After watching the program for the last week we knew that you had to stay away from the little delights that caught your eye and stick with what cost the most. Joan and I raced around the kitchen, gathering items, working together like a well-oiled machine. We stole a dishwasher, a bread maker, a deluxe microwave oven, a china set, a barbecue grill, and the Julia Child cookbook library, leaving behind wine glasses, a Presto Perfect potato cooker, a blender, a toaster oven, and most painfully, a generous supply of Healthy Choice frozen dinners.

We escaped through the window right before the alarm sounded.

Bill took our envelopes and with the help of Anke Mitmar totaled up our loot: $2,700. Anke handed Bill the envelope containing the destination of our bonus prize. Bill opened the envelope seductively.

"You're going to Puerto Rico!"

The theme music played. Bill shook our hands. The audience clapped at us. We waved good-bye to them. What can I tell you, it was a love fest.

On the drive home Joan was elated. She talked a mile a minute. *Wasn't Anke Mitmar pure enchantment? In a certain light doesn't she look a bit like Princess Di? Isn't it a coincidence that Yul Brynner is one of my favorite actors? I've always wanted to go to Puerto Rico! But this is just the beginning, Ben. From here there's no place but up. Is "Let's Make a Deal" still on the air?*

Let's just say that if this was musical theater Joan could have danced all night.

The next morning was spent catching up with friends, looking into a few new possible job assignments.

Joan called at 11:00. We have to get together to practice. We can't get too comfortable. She wanted to know if I've told anyone. I hadn't. Did she tell Martica? No.

"This must be what cheating is like," she sighed.

The rest of the week I found myself thinking about Matt. I ran a few scenarios in my mind. One involved calling him up to ask him about some clarification of the rules. *When the security alarm goes off do you have to be entirely out of the window, or just mostly out of the window?* My other idea had me stopping by the studio and ringing him at the front gate. *Joan and I were going to go for a romantic drive down the PCH and watch the sunset, but she couldn't make it . . . ?*

My friends Pete and Jose invited me to go dancing with them at the Probe. I said yes because I thought maybe I'd run into Matt, then I called back and said no for the same reason. I called back and told them to pick me up. When they pulled up in the driveway I ran out to their car and told them I had changed my mind. Halfway back to my door I changed my mind again and finally went with them. When we got to the Probe I couldn't enjoy myself. I spent most of my time looking over my shoulder, certain that every dark-haired guy across the room was Matt. Pete and Jose finally offered to pay my cab fare and begged me to go home.

"Breaking and Entering" had a short prep time (which Joan said meant that the network was probably always on the verge of canceling it), and shows were taped only about a week in advance. Our first show would air the day after the taping of our second show.

The morning of the taping Joan came to my house and we went for a run. We took turns showering and listened to some upbeat music. We'd been practicing all week and we felt confident about the day's taping. I thought to myself that this must be what it feels like to be Steffi Graff or Michael Jordan, to be the masters of your game.

Before the taping of the show I ran into Matt outside his office, where I had been standing for about fifteen minutes. Even though he tried to disguise it, I could tell that he was as thrilled to see me as I was to see him.

"Good luck today."

"Thanks." I extended my hand for him to shake, then when it was too late to be retracted, realized that there was no context for this handshake, except my desire to touch him.

"I'm sure you'll do great today." He smiled at me before ending the handshake. "I thought you guys did great last week. I was actually just watching the tape again . . ."

"You were watching our show?"

"Yeah," he said, embarrassed. "And if I don't see her, wish your fiancée luck."

"Of course. I will tell her. If I see her. Sometimes I don't see her, you know. Sometimes there are just . . . days where we just don't see each other," I stammered.

For the second show we were matched with Paula and Yancy. Their first win was on the previous day's show and Joan and I had noted their technique. Paula and Yancy were all about energy. Their opponents were intimidated by their loudness and their bounciness which made up for the fact that Paula and Yancy weren't the brightest contestants in the game-show constellation. They were all style, no substance. We knew we'd wipe the floor with them.

Joan and I really hit our stride. When asked to pantomime an eagle, Joan flapped her wings and ran all across the stage. I was amazed. She'd made progress that would've taken years in therapy. Years.

We also scored with the stunt that had me ordering from a menu for Joan while she stood behind a partition. We've had so many meals together I could order for this woman in my sleep. *French fries or baked potato? Baked potato. Hamburger or chef's salad? Chef's salad. Chocolate cake or fruit salad? Chocolate cake; she likes a little spice in her life.* The audience loved us. Twenty-five more points.

By the time the lightning round came along Paula and Yancy's

level of enthusiasm had dwindled. We didn't even need the lightning round, but it was played and we won.

During the commercial break we were visited by Lorraine Aqua
Viva Heidegger, who called us "Hall of Famers."

Our bonus round had us stealing from a living room. We made
off with a Laz-E-Boy, a CD player, a set of golf clubs, an oriental
rug, a wine rack, and a fireplace grill that we later fought over
even though neither of us owned a fireplace.

Our winnings easily surpassed $2,500. When Bill announced
that he was sending this lovely engaged couple to London, we
cried. We jumped up and down and cried. Then we went home in
a dark panic, hoping no one would ever find out what we were
doing.

The next day I made a point of not being home at 3:30 when our
first episode aired. I knew it would make me self-conscious to see
myself on television.

When I returned I glanced nervously at the answering machine. There was one message. I didn't expect to get off scott-free,
but I hoped that if any of my friends had seen the show it would
be someone who would keep the secret and not spread it around
to all our friends that I was on a game show posing as a straight
man. I pressed the button on the answering machine and the
voice that played back belonged to Matt. His voice was quiet and
low. He said that he knew it was somewhat unorthodox, but he
wanted me to join him for a drink tonight at some bar I had never
heard of in North Hollywood. Obviously he was nervous about us
being seen together. On the message he said if I didn't show up
he'd understand.

I dressed as if I were going on a date and on the drive to the
bar fantasized about what could possibly happen. I pictured myself walking straight up to him, taking him off guard, and kissing
him. After making out in the bar we'd go back to my house. No,
we'd go to his house, mine's too messy. Or perhaps we'd wait until
right after Joan and I finished our game show reign.

At this bar called the Watering Spot, I found Matt slumped at a
table in the back, picking at a plate of pretzels and drinking what
must have been his third or fourth beer, judging from his posture.

"You came." He looked happy, yet depressed to see me. Something had changed in his demeanor. He no longer looked like

someone out of a Tom Bianchi photograph but now like someone out of a William Inge play.

"Rough day at the office?"

"Rough," he laughed to himself. "You know my friends make fun of my job. They don't respect what I do for a living. I don't see anything wrong with game shows, do you?"

"Nothing that a frontal lobotomy couldn't fix," is what I wanted to say. But seeing Matt so despondent I could only shake my head no and tell him that I thought it was a proud profession.

Matt took another sip of his beer. "Queen for a Day."

"I beg your pardon?"

"The first game show I remember seeing. I must have been just a kid, but I ate it up. They had three women whose lives were in the toilet, but in thirty minutes one of their lives would be changed forever."

"What about the other two?" I asked.

He ignored my question. "That's the power of television. To entertain, to inform, to change. And the chance to be one of the greats. 'Hollywood Squares.' 'To Tell the Truth.' 'Wheel of Fortune.'" He finished his beer.

"Did something bad happen today?"

Matt glanced around the bar nervously. "I shouldn't even be meeting you here. I don't know what I'm doing. It's just that you seem like a . . . very nice person."

"What happened?"

Matt took a deep breath and continued. "There's these two people who had been on our show as a married couple. They did well and won a lot of stuff. We just found out today they've since appeared on another show as brother and sister and on another as co-workers. There's going to be an article about it in the paper. Lorraine was furious. She's going to sue the couple to get the prizes back. It's within our legal right. Of course she blames it all on me. I've got to be more cautious in the screening process. I almost lost my job today."

His message was starting to reach me.

"We're on the verge of getting canceled anyway and Lorraine told me that if we go down because of this that she'll blackball me all over town." He paused to let his point sink in. "So if I find out that anyone's not quite what they claim to be, it's my responsibility to pull them from the show. It's my job responsibility, and I guess my moral responsibility. Now, that's not to say that some people may not be what they claim to be . . ." He looked at me with his soulful eyes. "I just can't ever find out, that's all."

I parked and sat in front of Joan's house for a while and thought the situation through. Matt knew that Joan and I weren't engaged or even lovers. He wasn't going to tell, but in exchange it meant that nothing was going to happen between us. Was it worth losing the chance for the only significant relationship in my life for a few prizes? A trip to London? A television set? No. It wasn't. I decided I would tell Joan that I wanted to quit. We could confess to Lorraine and give the prizes back.

When Joan answered the door I could see she had been crying, something she doesn't do all that often. She took me to her living room and told me that Martica had broken off their relationship. An ex-girlfriend of Martica's had seen our game-show appearance, recognized Joan, and taped the show.

"She couldn't believe that I'd lie to her and that I would lie about myself to the world."

"Did you tell her that we're not talking about the March on Washington here, it's just a game show?"

"Three other people recognized me and called her. Urvashi Vaid called her and said, 'Isn't that the girl you're dating?' Urvashi Vaid! Who knew she watched game shows?"

"So it's completely over?"

Joan nodded. "She said, 'How can I chair National Coming-Out Day and as my date bring a woman who posed as a heterosexual on a game show just to win prizes?'"

I put my arm around her. "Maybe we should quit. Call the whole mess off. Give back the prizes."

Joan grabbed me by the shoulders. "Have you lost your mind? We can't give back the prizes. Can't you see that? It's over with Martica. The only thing that's helping me through this nightmare is thinking about that trip to Puerto Rico." Joan snuggled up next to me. "We're in too deep to pull out now."

Our second episode aired. My parents called wondering when they can meet Joan. They invited us both to fly to Seattle for Mom's birthday next month.

"We knew you'd get over the thing you were going through."

I had spent years and years trying to convince my parents that being gay was a permanent fixture in my life, and now that was completely fucked up just because of this thirty-minute game show.

"Joan and I are just friends. We're not really engaged."

"Oh, we just can't wait to meet her," my mother cooed.

A month ago I didn't even know this game show existed. Now I find out that my parents and Urvashi Vaid watch it.

During the course of my day three strangers stopped and said hello to me. The only other consequence of my new-found celebrity was that the guy in the laundromat gave me a dirty look when I smiled at him. It was a look that said, How could you even consider cheating on Joan?

Later in the day a friend invited me to a protest against Father Felice. Father Felice was going to be speaking out against a school in the valley that was trying to implement a gay and lesbian student organization.

At the protest I realized how great it felt to be out and open and part of the fifty or sixty other fags and dykes screaming at this priest. Of course he had more people there than we did but we were louder and angrier. There were queers there in office drag who had taken time off from work, and there was a good showing of the younger set, either from this school or other schools, there to show support. The most moving part of the afternoon was when our screams and shouts made it impossible for Father Felice to complete his speech. He stepped down off the podium and disappeared into a waiting limousine. On my way home an hour later I realized that this was the only thing I've done for a long while that I felt good about.

I received a phone call from Lorraine Aqua Viva Heidegger reminding us that our third and final appearance on the show would be filmed in two days.

"We're getting loads of calls about you two," she told me. "Our audience adores you two. Especially the girl, what's her name, Joanie." Lorraine told me that we were going to be playing against another couple that had won two games. "I never play favorites," Lorraine sighed, "but I've got something really special planned for you two if you win. Ratings have been in the crapper. God knows we need some excitement to goose things up and keep our heads off the chopping block."

One of the biggest misconceptions about game shows is that you'd think the winners would drive home with all their prizes that night. Apparently it takes months. We would not be receiving our prizes for months and months. I couldn't understand this. If they have it right in the studio why couldn't they just give it to us? If the show got canceled next week, would we still get our prizes? If the show got canceled and nothing ever arrived, who do we call? Are there special government agencies that look after the interest of game-show contestants? These are the questions I had.

One day to go. Joan and I practiced in the morning. She just wasn't the same though since the break up with Martica. She'd lost some of her verve. When we practiced pantomiming letters she was so listless that her curves all meshed together. Her *A* looked like a lower case *h.*

"Look," I said, "do you want me to talk to Martica? I'm sure she'd come around." I wanted to make Joan feel better but we both knew that Halley's comet would come back around before Martica did.

"Fuck her. I wasn't a girlfriend, I was an accessory. She doesn't want me if she can't show me off at National Coming-Out Day, well who needs that? I'll get over her while we're in Puerto Rico, how about that?"

Joan hugged me, told me that she was going to be fine, and we went back to work practicing being vowels.

That night I couldn't sleep so I went to the market. The super-markets in L.A. are as big as college campuses and something thrilled me about walking the aisles at 1:30 in the morning and having the place to myself. Not to mention the exercise. From the time you start at the bread section to the time you head out of the meat department you've had a real journey and a cardiovascular workout to rival any step class.

I turned the corner, entered another aisle, and saw Matt standing in the frozen-food section. He seemed to be deciding between Marie Calendar's frozen macaroni and cheese or her chicken casserole. He seemed as amazed at this chance meeting as I was.

"Couldn't sleep," he told me.

"Me either," I confessed. "You always come here?"

"I go to markets when I can't sleep. Plus I love supermarkets. Something very . . . American about them."

"Like game shows?"

He smiled. "Sort of like game shows."

I was starting to get numb standing in the frozen-food section. "Mind if I walk with you?"

"Not at all."

Matt seemed to be buying nonessential odds and ends like Eggo waffles, yogurt, and black olives. Out of all the carts in the conga line out in front of the market he picked the one suffering from mad-cart disease. We both tried to ignore it as we walked the aisles while one of the back wheels twirled in spasms, stalling our progress.

"Do you live alone?" I asked.

"Yes. And you?"

"Well, yes, I live alone too."

"Not with Joan?"

"Joan and I both live alone."

We came to the end of the aisles and hesitated before getting in line. Matt looked so forlorn in the middle of this supermarket with this barely filled shopping cart at nearly 2:00 in the morning. Of course I must have been his mirror image.

"This was fun," he told me.

"Wasn't it? We'll have to do this again. Let's say every Wednesday night at two A.M., aisle six."

Matt laughed. We checked out at the same time, four cash registers apart, walked out to the parking lot, then drove off in separate directions.

I woke up dreading the day. Robert Louis Stevenson once said that "Everybody, sooner or later, sits down to a banquet of consequences." If that was the case, I had the feeling as I left for the studio that I was on my way to a feast.

I found Joan in the make-up department. She looked like she hadn't slept much last night either.

"Excited?"

"Excited isn't big enough of a word for what I feel," she said wearily. "Did I tell you that another one of Martica's friends is doing a one-woman, multimedia performance piece about me? She's going to use clips from the show. It's going to be about how I sold my soul to the devil in exchange for a bread maker."

"Actually," I interrupted, "I thought I was getting the bread maker."

She gave me an evil look.

As we were leaving the make-up room we ran into the young couple that we had auditioned with back at the try-outs. They were introduced to us as Cliff and Betsy, our opponents.

"Those two worry me," I told Joan as the couple hopped up in the make-up chairs.

"Them? Those virgins don't stand a chance against us," Joan said, loud enough for them to hear.

Walking down the hallway, the show's hairdresser stopped Joan and started to mess with her hair.

"I like it how it is. Don't touch me," Joan snapped.

I couldn't believe what was happening before me. "You're turning into a game-show diva," I told her. We settled into the green room and I took this opportunity to talk to her. "I know this has been stressful, but by the end of this day the whole ordeal will be over and life will go back to the way it used to be." I told Joan that I loved her, and I did. She had become my best friend, my family, and at least until the end of the day, my fiancée.

We settled into the green-room couch and drank sodas. At one point Anke Mitmar passed through the room. I'd noticed that there had been some kind of flirtation going on between the two of them. Anke walked up to us, ignored me, and wished Joan good luck. It wouldn't be exaggerating to say that it helped lift Joan's spirits.

We had a half an hour before the show started so I excused myself and snuck toward the set. I saw Matt going over some notes with a camera operator. When he finished I followed him back toward his office. In front of his door he turned and noticed me.

"Ben, you're not supposed to be back here."

"Where do you think I should be?"

"In the green room with your fiancée," he said sharply.

"I'll go then."

He stopped me before I was halfway down the corridor. "I guess there is something to say. I owe you an apology. I shouldn't have called you up last week and invited you out for drinks. It was inappropriate."

A crew person walked toward us and Matt stopped the conversation until the person passed us and disappeared down the hall.

"Do you want to go out and celebrate with me and Joan after the show?"

"I don't think so. I doubt we'll see each other after today." He shook my hand and I walked back to the green room. I knew this would be a moment I'd regret and rewrite in my mind for a long time.

The show was about to begin, and Joan and I stood in the wings until our names were called out by the announcer. On cue we ran to the stage, waving at the audience.

"Rarely have we had such dynamite teams playing against each other," Bill Modell told the studio audience. "Ben and Joan, have you two set a date yet?"

"We've been too busy with the show to think about it," Joan announced.

He shifted his attention to our opponents. "And Cliff and Betsy, I just heard backstage that you two make sculptures out of soap."

"Yes, Bill," Betsy explained. "We mostly carve out different types of animals although last winter we shaped one like the state of Texas!"

Cliff and Betsy got the first pantomime. It took Cliff all of fourteen seconds to guess the word "bubble."

Joan looked troubled when she saw the word she had to act out. She hated this round, but like the trouper that she was she gave it all she had. She dropped to all fours, making a chewing motion with her mouth. I yelled out, "Cow." Then she collapsed and I yelled out, "Dead cow." Joan jumped to her feet and acted out eating something. In twenty-two seconds I had correctly guessed that the word was "hamburger." But the other team won the round and the twenty points by eight seconds.

Joan and I moved ahead in the stunt round where Cliff and I raced to see who could take a pile of clothes and separate the whites from the colors faster. Cliff obviously hadn't washed enough of his own laundry in the past because he hesitated when he reached those between-colors like beige and tan. Those twenty-five points were ours.

During the commercial break Joan and I huddled together.

"They're tough," she said.

"We're tougher though. Or at least more evil. That has to count for something."

Joan stretched and took a sip from a nearby glass of water.

"Do you still want to win?" I asked.

She paused and considered the question. "I don't want to lose."

"Let's finish them virgins off."

Bill welcomed back the audience and told them that we were going into the lightning round and either team could win.

I took a deep breath. At this point I agreed with Joan completely. I didn't want to lose. We both went into the round with this mindset. It didn't hurt that we knew that Lake Titicaca was the deepest lake in the world or that a form of Japanese poetry composed of seventeen syllables in three lines is called a haiku.

"Ben and Joan have won the game!" Bill announced to the audience.

Joan hugged me. If nothing else, we had finished what we started and now it was almost over. Cliff and Betsy congratulated us, then were quickly shuffled off the stage.

By winning three games we didn't have to go through the breaking and entering ordeal again. We instantly were entitled to the grand prize selected just for us. With any luck we'd be home in an hour. I started feeling silly for expecting today to be any kind of disaster.

Lorraine Aqua Viva Heidegger rushed over to us at the commercial break.

"Applause, applause, applause, applause," she said, patting her hands together. "And wait till you see what we've got planned. Some people thought it was too much. But you don't get anywhere in the business if you don't take chances." Then she was gone as quickly as she came.

We were herded over to the middle of the stage. Just before the cameras rolled, Bill and Anke ran over and stood next to us. Bill Modell, whom I had failed to bond with during the course our appearances, actually put his arms around us.

"And what do we have for Ben and Joan, three-time 'Breaking and Entering' champs? We have a dream honeymoon vacation!"

The announcer's voice came on again and told us that we were going on a honeymoon cruise to Norway. Plus luggage. Plus spending money. Plus a camcorder. Joan and I shook our heads in disbelief. But then that's when the feeling started. The same feeling that I had had at the garlic festival just before Joan passed out. The same feeling just as we were about to cross the border to Mexico. It was a feeling of dread I couldn't justify. Nothing bad was happening. These people were throwing prizes at us. We just had to hold hands, maybe peck each other on the cheek, thank them, then leave.

"But there's still more," Bill added. "Ben and Joan, we know you haven't been able to afford a wedding. So we're going to give you one ourselves, right here and right now!"

"I beg your pardon?" I asked.

"That's right, a wedding. And we haven't forgotten a thing."

They opened up the side of the set, usually reserved for the breaking and entering segment, and it was dressed up like a chapel. The crew handed out bags of rice to the studio audience. Bill walked us over to the chapel.

"What should we do?" Joan whispered. "I don't want to marry you! And I don't want to get married in this!" She pointed to the costumes we were wearing.

Once we were in the chapel set, organ music started playing. Bouquets of plastic flowers lined the walls. I searched my mind frantically for a gracious way to get out of this predicament.

"Are you thinking?" I asked Joan.

"We could just refuse. Tell them we're not ready."

I started to get more frantic as the music continued. Then a thought occurred to me. Why not just do it? We'd gone to such ridiculous lengths already, why stop here? There was such a thing as divorce.

"Let's just do it!" I whispered back to Joan as Anke Mitmar started singing "Oh Promise Me."

"What? Are you crazy?"

"No. We'll do it, go to Norway, come back and get divorced. What does it really matter?"

Joan shot me a menacing look that told me she that she'd never fall into one of my schemes again. "OK," she whispered, "but we are *not* going to be one of those gay couples that sleep together then write one of those ponderous articles about it for the *L.A. Weekly*, you hear me? No sex, just prizes."

The song was finished and Bill Modell walked offstage for a

moment, then returned with a priest. When the priest was finally
standing in front of me I saw that it was Father Felice, making another one of his television appearances. He started a short version
of the wedding vows. There was a pounding in my head. I glanced
around the studio and saw audience members poised to clobber
us with cheap Minute Rice. *We're going to take the prizes and run.*
We're going to take the prizes and run. Then I remembered Father
Felice from all of his televised appearances, lashing out against
the queer community. It couldn't have been randomness that
brought him here to bind Joan and I in his web of hate and big-
otry. *At some point I have to say no.*

"Do you take this woman to be your lawfully wedded wife?"

"Could you repeat that please."

"I said, do you take this woman to be your lawfully wedded
wife?"

Sweat was dripping down my brow. I felt paralyzed. "Could you
repeat that one more time please."

Father Felice gave me a disapproving glare; the same look I
had seen in from him in his speeches about gay marriages and
equal rights for gays and lesbians. "Are you going to take her or
not?" he snarled.

"No."

"Did I hear you correctly, son?"

"I said no."

"I say no, too," Joan added.

Father Felice looked around the stage, confused as to what to do.
Bill Modell walked over to us and tried to downplay the situation.

"Our little lovebirds having a case of the jitters?"

"We're just not going to do it."

Father Felice put his hand on my shoulder. "I don't understand
what's going on."

I realized that I had gotten us this far but I had no idea what to
do next.

"What's going on," Joan said loudly, "is that Ben and I are not
engaged. We're not lovers. We're best friends and we're both gay."

"What's going on here?" Father Felice repeated, looking for some
help offstage. "Can somebody tell me what the hell is going on?"

"This is what's going on," I said, walking over to Bill Modell
and kissing him on the lips.

What happened next is mostly a blur, something I'll remember one day through therapy or hypnosis. Best as I can recount, it went like this. Bill Modell shrieked, pushed me away, and retreated off the stage. Father Felice started screaming "sinners, sinners, sodomites, sinners." Lorraine Aqua Viva Heidegger stormed out onto the stage and stopped the cameras from rolling. Joan and I ran off the stage and through the aisles past the confused studio audience who threw rice at us just the same.

Joan and I felt exhilarated for the first few hours after leaving the studio. Then depression set in. I started calculating how much, in cash and merchandise, we had walked away from. It was too much for Joan to handle so she sent me home.

We didn't speak for a few days. Joan said she needed her space, but I knew that she was rethinking our association and where it had finally lead us. I received a registered letter from Lorraine Aqua Viva Heidegger that our winnings had been forfeited and that if we wanted to fight it she'd see us in court.

I tried calling Matt at the studio but was told that he was no longer an employee of the show.

We had lost it all. Love. Money. Dignity. We weren't even going to get the meager year's supply of Listerine or cough drops that the losing team usually received.

Wednesday night I could not sleep. There was nothing on television and no one to phone at 2:00 in the morning since I couldn't call Joan. I put on my clothes and drove to the supermarket. I thought that maybe if I bought myself some of my own parting gifts I'd feel better.

I roamed the aisles, picking up things like marshmallow fluff and fruit rolls. Soon I had a cart full of this stuff. There was a sale on applesauce so I pulled out a case of them and carried them over to my cart. It was at that point that I saw Matt. The case of applesauce went crashing to the ground. I followed my instinct, the instinct I had the very first time I met him, the only instinct I should have ever paid attention to, and walked over and kissed him. He put his arms around me and kissed me back.

"I want to take you home," I told him, "but I don't know if I can fit you in my cart."

Matt and I spent the night together. It was an amazing evening, the most tender night of lovemaking I had ever experienced.

Afterward I knew I had to make my peace with Joan. The next day I drove to her house and rang the bell. She opened the door dressed in a white T-shirt and sweatpants. I told her about what happened between me and Matt and she seemed genuinely glad about it. I told her I didn't want to lose her friendship.

"Of course we're going to stay friends, Ben, but things are going to be different. I need some stability in my life. No more craziness. No more running off on any of your bizarre schemes."

"I understand that."

"We're too old for that."

"I understand that, too."

"I mean, my God, we were standing there, about to be married."

"Imagine."

Just then the phone rang. Joan answered it and seemed surprised by the content of the call.

"How'd you get my phone number?" she asked the person she was speaking to. "When? For how long? Are you kidding, I'm flattered!" She started scribbling down some information. Then she hung up the phone and rushed to the bedroom and pulled out a suitcase.

"What's going on?"

"Ben," she panted, "you're not going to believe this. That was Anke Mitmar."

"*The* Anke Mitmar?"

"She's doing a modeling session in the south of France and she's inviting me to go with her. Thank God I have my passport. I have to stop at the bank. The magazine she's modeling for is paying for everything though."

Joan started running from room to room, pulling things frantically out of drawers and closets.

"No more craziness in your life, huh?" I asked, flatly.

"What's that?"

"No more running off on crazy schemes."

"Are you saying something?" Joan asked, turning on the radio. "I can't hear you."

I turned off the radio, gave her a hug, helped her pack, then drove her to the airport.

Whose Song?

THOMAS GLAVE

Yes, now they're waiting to rape her, but how can they know? The girl with strum-vales, entire forests, behind her eyes. Who has already known the touch of moondewed kisses, nightwing sighs, on her teenage skin. Cassandra. Lightskinned, lean. Lovelier to them for the light. How can they know? The darkskinned ones aren't even hardly what they want. They have been taught, have learned well and well. Them black bitches, that's some skank shit, they sing. Give you VD on the woody, make your shit fall off. How can they know? Have been taught. Cassandra, fifteen, in the light. On her way to the forests. In the light. Hasn't known a man yet. Hasn't wanted to. How can they know? She prefers Tanya's lips, the skin-touch of silk. Tanya, girlfriend, sixteen and fine, dark glider, schoolmate-lover, large-nippled, -thighed. Tanya. Who makes her come and come again when the mamas are away, when houses settle back into silent time and wrens swoopflutter their wings back down into the nightbird's song. Tanya and Cassandra. Kissing. Holding. Climbing and gliding. What the grown girls do, they think, belly-kissing but shy. Holding. She makes me feel my skin, burrowing in. Which one of them thinks that? Which one flies? Who can tell? Climbing and gliding. Coming. Wet. Coming. Fast. Laughing. Smelling. Girlsex, she-love, and the nightbird's song. Thrilling and trilling. Smooth bellies, giving face, brushing on and on. Cassandra. Tanya swooping down, brown girls, dusky flesh, and the nightbird's song. How can they know? The boys have been watching them, have begun to know things about them watchers know or guess. The boys, touching themselves in nightly rage, watching them. Wanting more of Cassandra because she doesn't want them. Wanting to set the forests on fire, cockbrush those glens. How can they know? They are there and they are there and they are watching. Now.

Sing this tale, then, of a Sound Hill rape. Sing it, low and mournful, soft, beneath the kneeling trees on either side of the rusty bridge out by Eastchester Creek; where the sun hangs low over the Sound and water meets the sky; where the departed walk along Shore Road and the joggers run; where morning rabbits leap away from the pounding joggers' steps. Sing it far and wide, this tale of pain and regret, of rage, this sorrow song woven into the cresting nightbird's blue. Sing it, in that far-off place, far up away from it all, where the black people live and think they've at last found peace; where there are homes, small homes and large, with modest yards, fruit hedges, taxus, juniper trees; where the silver hoses, coiled, sag and lean; where the withered arms hanging out of second-story windows are the arms of that lingering ghost or aging lonely busybody everybody knows. In that place, that northerly corner of the city where no elevated IRT train yet comes; where the infrequent buses to Orchard Beach and Pelham Bay sigh out spent lives and empty nights when they run; where the Sound pulls watersmell through troubled dreams and midnight pains, the sleeping loneliness and silence of a distant place. Sound Hill, beneath your leaning trees and waterwash, who do you grieve for now? Sound Hill girl of the trees and the girlflesh, where are you now? Will those waters of the Sound flow beside you now? Caress you with light-kisses and bless you now? The City Island currents and the birds rush by you now? O sing it. Sing it for that yellow girl, dark girl, brown girl homely or fine, everygirl displaced, neither free nor named. Sing it for that girl swinging her axe through the relentless days, suckling a child or selling her ass in the cheap hotels down by the highway truckers' stop for chump change. Sing it for this girl, swishing her skirt and T-shirt, an almost-free thing, instinctual, throwing her head back to the breeze. Her face lifted to the sky. Now, Jesus. Walk here, Lamb. In thy presence there shall be light and light. Grace. Cadence. A witness or a cry. Come, now. All together. Sing it.

How could we know? Three boys in a car, we heard, but couldn't be neighbors of ours. Had to be from some other part of the world, we thought; the projects or the Valley. Not from here. In this place every face knows every eye, we thought, what's up here in the heart always is clear. But they were not kind nor good, neither kin nor known. If they were anything at all besides unseen, they were maimed. Three boys, three boys. In a car. Long legs, lean hands. In a car. Bitter mouths, tight asses, and the fear of fear. Boys or men and hard. In their car. Who did not like it. Did not like the way those forest eyes gazed out at those darker desert ones, at the eyes of that other who had known what it was to be dark and loathed. Yo, darkskinned bitch. So it had been said. Yo, skillet ass. Don't be cutting your eyes at me, bitch, I'll fuck your black ass up. It had been said. Ugly black bitch. You need some dick. Them eyes gone get you killed, rolling them at me like that. It had been said. Had to be, *had* to be from over by Edenwald, we thought. Rowdy, raunchy, no kind of class. Nasty homies on the prowl, not from this 'hood. How could we know? Three boys, fretful, frightened, angry in a row. The burning rope had come to them long ago in willed and willful dreams, scored mean circles and scars into their once-gorgeous throats. The eyes that had once looked up in wonder from their mother's arms had been beaten, hammered into rings, dark pain-pools that belied their depth. Deeper. Where it hurt, where they lived, named and unnamed. How could they know? Know that those butterflies and orchids of the other world, that ice-green velvet of the other world, the precious stones that got up and wept before the unfeeling sky and the bears that slept away entire centuries with memories of that once-warm sweet milk on their lips, were not for them? So beaten, so denied, as they were and as they believed, their own hands had grown to claws over the years; savaged their own skin. Needles? Maybe, we thought. In the reviling at large, who could tell? Pipes, bottles? Vials? So we thought. Of course. Who could know, and who who knew would tell? Who who knew would sing through the veil the words of that song, about the someone-or-thing that had torn out their insides and left them there, far from the velvet and the butterflies and the orchid-time? The knower's voice, if voice it was, only whispered down bitter rains when they howled, and left us only the curve of their skulls beneath the scarred flesh on those nights, bony white, when the moon smiled.

And she, so she: alone that day. Fresh and wet still from Tanya's arms, pajama invitations, and TV nights, after-dark giggles and touches, kisses, while belowstairs the mama slept through world news, terrorist bombings, cleansings ethnic and unclean. Alone that day, the day after, yellow girl, walking out by the golden gray-swishing Sound, higher up along the Shore Road way and higher, higher up where no one ever walks alone, higher still by where the dead bodies every year turn up (four Puerto Rican girl-things cut up, garbage-bagged, found there last year: bloated hands, swollen knees, and the broken parts); O higher still, Cassandra, where the fat joggers run, higher still past the horse stables and the smell of hay, higher yet getting on to where the whitefolks live and the sundowns die. Higher. Seeking watersmell and sheen for those forests in her eyes; seeking that summer sundown heat on her skin; seeking something away from 'hood catcalls and yo, bitch, let me in. Would you think she doesn't already know what peacefulness means, contains? She's already learned of the dangers of the too-high skirt, the things some of them say they'd like to put between her knees. The blouse that reveals, the pants that show too much hip. Ropes hers and theirs. Now seeking only a place where she can walk away, across the water if need be, away from the beer cans hurled from cars, the What's up, bitch yells and the burning circle-scars. Cassandra, Cassandra. Are you a bitch out here? The sun wexing goldsplash across her now says no. The water stretching out to Long Island summerheat on the other side says no, and the birds wheeling overhead, *okay, okay,* they cry, call down the skytone, concurring: the word is no. Peace and freedom, seasmell and free. A dark girl's scent riding on her thighs. Cassandra. Tanya. Sing it.

But they watching. The three. Singing. Come, now, listen: a bitch ain't nothing but a ho, sing those three. Have been taught. (But by whom?) Taught and taut. Taught low and harsh, that rhythm, brutal melody. Melodylessness in mixture, lovelessness in joy. Drunk on flame, and who the fuck that bitch think she is anyway? they say—for they had seen her before, spoken to her and her kind; courted her favor, her attentions, in that car. Can't talk to nobody, bitch, you think you all a that? Can't speak to nobody, bitch, you think your pussy talks and shit? How could they know then?—of her forests, smoldering? Know and feel?—how in that growing silent heat those inner trees had uprooted, hurled stark branches at the outer sky? The firestorm and the after-rain remained unseen. Only the lashes fluttered, and the inner earth grew hard. With those many ropes choking so many of them in dreams, aware of the circles burnt into their skins, how could they know? How could they not know?

Robbie. Dee. Bernard. Three and three. Young and old. Too old for those jeans sliding down their asses. Too young for the rope and the circle's clutch. Too old to love so much their own wet dreams splashed out onto she they summoned out of that uncentered rolling world. She, summoned, to walk forth before their fire as the bitch or cunt. So they thought, would think and sing: still too young for the nursing of that keening need, the unconscious conscious wish to obliterate through vicious dreams who they were and are, have been, and are not. Blackmenbrothers, lovers, sons of strugglers. Sharecroppers, cocksuckers, black bucks, and whores. Have been and are, might still be, and are not. A song. To do away with what they have and have not; what they can be, they think, are told by that outer pounding chorus they can be—black boys, pretty boys, big dicks, tight asses, pretty boys, black scum, or funky homie trash—and cannot. Their hearts replaced by gnashing teeth, dirt; the underscraping grinch, an always-howl. Robbie Dee Bernard. Who have names and eyelids, fears, homie-homes. Watching now. Looking out for a replacement for those shredded skins. Cause that bitch think she all a that, they sing. Word, got that lightskin, good hair, think she fly. Got them titties that need some dick up in between. The flavor. Not like them darkskinned bitches, they sing. (But do the words have joy?) Got to cut this bitch down to size, the chorus goes. A tune. Phat pussy. Word, G! Said hey-ho! Said a-hey-ho! Word, my brother. My nigger. Sing it.

So driving. Looking. Watching. Seeing. Their words a blue song, the undercolor of the nightbird's wing. Is it a song you have heard before? Heard it sung sweet and clear to someone you hate before? Listen:—Oh shit, yo, there she go. Right up there. Straight on. Swingin her ass like a high-yellow ho. Said hey-ho! Turn up the volume on my man J Live J. Drive up, yo. Spook the bitch. Gonna get some serious pussy outa this shit.—Driving, slowing, slowing down. Feeling the circles, feeling their own necks. Burning skins, cockheads fullstretched and hard. Will she have a chance, dreaming of girlkisses, against that hard? In the sun. Here. And.

Pulling up.—So, Miss Lightskin, they sing, what you doing out here? Walking by yourself, you ain't scared? Ain't scared somebody gonna try to get some of your skin? Them titties looking kinda fly, girl. Come on, now. Get in.

Was that, then, the one mistake she made? Feeling the smoldering in those glens about to break? The sun gleaming down silver whiteheat on her back? *And O how she had only longed to walk the walk.* To continue on and on and on and through to those copses where, at the feet of that very old and most wise woman-tree of all, she might gaze into those stiller waters of minnow-fishes, minnow-girls, and there yes! quell quell quell quell quell the flames. The gravest error?—as one of them then broke through her glens, to shout that she wasn't nothing anyway but a yellow bitch with a whole lotta attitude and a skanky cunt. As (oh yes, it was true, rivers and fire, snake daggers and black bitches, she had had enough) she flung back words on what exactly he should do with his mother's cunt, cause your mother, nigger, is the only mother-fucking bitch out here. And then? Who could say or know? The 5-0 were nowhere in sight; all passing cars had passed; only the wheeling birds and that drifting sun above were witnesses to what they could not prevent. Cassandra, Cassandra. —Get in the car, bitch.— —Fuck no, I won't. Leave me alone. Leave me— —trying to say Fuck off, y'all leave me the fuck alone, but whose hand was that, then, grabbing for her breast? Whose hand *is* that, on her ass, pressing now, right now, up into her flesh? —Stop it, y'all. Get the fuck off before—screaming and crying. Cursing, running. Sneakered feet on asphalt, pursuit, and the laughing loud. An easy catch. —We got you now, bitch.— Who can hear? The sun can only stare, and the sky is gone.

Driving, driving, driving on. Where can they take her? Where will they? They all want some, want to be fair. Fair is fair: three dicks, one cunt. That is their song. Driving on. Pelham Bay Park? they think. But naw, too many people, niggers and Ricans with a whole buncha kids and shit. (The sun going down. Driving on.) How about under the bridge, by Eastchester Creek? That's it, G! Holding her, holding, but can't somebody slap the bitch to make her shut up? Quit crying, bitch. Goddamn. A crying-ass bitch in a little funky-ass car. Now weeping more. Driving on.—Gonna call the police, she says, crying more; choking in that way they like, for then (oh, yes, they know) in that way from smooth head to hairy base will she choke on them. They laugh.—What fucking 5-o you gonna call, bitch? You lucky we ain't take your yellow ass over to the projects. Fuck your shit in the elevator, throw your ass off the roof. These bitches, they laugh. Just shut up and sit back. Sit back, sit back. Driving on.

Now the one they call Robbie is talking to her.—Open it, he says. Robbie, O Robbie. Eager and edgy, large-eyed and fine. Robbie, who has a name, unspoken hopes; private dreams. How can they know? He'll be dead within a year like so many others, mirrored images in a mirror that shows them nothing, shattered glass and regret: a wicked knife's slide from a brother's hand to his hidden chewed-up heart. Feeling now only the circle around his neck that keeps all in thrall. For now he must be a man for them. Must show the steel. Robbie don't be frontin, he prays they think, Robbie be hard. Will they like you better, Robbie, then, if you be hard? Will the big boys finally love you, take you in, Robbie, if you be hard? But it's deep sometimes, isn't it, Robbie, with all that hard? Deep and low. . . . —He knows. Knows the clear tint of that pain. Alone and lonely . . . unknown, trying to be hard. Not like it was back then when *then when he said you was pretty*. Remember? All up in his arms . . . one of your boys, Darrell J. In his arms. Where nobody couldn't see. Didn't have to be hard. Rubbing up, rubbing. Kissing up on you. Licking. Talking shit about lovelove and all a that *But naw man* he said the first time (Darrell J., summertime, 10 P.M., off the court, hotwet, crew gone home, had an extra 40, sweaty chest neck face, big hands, shoulders, smile, was fine), *just chillin whyn't you come on hang out?*—so said Darrell J. with the hands and the yo yo yo yo going on and on with them eyes and *mouth tongue up in his skin* my man—: kissing up on Robbie the second time, pretty Robbie, the third time and the fourth and the *we did and he* kissing licking holding y'all two and O Robbie Robbie Robbie. A homie's song. Feeling then. Underneath him, pretty. In his arms. *Where nobody couldn't see   didn't have to be hard   kissing up on him shy shy and*   himinyou youinhim   Robbie, Robbie. Where has the memory gone? Back then, straddling hips, homie-kisses and the nightbird's song. But can't go back there, can you? To feel and feel. Gots to be hard. Can't ever touch him again, undress him, kiss his thing . . . feel it pressing against the teeth and the slow-hipped song. Black skin on skin and

— *but he was holdin onto me and slidin, slidin way up inside suckin comin inside me in me in hot naw didn't need no jimmy aw shit now hold on holdin him and I was I was Robbie Robbie Robbie Darrell J. together we was and I we I we came we hotwet on his belly my side slidin over him under him holdin and we came we* but naw, man, can't even be *doing* that motherfucking punk shit out here. You crazy? You buggin? Niggers be gettin smoked dusty for that shit. Y'all ain't never seen *me* do that. Gots to be hard.—So open it, bitch, he says. Lemme get my fingers on up in there. Awright, awright. Damn, man, he says, nobody don't got a jimmy? This bitch stinks, man, he says, know I'ma probably get some VD shit on my hands and shit. They laugh.—He a man, all right. Robbie! Ain't no faggot, yo. Not like we *heard.* They laugh.—Just put a sock on it, the one they call Dee says. Chillchill, yo. Everybody gonna get their chance.

And the sun. Going down, going down. Light ending now, fire and ice, blue time watersheen and the darkened plunge. Sink, golden sun. Rest your bronze head in the Sound and the sea beyond. The birds, going down, going down. Movement of trees, light swathed in leaves. Going down, going down. And.

Hard to see now, but that's OK, they say. This bitch got enough for everybody here under the bridge. No one's around now, only rusty cars and rats. Who cares if they shove that filthy rag into her mouth and tie it there? It's full of turpentine and shit, but the night doesn't care. The same night that once covered them in swamps from fiery light. Will someone come in white robes to save a lightskinned bitch this time?

Hot. Dark. On the backseat. Burning bright. Burning. On the backseat. Fire and rage. —Naw, man, Robbie, not so hard, man. You gone wear the shit out fore I get my chance. Who said that? Which one in the dark? O but can't tell, for all are hidden now, and all are hard. The motherfucking *rig*orous shit, one of them says. Shut up, bitch. Was that you, Bernard? Did you miss your daddy when he went off with the one your mama called a dirty nigger whore, Bernard? Was that where you first learned everything there was to learn, and nothing?—there, Bernard? When he punched you in the face and left you behind, little boy Bernard? You cried. Without. A song unheard. A song like the shadowrain—wasn't it? The shadowrain that's always there so deep, deep

down inside your eyes, Bernard. Cold rain inside. Tears and tears.
Then fists and kicks on a black shitboy's head. Little punk-looking
nigger dumped in a foster home, age ten, named Bernard. Fuck-
head faggot ass, the boys there said. The ones who stuck it up in
you. Again and again. The second and the third . . . — don't hurt
me, don't!—screamed that one they called the faggot ass pussy
bitch. You, Bernard. How could they know? Know that the little
bitch punk scrunched up under the bed had seen the whole night
and afterward and after alone? Bernard? *Hurts, mama. Daddy—:*
Rain. Rain. Little faggot ass punk. Break his fucking face, yo. Kick
his faggot ass down the stairs. Then he gone suck my dick. Suck it,
bitch, fore we put this motherfucking hammer up your ass. The
one you trusted most of all in that place, in all those places . . .
everywhere? Bernard? The one who said he'd have your back no
matter what. Little man, my man, he said. Smiling down. His teeth
so white and wide. Smiling down. Smiling when he got you by the
throat, sat on your chest and made you swallow it. Swallow it,
bitch, he sang. Smiling down. Choking, choked. Deep inside the
throat. Where has the memory gone? Something broken, then a
hand. A reaching-out howl within the rain. A nightbird's rage. A
punk, used up. Leave the nigger there, yo, they said. Till the next
time. And the next. On the floor. Under the bed. Under. Bleeding
under. You, Bernard.

The words to every song on earth are buried deep somewhere.
Songs that must be sung, that must never be sung. That must be
released from deep within the chest yet pulled back and held.
Plaintive and low, they rail; buried forever beneath the passing
flesh, alone and cold, they scream. The singer must clutch them
to the heart, where they are sanctified, nurtured, healed. Songs
which finally must be released yet recalled, in that place where no
one except the singer ever comes, in one hand caressing the keys
of life wounded, ravaged, in the other those of the precious skin
and life revealed. The three of them and Cassandra know the
words. Lying beneath them now and blind, she knows the words.
Tasting turpentine and fire, she knows the words. —Hell no, yo,
that bitch ain't dead.— A voice. —Fucked up, yo. The rag's in her
mouth, how we gone get some mouth action now?— —Aw, man,
fuck that shit.— Who says that? —My turn. My turn.— They know
the words.

Now comes Dee. Can't even really see her, has to navigate. Wiggles his ass a little, farts softly to let off stress. —Damn, Dee, nasty motherfucker! they laugh. But he is busy, on to something. Sniffs and sniffs. At the bitch's asshole. At her cunt. —Cause yeah, yo, he says, y'all know what's up with this shit. They be saying this bitch done got into some bulldagger shit. Likes to suck pussy, bulldagger shit. —Word? —The phattest bitch around, yo, he says. Bulldagger shit.

Dee. DeeDee. Someone's boy. Has a place that's home. Eastchester, or Mount V. Has a heart that hates his skin and a mind half gone. Is ugly now, got cut up, but smoked the nigger who did it. Can't sleep at night, wanders seas; really wants to die. The lonely bottle might do it if the whiffs up don't. The empty hand might do it if the desire can't. What has been loved and not loved, what seeks still a place. The same hand, pushed by the once-winsome heart, that before painted angels, animals, miraculous creatures. Blank walls leaped into life, lightspeed and light. When (so it seemed) the whole world was light. But was discouraged, led into tunnels, and then of course was cut. The eyes went dim. Miraculous creatures. Where have the visions gone? Look, now, at that circle around his neck. Will he live? Two young ones and a dark girl waiting back there for him, frightened—will he live? Crushed angels drowned in St. Ides—will he live? When he sells the (yes, that) next week to the undercover 5-o and is set up, will he live? When they shoot him in the back and laugh at the stain that comforts them, will he live?

But now he's happy, has found it!—the hole. The soft little hole, so tight, down there, as he reaches up to squeeze her breasts. Her eyes are closed but she knows the words. *That bitch ain't dead.* How can they know? When there is time there's time, and the time is now. Time to bang the bulldagger out of her, he sings. Listen to his song:—I'ma give you a baby, bitch. (She knows the words.) Got that lightskin, think you all that, right bitch? Word, I want me some lightskin on my dick, yo. When I get done this heifer ain't gone be *half* a ho. You know know? Gonna get mines, til you know who you dis and who you don't. Til you know we the ones in *con-trol*, sing it! Got the flavor.— Dim-eyed, banging out his rage. Now, a man. Banging out his fear like the others, ain't even hardly no faggot ass. Def jam and slam, bang bang shebam. On and on as he shoots high, shoots far . . . laughter, but then a sense of falling, careening . . . sudden fear. It doesn't matter. The song goes on.

Night. Hell, no, broods the dim, that bitch ain't dead. Hasn't uttered half a sound since they began; hasn't opened her eyes to let the night look in again; hasn't breathed to the soft beating of the nightbird's wing. The turpentine rag in place. Cassandra, Cassandra. The rag, in place. Cassandra. Is she feeling something now? Cassandra. Will they do anything more to her now? Cassandra, will they leave you there? Focusing on flies, not meeting each other's eyes, will they leave you there? Running back from the burning forests behind their own eyes, the crackling and the shame? Will they leave you there? —Push that bitch out on the ground, the one they call Dee says. —Over there, by them cars and shit.— Rusty cars, a dumping ground. So, Cassandra. Yes. They'll leave you there.

Were they afraid? Happy? Who can tell? Three dark boys, three men, driving away in a battered car. Three boy-men, unseen, flesh, minds, heart. Flame. In their car. O my God, three rapists, the pretty lady in her Volvo thinks, locking her doors at the traffic light. In their car. Blood on the backseat, cum stains, even hair. Who can tell? It's time to get open now. Time to numb the fear. — Get out the whiff, yo. —40s and a blunt. —That bitch got what she deserved. —Those words, whiffs up, retreat, *she deserved it, deserved it*—and they are gone. Mirrored images in shattered glass, desire and longing, chill throbbing, and they are gone. The circles cleaving their necks. Flesh, blood and flame. A whiff and a 40. —We fucked that bitch good, G. —Night. Nightnight. Hush dark silence. Fade. They are gone.

Cassandra. What nightbirds are searching and diving for you now? What plundered forests are waiting for you now? The girl-trees are waiting for you, and so is she. Tanya. The girl-trees. Mama. How can they know? Their eyes are waiting, searching, and will soon be gray. The rats are waiting. They are gray. Cassandra, Cassandra. When the red lights come flashing on you, will they know? Fifteen, ripped open. Will they know? Lightskinned bitch nigger ho, went that song. Will they know? Girl-trees in a burning forest . . . they will know. And the night . . . .

Where is she, they're wondering, why hasn't she come home? They can't know what the rats and the car-carcasses know.

Cassandra? they are calling. Why don't you answer when night-voices call you home?

Night . . . .

Listen now to the many night voices calling, calling soft, *Cassandra. Come.* Carrying. Up. *Cassandra. Come. Out* and *up.* What remains is what remains. *Out* and *up.* They will carry her. A feeling of hands and light. Then the red lights will come. *Up* and *up.* But will she see? Will she hear? Will she know?

The girl-trees are screaming. That is their song.

It will not appear on tomorrow's morning news.

But then—come now, ask yourself—whose song, finally, shall this be? Of four dark girls, or four hundred, on their way to lasting fire in Sunday school? Of a broken-backed woman, legs bent? Her tune? Of a pair of hands, stitching for—(but they'll never grow). Of four brothers rapping, chugging?—a slapbeat in the chorus? Doing time? Something they should know?

A song of grieving ships, bodies, torch-lit roads?

(*—But then now O yes remember, remember well that time, face, place or thing: how those ten thousand million billion other ashes eyelids arms uncountable dark ceaseless burnt and even faces once fluttered, fluttered forever, in someone's dream unending, dream of no escape, beneath a black-blueblack sea; fluttered, fluttered forever, flutter still and descend, now faces ashes eyelids dark reflection and skin forever flame: descend, descend over laughing crowds.*)

A song of red earth roads. Women crying and men. Red hands, gray mouths, and the circle's clutch. A song, a song. Of sorrowing suns. Of destruction, self-destruction, when eyes lay low. A song—

But whose song is it? Is it yours? Or mine?

Hers?

Or theirs . . .—?

—But a song. A heedless, feckless tune. Here, where the night-time knows. And, well—

Yes, well—

—So, Cassandra. Now, Cassandra.

Sing it.

The Gospel of
Bartholomew
Legate:
Three
Fragments

RICK SANDFORD

On March 18, 1612, Bartholomew Legate became the last man to be burnt at the stake for saying that Christ was not divine. Reports of his trial mention a "blasphemous, heretical"[1] book that he wrote about the life of Christ, but until recently this writing was not thought to exist. However, some manuscripts have recently come to light that suggest that they may indeed be from Legate's book.

According to T. B. Howell, Legate was a native of county Essex, and of a "comely" appearance. Howell says he was of "a bold spirit, confident carriage, fluent tongue, excellently skilled in the Scriptures; and well had it been for him, if had known them less, or understood them better; whose ignorance abused the word of God, therewith to oppose God the word."[2]

The three fragments presented here were found in a storeroom of an estate that was being liquidated in the northwest of England. They had been set in type and printed, a rather amazing occurrence as the printers themselves must have known the dangers involved in abetting such a project (they were, in fact, later

---

[1] J. Payne Collier, ed., *The Edgerton Papers: A Collection of Public and Private Documents, Chiefly Illustrative of the Times of Elizabeth and James I* (John Bowyer Nichols and Son, 1809).

[2] T. B. Howell, ed., *A Complete Collection of State Trials and Proceedings for High Treason and Other Crimes and Misdemeanors from the Earliest Period to the Year 1783* (T. C. Hansard, 1816).

tried and imprisoned). On one of the sheets is a signature, "Bartholomew Legate," but whether this is in Legate's hand is not known for certain.

The three fragments seem to represent the beginning and end of the piece, with a longer central portion recounting a part of "the last supper." It is to be hoped that the rest of the manuscript may come to light and the full extent of Legate's "blasphemous, heretical" book may at last find its proper recognition.

Fragment One:

IN the beginning was the Seede, & the Seede was in Silence, and the Seede *was* Him.

2 The same was in the beginning Hee.

3 All things were made of Seede, and without Him was not any thing made that was made.

4 In the Seede was life, and life was the light of men.

5 And the light shineth in Silence, and the Silence comprehended it not.

Fragment Two:

NOW when the even was come, he sate downe, and the disciples with him.

2 And he said unto us, Verely I say unto you, that I shall not be with you long.

3 And we were exceeding sorowfull, and began every one to ask of him where he was going, but he answered us not.

4 And we said to him, Are you leaving because you feel we have betrayed you?

5 And he answered and said, The sonne of man goeth as it is determined: but he that shall lift up his rod in remembrance of mee shall be magnified.

6 And we began to enquire among ourselves, what this might meane, and to aske of him, What shall we doe, that we might worke the workes of God?

7 Labour not for the meat which perisheth, but for that meat which endureth unto everlasting life, which the Sonne of man shall give unto you.

8 Thomas said therefore unto him, What signe shewest thou then, that we may see, and beleeve thee? What does thou worke?

9 And hee tooke bread, and gave thankes, and brake it, and gave unto us, saying, Man shall not live by bread alone, but by the seede that proceedeth out of the mouth of God.

10 And laying aside his garments, he displayed himselfe and said, Verely, verely I say unto you, he that receiveth whatsoever I give, receiveth me: and he that receiveth me, receiveth the Father.

11 Take, eate, this is my body which is given for you.

12 And the disciples began to enquire amongst themselves, what this might meane.

13 And Iesus said unto them, I am the bread of life.

14 Your fathers did eate Manna in the wildernesse, and are dead.

15 This is the bread which cometh down from heaven, that a man may eate thereof, and not die.

16 The disciples therefore strove amongst themselues, saying, How can our master give us his flesh to eate?

17 And Simon Peter saith unto him, Shalt not I rather washe thy feete, and not thy feete only, but also thy hands and face?

18 Jesus answered, and said unto him, If thou doest not regard the miracle of my body, of what worth is thy comfort?

19 And Peter saith unto him, Lord, I am ready to goe with thee both into prison, and to death.

20 But hee said unto him, I tell thee, Peter, before this day is done, thou shalt know me in the issue of mine owne most inner selfe. Thou hast already twice denied me, shalt thou do so more?

21 And Iesus took the cup, and when he had given thankes, he offered of his person againe, saying, Wilt not this vessel quench a longer thirst?

22 Verely, verely I say unto you, Except yee eate the flesh of the sonne of man, and drinke his blood, yee have no life in you.

23 Whoso eateth my flesh, and drinketh my blood, hath eternall life.

24 For my flesh is meate indeed, and my blood is drinke indeed.

25 He that eateth my flesh, and drinketh my blood, dwelleth in me, and I in him.

26 Many of the disciples, when they had heard this, said, This is an hard saying, who can heare it?

27 And when Iesus knew in himselfe, that his disciples murmured at it, hee said unto them, Doeth this offend you?

28 What and doe yee not see the sonne of man ascending up where he was before? Is not this the Father's will?

29 But Philip said unto him, Lord, shew us the Father, and it sufficeth us.

30 Iesus said unto him, Have I bin so long time with you, and yet hast thou not knowen me, Philip? He that sees me thus, sees the father, and how sayest thou then, Shew us the father? Beleevest thou not that this is the father?

31 And Philip cast aside his robe, disclosing his nakednesse, and holding himselfe he cried, Is this also the father? Am I my own begetter?

32 Iesus saide, The words that I speake unto you, I speake not only of myself: but of the father that dwelleth in all of us. Beleeve me that I am in the father, and the father is in me:

33 Verely, verely, I say unto you, he that beleeveth on me, shall receiveth of me: This is the worke of God.

34 And Philip knelt before him, crying, Truely, thou art mine owne most precious vessel: of water of gold and milk of pearls.

35 And Iesus saide to him, Drinke ye all of it: for this my seede shall spew forth in thee as the remission of all thy feare.

36 And as Philip beganne to kisse him, Iesus closed his eyes and said, With desire I have desired thy desire.

Fragment Three:

STILL I dreame and even see in waking hours: My God why hast thou forsaken me?

2 And in that colde and day time darke, no longer fearefull, I climbe his tree.

3 Holding on and pulling up, I am come, I whisper, I am with thee, Lord.

4 And from that beame my arms let downe, to impart myself upon his crowne.

5 Thus is hee risen harde within me, his life rejoycing mortalitie, his eyes enlightened to trinity: hee his selfe and I and Wee:

6 For that thy mercy shall not forfeit, unto thy bowles I commend my spirit.

7 And witha cry he suddenly tears forth himselfe from off

the crosse, breaking sinew bone and fleshe, flinging us twined into the skie.

8 And thus ascend we above the clouds, as he enioynes his bloode about mee:

9 Hee my matrix, and I his God:

10 Quickening now desire: to die:

Notes
on the
Contributors

Eitan Alexander

Eitan Alexander, 33, lives in Los Angeles, which helps blur the line between fact and fiction.

Kevin Bentley

Kevin Bentley is a writer and editor living in San Francisco whose work has appeared in *Diseased Pariah News, ZYZZYVA,* and the *James White Review,* as well as being included in the forthcoming *Flesh and the Word 4. "Why do you have to tell everything?* I write for love, and revenge: I want the last word. As a gay man, I have a terrific drive to tell what had to be kept secret, and to find the meaning in it. Also, I have an imperative to make something out of so many scenes of which I'm the only survivor. Memory is everything."

Peter Cashorali

In the final half year of my lover Caesar Bonilla's life, a sudden rebirth of desire between us cut through much of the depression and despair he experienced. The Grimm brothers in their collection offer a fairy tale called "The White Snake." This content and that form came together and produced the fairy tale in this anthology. Your life follows pathways hundreds, even thousands of years old, and yet has never been lived before. Your life is heroic, terrifying, an astonishment to someone observing it as it occurs, unable to imagine what will happen next.

Gil Cuadros

"I want to write about AIDS spiritually, symbolically, out of context of time and reality. Our communities are heartbroken, burned out, attacked, enemies ready to deny our civil rights. Families would see their son's lover punished by tossing him to the street. These horrors have become commonplace, we are nearly emotionless. I wanted to write a book with my beloved Marcus and me as the main characters, as a tribute to our love. He died March 29, 1996. The pain is so intense I'm close to not wanting to write again. The book is on hold."

Gil Cuadros died on August 29, 1996.

Jay Ruben Dayrit

Jay Ruben Dayrit is originally from Kolonia, Pohnpei in the Federated States of Micronesia. He is a graduate of Yale University and the Creative Writing Program at San Francisco State University. His work has recently appeared in *XY Magazine* and *Sumtin' To Say/Behind Our Backs,* a gay men's resource guide published by the San Francisco AIDS Foundation. "'Drinking Water Lilies' began as a few choppy paragraphs, written in haste, out of the need to encapsulate the events of a particular weekend, like if I didn't write something down that very second, it would slip away forever. And then those few paragraphs sat in a notebook for about six years. In graduate school, I finally built them into a story. By then, enough time had passed for me to fictionalize what was once reality, so much so that I now have difficulty recalling what really happened and who was actually there. And yet, the emotions remain intact. Perhaps this defines successful fiction. Of my completed stories, 'Drinking Water Lilies' is my favorite."

Viet Dinh

Viet Dinh doesn't eat much sushi, because, being an aspiring writer, he can't afford it. A graduate from the Johns Hopkins University with a double major in biology and writing, he currently lives in Denver, which boasts a large Vietnamese community. Homosexuality within Asian communities isn't discussed, but silently adopts the dreaded "don't ask, don't tell, don't pursue" policy, thus increasing the invisibility of Asian queers everywhere. That doesn't mean they're not there, but you just have to look that much harder. The Vietnamese word for homosexual is *lai cái.* Use it often and well.

Robert Drake

"The Man was created so that I could exorcise some personal demons of violence and anger via pure fantasy. I'm a Quaker—like Adam's life-partner Matthew was—and I don't believe in violence as a means to an end. This understanding plagues Adam/The Man as well: if The Man was created in great part to avenge Matthew's death, does it honor the memory of a peaceful man to exercise violence in the course of retribution? The answer is that it doesn't—but in this instance, it helps to salve the pain of the living. Adam's not a Quaker (obviously) but he is haunted by the Quaker testimony of Matthew's life. The Man is never 100 percent certain that what he is doing is morally the right thing—although he desperately wants it to be. The first three novels of The Man hang upon the heroic myth structure as outlined by Joseph Campbell. This story is separate from that."

Thomas Glave

Thomas Glave has been a Fellow of the New York Foundation for the Arts and of the Fine Arts Center in Provincetown. A graduate of Bowdoin College, he is currently enrolled in the M.F.A. creative writing program at Brown University.

G. Winston James

G. Winston James is a member of the Other Countries: Black Gay Expression literary collective. His prose is featured in *Shade: An Anthology of Short Fiction by Gay Men of African Descent* (Avon Books) and *Waves: An Anthology of New Gay Fiction* (Vintage Books). His poetry appears in *Milking Black Bull: 11 Gay Black Poets* (Vega Press), *Sojourner: Black Gay Voices in the Age of AIDS* (Other Countries Press), and *The Road Before Us: 100 Gay Black Poets* (Galiens Press). The short story "Storm" is a part of the author's attempt to observe the ongoing AIDS crisis from a nongay vantage point—especially from that of individuals who are related to closeted gay and seropositive men. His writing is concerned with revealing how each of us in our interrelated communities deals with the truth and loss.

Alex Jeffers

"A Handbook for the Castaway": Composed September 1995, Boston, Massachusetts, with special thanks to Michaels Ford, Bronski, and Lowenthal. Dedicated, after the fact and with some rue, to

Larry Hyman: in a previous life a pirate's boy. Anachronisms, implausibilities, and extravagances intended. See also Daniel Defoe: *Robinson Crusoe*; R. M. Ballantyne: *The Coral Island*; Johann David Wyss: *The Swiss Family Robinson*; J. M. Barrie: *Peter Pan*; William Shakespeare: *The Tempest*; Armstrong Sperry: *Call It Courage*; B. R. Burg: *Sodomy and the Pirate Tradition*. Note that most of these works are (or are generally read as) "children's books."
    <http://www.people.hbs.edu/ajeffers/>

Drew Limsky

Drew Limsky was educated at Emory University (B.A.), New York University (J.D.), and American University (M.A.). His work has appeared in the *Washington Post*, the *Baltimore Sun*, the *Atlanta Journal-Constitution*, *The James White Review*, the *New York Native*, *Lambda Book Report*, and the *Washington Blade*. He has taught writing at American University and the Writer's Center in Bethesda, Maryland. "After looking at my earlier stories and discovering that all my romantic scenes could be characterized as comic and/or humiliating, I decided to try my hand at a relatively healthy romantic involvement. This story is an homage to John Cheever's 'The Swimmer,' and a tribute to Luis F., who looked better than good in my bathtub."

William J. Mann

William J. Mann is the author of the novel *The Men from the Boys* (Dutton) as well as *Wisecracker: The Life & Times of Billy Haines*, the biography of the openly gay actor and designer due in 1998 from Viking. A widely syndicated journalist for the queer and alternative press, he is the winner of a 1996 fiction-writing grant from the Massachusetts Cultural Council. His fiction has appeared in *Men on Men 6*, *Happily Ever After*, and *Shadows of Love*. His essays have been included in the anthologies *Sister & Brother* and *Looking for Mr. Preston*, as well as in *The Advocate*, the *Harvard Gay & Lesbian Review*, *Frontiers*, and numerous other publications. The story included here, "Say Goodbye to Middletown," is partly a homage to Sherwood Anderson, and was originally conceived as part of a collection of interrelated short stories.

David A. Newman

David A. Newman grew up in Michigan, the youngest of seven children, all of whom scooped cones at the local ice-cream store. "What opened 'Ice Cream' up for me was remembering that the flip side of desire is pain. That feeling, combined with everything else you feel when you're barely fifteen, is what I wanted to capture." An award winner in the 1995 Hemingway Short Story contest with "Lesser Known Toys," Newman lives in Los Angeles, where he is at work on a collection of stories.

Joe Resjan

My stories have always come out of a few words that settle in me. One summer, I drove with a friend through a part of Michigan I'd never known: small, poor towns with, I learned, a rich history. The next night, back in Detroit, I watched a drag queen doing Cher. Later, at the airport, sitting at the Northwest gate, I mouthed the first six words of this story. That's how I came to live with A-Tone. I like to write about lost and forgotten people. Like A-Tone. I'm a teacher by profession, and they sit in my classroom. Summers I travel, and they walk by me in the streets of Jerusalem or Budapest. When I return home, they show up on my computer screen.

Rick Sandford

Rick Sandford began his bio in *His* with, "I am a gentile man who is currently working on the third part of what I like to think of as my Jewish trilogy." The writing he referred to is "The Gospel of Bartholomew Legate." He went on to say that, "As a person with AIDS, I believe that this affliction is a symptom, a sore of the Judaic/Christian disease that permeates our society." Rick died from complications relating to AIDS in 1995. From 1971 to 1972 he had been a "born-again" Christian—the experience made him an atheist. He is loved, and missed.

Mark A. Shaw

"The Loneliest Gentleman" is excerpted from my first novel, *The Province of Joy,* which should be finished by the time you read this (with the kind intercession of the Sts. Jane Bowles, Mary Flannery O'Connor, and the Hon. Nancy Mitford). After a grueling education in effective cocktail chatter provided by the heiresses at

Bennington College, I've spent ten years in Baltimore, Maryland. While my pleas for a pardon have not been granted, the state of Maryland was generous enough to provide me with an Individual Artist Award in 1990. They are grudgingly thanked.

David Vernon

David Vernon's fiction has appeared in *Men On Men 4* and *6, His, Blood Whispers 1* and *2, Indivisible,* and *Frontiers* magazine. He lives in New York and is currently working on a novel and a collection of his short fiction. "When I was seven years old I was on a show called 'Wonderama' and won a package of hot dog franks and an 8 x 10 of Wonderama's host, Bob Macalister. That same year I was also on 'The Soupy Sales Show' and won a Kenner Close and Play record player. I've been fascinated with game shows ever since. My father was a writer and a comedian and taught me the great value in making people laugh. I wrote 'Parting Gifts' as a vacation from my other writing, in an attempt to write something fun that still might have some meaning to the community."

David Watmough

"Evesham Encounter" demonstrates just how confusing an author can be. When my fourth novel, *The Time of the Kingfishers,* appeared two years ago I spent much time suggesting I had abandoned stories and that my next novel would be about gay middle age. So what did I do? Irritated by the assumption that gay life only began with Stonewall, I wrote this tale of adolescence set in 1952. I enjoyed writing it and when not tackling inversion on the Internet as in my current volume, *Hunting with Diana,* I'll return again to the distant, personal past. Or will I?

Richard C. Zimler

I live with my boyfriend Alex in Porto, Portugal, a few blocks from the sea. My second novel, *Unholy Ghosts,* was published in September by GMP Publishers. When I started writing "Stealing Memories," I was thinking a good deal about several sadistic and mendacious letters that a family member had sent me following the death of one of my brothers from AIDS. My anger toward this person started to come out as I developed the story. It also petrified me that someone I'd known all my life could write me something so cruel and demented. I tried to put that fear into the story.

About
the
Editors

Robert Drake

Robert Drake is the author of the popular fiction series, *The Man: A Hero For Our Time,* and coeditor of the anthologies *Indivisible, His,* and *Hers.* Since 1984 he has worked as a literary agent, representing, among others, Robert Rodi and Christian McLaughlin. He is also the book review editor for the *Baltimore Alternative,* a position he has held since 1993. A Quaker, he lives in Philadelphia with his family—a bull terrier named Pudsey Dawson, two cats named (pro)Zac and Brady, and The Most Understanding Man In the World, E. Scott Pretorius, to whom he dedicated his work on the first volume of *His* and would have dedicated this volume were it not for tragedy's damnable interference.

Terry Wolverton

Terry Wolverton is the author of *Bailey's Beads,* a novel (Faber and Faber) and *Black Slip,* a collection of poetry (Clothespin Fever Press). She has also edited several successful compilations, including: *Blood Whispers: L.A. Writers on AIDS, Volumes* 1 and 2 (Silverton Books), and, with Robert Drake, *Indivisible* (Plume) and the first volumes of *His* and *Hers.* Since 1976 Terry Wolverton has lived in Los Angeles, where she has been active in the feminist, gay and lesbian, and art communities. Since 1988 she has been a writer-in-residence at the Los Angeles Gay and Lesbian Center, where she directs the Perspectives Writing Program. Terry lives with her lover, visual artist Susan Silton.

Acknowledgments

The editors would like to thank Valerie Cimino, Mary Bisbee-Beek, and Betsy Uhrig for their belief in these books and their tireless efforts on our behalf. Robert Drake would also like to extend a special nod to Catherine Carter, Liz Wolfson, and Adrian Wood for providing a home away from home (in a literary sense) during the 1996 ABA convention, and for promoting these anthologies so earnestly to booksellers.

We once again extend our deepest thanks to Susan Silton for her stunning cover designs and to John Dugdale, whose eye-catching photography establishes the tone of the collection. In addition, Terry Wolverton would like to offer a belated but no less heartfelt acknowledgment to Ana Castanon, whose thought-provoking suggestions led us to the titles of this series.

We are fortunate to have been able to work with the talented writers whose stories are collected within these books. To them, most of all, we offer our gratitude.

All stories are printed by permission of the authors.